Classic Chinese Cuisine

The secret of Chinese gastronomy is a simple one: flavors should blend and textures should vary. Ways to modify and control these all-important elements of flavor and texture are fully outlined in this complete guide to classic Chinese cuisine.

Together with practical advice on cooking utensils and methods, the authors also provide a colorful culinary journey into the history and customs surrounding each dish.

Interwoven in the delightful text are recipes for regional specialties (Peking Duck), "curiosities" (Happy Family), plain and classic cooking (Chicken 4-4-4-4, Shark's Fins in Crab Sauce), and a Gastronomic Calendar with traditional dishes of the Chinese feast days.

"To eat well requires a sense of fitness . . . and an adventurous spirit"—plus this collection of outstanding recipes and fascinating Chinese lore.

知
味

Chinese Gastronomy

by Hsiang Ju Lin and Tsuifeng Lin
with an introduction by Lin Yutang

Charles E. Tuttle Co., Inc.
Boston • Rutland, Vermont • Tokyo

ACKNOWLEDGMENTS

We are most grateful to George Lang for reviewing the manuscript and for contributing his discerning and knowledgeable suggestions.

H. J. L.
T. F. L.

Library of Congress Cataloging–in–Publication Data

Lin, Hsiang-ju, 1931-
    [Chinese gastronomy]
  The art of Chinese cuisine= [Chih wei] / by Hsiang Ju Lin and Tsuifeng Lin : with an introduction by Lin Yutang.
    p. cm.
  Originally published: Chinese gastronomy. New York : Harcourt Brace Jovanovich, 1969.
  Includes index.
  ISBN 0-8048-3089-4
  1. Cookery, Chinese. I. Lin, Tsuifeng. II. Title. III. Title: Chih wei
TX724.5.C5L549 1996
641.5951—dc20   95-49557
                                                    CIP

Published by Charles E. Tuttle Co., Inc. of Rutland, Vermont,
and Tokyo, Japan, with editorial offices at
153 Milk Street, Boston, MA 02109

First Tuttle edition 1996

1 3 5 7 9 10 8 6 4 2   01 00 99 98 97 96

Printed in the United States of America

CONTENTS

MEASURES

This book was designed to be used by both British and American readers. British and U.S. measures differ on the terms cup, pint and quart. Where there is a discrepancy between these two systems, the British measure is given first followed by the U.S. equivalent in brackets ( ). Thus, 2 pints (5 cups) means 2 British pints *or* 5 cups by U.S. measure.

Some British and U.S. cookery terms differ. The British term is followed by the American term in brackets on the first occasion in each recipe. Thereafter the British term is employed.

RECIPES

Recipes which are relatively simple and easily prepared are starred (*).

Convenient stopping points in each recipe are indicated by three stars (***).

Recipes are referred to in the text by number and not by page.

As a rule each recipe serves 2 to 3 persons. The standard meal, composed of four dishes and a soup, would serve 6 to 8 persons.

THE USE OF MSG

Those who do not wish to use MSG can omit it from recipes where it appears as an ingredient. Since MSG is merely a flavor enhancer, omitting it will not change the basic taste of the dish.

Foreword

BY LIN YUTANG

THIRTY YEARS AGO I wrote in *My Country and My People* that "if there is anything [the Chinese] are serious about, it is neither religion nor learning, but food," and I added that "preachers should not be afraid to condemn a bad steak from their pulpits and scholars should write essays on the culinary art as the Chinese scholars do." My opinion has not changed since. I suppose that the pleasures of the table can be called "carnal" pleasures, and the Chinese people with their down-to-earth philosophy have always regarded eating as one of the things which reconcile us to this earthly life. It is this philosophy which enables the Chinese to discuss pork and philosophy under the same rubric and praise a man's philosophy but condemn his fillet. It takes a Latin temperament to appreciate this.

This Chinese culinary genius is often appreciated rather than understood. I have witnessed China's culinary conquest of the West in the last decades. However, Chinese food has remained a mystery. As the average Westerner progressively explores the rarer dishes, he has the feeling of coming to a continent unknown, with its exciting new flavours, new textures and new sauces and relishes. As he progresses from chicken chop suey to Peking duck, he becomes aware of a whole field of gustatory experiments of the Chinese world, vast and unknown.

There has been a flood of Chinese cookery books, but there has never been a Chinese Savarin in English. Recipes can be followed, but the whys and wherefores are not gone into. Tactile and gustatory sensations can be experienced directly, but the *raison d'être* and the critical standards are unknown. This is, I believe, the first book on Chinese gastronomy in English which gives a broad survey of the development of the Chinese culinary art. It not only gives a historical and geographical survey, but comments on the difference of taste of regional cuisines, on classical cuisines and plain home cooking, on food snobs, and occasionally on instances when the Chinese forget the difference between good and bad taste. I am particularly interested in the authors' opinions on these points. Taste can be good or bad, instinctive or cultivated, ostentatious or sophisticated and restrained. Also there is personality about types of cuisine, about certain types of preference. It varies like the music of composers. In dealing with the art and science of tastes, this book is rightly called *Chinese Gastronomy*. While it contains plenty of recipes, these are rather presented as illustrative of certain culinary principles, and of the goals, motives and methods of the Chinese cook.

For about two years, a unique research and experiment has been going on in my home, of which I have become the unwitting partner, happily on the eating end. I remember the perfecting of Su Tungpo pork or of the Singapore crunchy fish balls; the breakthrough came after a series of trials and experiments. It was a search for perfection. This must be so in cooking as in music; the supposed *coq-au-vin* may be commendable, but not just "quite right", quite *comme il faut*. As the search for perfection went on, I was presented, week after week, with exotic dishes of whose names I was only vaguely aware. Cooking at home became more and more recherché, and the delight of tasting novel concoctions was compounded by the knowledge of what had been done centuries before. For the authors insisted that they should not put down recipes until they had, in a scientific sense, verified repeatedly the exact measurements and procedures.

The work has entailed an immense amount of reading and research. The earliest Chinese cookery book with measurements, by one Madame Wu of Kiangsu, goes back to the Sung dynasty (A.D. 10th to 13th century). The unquestioned best gourmet's book is that by Yuan Mei, the poet of the eighteenth century. Hsiang Ju has systematically tested every recipe mentioned by Yuan Mei, and in the process has had occasion to admire the orthodoxy of Yuan's taste, while she has a lower opinion of Li Liweng, the seventeenth-century epicure. The earliest historical part goes back to the chapter on "Home-making" (*Neitseh*) in *Li Ki,* one of the Confucian classics. Another good philological method was to take the *Shuowen,* an authoritative study on the evolution of the Chinese script written in the second century, and check through the over 9,000 characters bearing information on Chinese foods, drinks and methods of cooking. (*Shuowen* is important for establishing dates; for instance, tea was not known as a drink at the time the book was compiled.) One finds various words for grilling (broiling), steaming, double-saucepan (double-boiler), minced herbs, relishes, parched rice, etc. Other references to cooking and food and drinks were culled from poetry of the various periods, and from special books, such as the book on food by the court physician prepared for the health of the emperor in the fourteenth century (*Yinshan Chengyao*) and the book on seasonal customs of Soochow (*Chingchialu*), compiled in 1831. The present book is the result of years of research and experience and thinking on the subject, and I am happy to add a few words as I see the conscientious work by my daughter and my wife brought to an end.

Hsiang Ju has a prodigious gustatory memory. Years after a dinner we once had at the renowned Provençal restaurant at Les Baux, she still remembers the ingredients and the *tastes* of the dishes. She is a born gastronome. She has done most of the research, while my wife provides the expert knowledge and skill and guidance. Having been a witness at the exciting drama that has been going on in the kitchen for the past two years, I have confidence that this book will contribute to a truer and deeper understanding of Chinese cuisine. With the increased knowledge, one can not only enjoy Chinese cooking, but also discuss it and be more critical when it goes wrong. And when it goes wrong with some of the dishes being served in the restaurants, one groans.

The author's previous book, *The Secrets of Chinese Cooking,* received the award of the Gastronomische Akademie Deutschlands at Frankfurt in 1960. It is hoped that we may all eat better and enjoy it more critically.

Introduction

If something is not right, this is due to carelessness, and it is the cook's fault. If something is good, say why, and when it is bad, pick out its faults. If one does not keep the cook in line, he becomes insolent. Before the food comes, send word down that the food tomorrow must be better.

YUAN MEI

THE COOK AS GASTRONOME

The Chinese cuisine is a world in itself. We have attempted the difficult task of showing what it is like. We have tried to show by example and explanation where the artist, the peasant, the food snob and the gourmet made their contributions, and so made it a thing of many parts. Its qualities are not readily summed up by generalizations: they are learnt one by one.

Why do we eat? In order to pursue the flavour of things. The word *gastronomy* now suggests a sensual indulgence, but the roots of the word mean *stomach* and *rule*—rules for the stomach. The art of eating has always been a disciplined habit. To eat well requires a sense of fitness (taste) and an adventurous spirit. Like good explorers, we must know when we have found something, then return to it, charting the approaches, so that it will be known to others. In this joyous adventure each person could travel alone, but the best team is made up of the gastronome and his cook. We have noted elsewhere in this book that the cuisine did not come into its own until the critics became articulate. They found fault with the food. They developed ideas and harassed their cooks. The gastronomes contributed their sense of form to the cuisine. Their prompting made the cooks masters of flavour and texture.

We had to learn how to eat before we could learn how to cook, and for this reason we have treated the arts of eating and cooking as a single subject, each supporting the other. We have emphasized the perfectly definite taste, texture and look of each dish, the joint creation of cook and gourmet, in order that the subtle judgments of the intelligent cook may be brought into play.

CHARACTER OF THE CUISINE

中
國
菜
的
特
點

Chinese cuisine is known to some only by its curiosities, but it actually differs from Western cuisine in a number of fundamental aspects. Its peculiar character comes from the realization that cooking is a form of artifice. This attitude accounts for its triumphs, its faults and its sophistications. Because of the trickery involved, the psychology of eating is different. The criteria of excellence in cuisine are somewhat different and are discussed as a lesson in Chinese. The pursuit of flavour has resulted more often in the blending of flavours, sometimes successful, often mismatched. Chinese cuisine is uniquely distinguished by textural variation, which has also led to the use of parts. And it is one of the few cuisines in which some kinds of fat are treated as delicacies.

Cooking is a form of artifice, because the taste of food is both good and bad. Good taste cannot be achieved unless one knows precisely what is bad about each ingredient, and proceeds to correct it. The curious, omnivorous cook knows that the taste of raw fruit is quite delicious and cannot be improved upon. Raw fish is insipid, raw chicken metallic, raw beef is palatable but for the rank flavour of blood. It is pointless to talk about the natural taste of these things, as many people like to do. We take it to mean the characteristic flavour of each thing, which is mainly in the fat and in the juices. This is brought out by artifice and appreciated as the *hsien* and *hsiang*, the flavour and aroma. They are to food what soul is to man. Cooking is essentially the capturing of these qualities, gastronomy the appreciation of them. *Hsien* and *hsiang* are not associated with any form of cooking. Here is the pivotal point where Chinese cuisine swings away from the others and takes off on its own. Note that Western pastry-making is a departure from the natural form and perhaps the "natural taste" of food. The *pâtissier* works only with butter, eggs, flour and sugar. But because he does not feel compelled to preserve the natural form, and present the flavour of each ingredient individually, he is often able to evolve something better. The palate can then perceive the taste of the ingredients interlocked in his inventions. The Chinese cook has done the same for food in general. (But Chinese sweet pastry is deplorably heavy and monotonous, often made up of glutinous rice, fat pork and sweet bean paste.) One discerns the *hsien* and *hsiang* of each ingredient in dishes of novel texture and appearance, these qualities having been brought out by artifice.

Criteria of Excellence

The unique qualities of the cuisine are contained in some almost untranslatable words. The words *hsien, hsiang, nung* and *yu-er-pu-ni* are the criteria of excellence in flavour. "Flavours must be rich and robust, never oily, or they must be delicate and fresh without being too thin. A flavour which is *nung* means that the essences are concentrated and the scum has been removed. Those who like greasy food might just as well dine on lard. When some dish is *hsien*, its true flavour is present. Not the least particle of error can be tolerated or you will have missed the mark." (Yuan Mei)

Hsien (鮮) Sweet natural flavour. *Usage:* to describe the delicate taste of fat pork, or the taste of butter; the taste of fresh fish, bamboo and prawns (shrimps). It may be simulated by a combination of seasonings, principally sugar. In an exceptional case, the *hsien* of fish is simulated by a mixture of seasonings and pork (Mock Fish, 66).

Hsiang (香) Characteristic fragrance; aroma. *Usage:* applied to those dishes which can give pleasure by their smell as well as their taste; characteristic fragrance of chicken fat, of roasted meats, of mushrooms, of sautéed onions, etc. *Hsiang* is almost impossible to duplicate by artifice, for it depends mainly on the oils present in each ingredient.

Nung (濃) Rich, heady, concentrated. *Usage:* in contrast to *hsien*, which must always appear natural and effortless, dishes which are *nung* are strongly flavoured with meat essences or spices. Applied to richly aromatic food (Glazed Duck, 121); to Cream Stock (16), composed of three kinds of meat. *Nung* is not always used in a complimentary sense: it may mean too rich, like overripe cheese.

Yu-er-pu-ni (油 而 不 膩) To taste of fat without being oily. *Usage:* applicable to the yolks of preserved eggs, to roe, to properly cooked belly pork. Compare the taste of these: caviar, cold fresh unsalted (sweet) butter or avocado. This phrase occurs frequently because of the importance of solid fat in the cuisine. Always used as a compliment.

The two following words describe texture. They are interesting because cooks try to achieve *tsuei* and *nun* textures with foods that do not naturally have them.

Tsuei (脆) Crisp, crunchy. A texture often brought out or concocted. *Usage:* applicable to dipped and sautéed snails, tripe, squid, Dipped Snails (93), Blanched Kidneys (124), prawns (Rule for Prawns, 25) and Fish Balls (31); pork crackling, roasted skin of fowl (Peking Duck, 57).

Nun (嫩) Soft and tender; non-fibrous. A somewhat resilient texture brought out by skilful cooking, to be distinguished from another word *ruan* (軟) meaning soft and loose-textured. *Usage:* applied to texture of a perfect soft-boiled egg, Velvet Chicken I (29), texture of *quenelles de brochet*.

These words are by no means sufficient to describe the range of flavours and textures, but they are most important and interesting words which have provoked a lot of thought. They embody qualities aimed at in cooking. The most famous dishes of Chinese cuisine combine several of these qualities. The skin of Peking duck is fragrant, crisp and rich without being oily (*hsiang, tsuei, yu-er-pu-ni*). Fish balls are at once fresh, crisp and tender (*hsien, tsuei* and *nun*). The combination of these qualities in a single dish suggests the complexity of classic Chinese cuisine. Note how no one quality contradicts any other.

Blending of Flavours

Plain flavours. The plain flavour appears simple because all the seasonings blended into it are undetectable. Cooks are satisfied when people appreciate the "natural" fragrance and taste of the food, unaware of the seasoning that has gone into it. They keep perfectly quiet about the amount of art that went into bringing out the "natural" taste. The fragrance and taste (*hsiang, hsien*) of many foods are brought out by the use of supporting ingredients which should merge into a single flavour. It was once suggested that bamboo be sautéed with marbled pork to extract its *hsien* juices, and then the pork be discarded before serving (Li Liweng). This is an extreme case to illustrate the importance of undetected seasoning.

Once supporting ingredients have done their job, they should be removed from view. If wine or vinegar is added, it can be evaporated away. If ginger and spring onions (scallions) are included, it is better to remove them before serving the dish. Light soy sauce should be used when seasoning prawns (shrimps) or vegetables. Sugar must not be detected in grains, nor should salt, unless it is served in a separate dish. Things are served either with or without sauce. Make it very obvious which you are doing.

Complementary flavours. Chinese cooking has been called "the marriage of flavours". This is very apt, for the individual ingredients should preserve their identity while complementing each other. This principle is discussed at length in Chapter 2. Unlike the subtle alterations of flavour discussed above, the second type of blending depends on showing up the flavours of individual ingredients by contrasting them with similar or totally different ingredients. The delicate taste of bird's nest is matched with very finely chopped winter melon (blending of similar flavours) or with minced ham (matching of contrasting flavours). This is comparable to matching several shades of white to each other, or contrasting black with white. The combination of cheese with other ingredients in French cooking comes closest to this idea of mutual support.

Variation of Texture

The refinement of the cuisine is most obvious in its control of texture. Classic cuisine stresses the creation of crisp or tender textures, demanding of the cook a certain virtuosity. Fundamentally, textural variation is an effort to improve upon nature. For example, every piece of meat is encased in invisible membranes, with sinewy connections and silky ligaments. Even after all these substances have been cleared away, the texture of meat remains a problem. The beginner knows well that it is difficult to keep meat tender while cooking it. Any error will make the meat fibrous and dry and all the tricks used in cooking it have the common aim of keeping it tender.

Variation of texture runs like a minor theme throughout the whole of Chinese gastronomy. At the most sophisticated tables it became an end in itself. It led to the search for texture-foods, things that have interesting textures but no taste. Today, there is no banquet without bird's nest or shark's fins, both texture-foods. These ingredients brought on yet another development in the cuisine. The cook was confronted with the problem of creating flavours for things which had no flavour in themselves. In Chinese cooking at its most sophisticated, substances with texture but no flavour were wedded to stocks of great flavour but no substance.

Use of Parts

The search for new flavours and textures led naturally to the use of parts. This was carried to an extreme. People distinguished between the cheeks of the fish, its soft under-belly, the jelly-like tissue at the base of the dorsal fins. Country-style cooking was by necessity a cooking of parts, quite aside from the art of eating. The inherent textural variation of innards is interesting to gourmets. Chinese tongues and teeth are perhaps rather unusual. Many people can split a watermelon seed, extract the meat and carry on a rapid conversation at the same time, pausing only to expel the shell. Others, with a little practice, are able to tie one or two knots in a cherry stem with tongue and teeth. The Chinese tongue is a sensitive thing. So the grainy quality of liver, the unctuous intestine, the fibrous gizzard, the spongy maw and crunchy tripe all stand apart from each other, to be appreciated as delicacies, each with its unique texture.

The use of parts is also favoured by the cook, who knows that the white meat of chicken is done earlier than the dark, and that the wings must be stewed, the legs fried, the skin roasted or fried, the breast meat sautéed or minced. Each part must be cooked differently to bring out the best, and by separating the parts one can bring out the best in each.

Use of Fat

Fat is a delicacy. Despite the term *yu-er-pu-ni* (to taste of fat without being oily), which belongs to gastronomy more than to common taste, all oil is considered good. Pork fat can be made to soak up juices, chicken and duck fat to flavour vegetables. Sesame oil is used to suppress the fishy taste of seafood, to fry sweets and to flavour food. Sesame, peanut and vegetable oils are used in vegetarian cooking. The flavour of meat and fish is in the fat. Hence, the cooking of fat as such has developed in step with the techniques for cooking meat. The use of fat is particularly appreciated when the main substance is rice or wheat. The lean food of peasants was enriched by fat. "The fat in meat, fish, ducks and chicken must be kept in the meat and not allowed to run out, else the flavour is all in the juices." (Yuan Mei)

做 法 KITCHEN ARTS

A number of methods for producing those particular tastes and textures we have just discussed are summarized in the four tables below. These are nothing but tricks of the cuisine, but without them the most patient and energetic cook would be misdirecting his efforts towards achieving the best. On the other hand, if he only knew these techniques but had no taste, the result would be equally sad. The application of each of these methods is limited to certain kinds of ingredients, as indicated in the second column of each table. It would be unwise to use some of these rather drastic procedures on unspecified ingredients. Details of the methods are described in the illustrative recipe.

Note the number of procedures concerned with removal of rank flavours, scum and other bad qualities of food. This is quite as important as the bringing out or creation of new flavours and textures.

Common Practices for Control of Flavour

METHOD	INGREDIENTS	PURPOSE	ILLUSTRATIVE RECIPE
Breaking of marrow bones followed by rapid boiling	spare ribs; pork, duck, chicken bones	To expose marrow, to enrich stock or juices.	Cream Stock (16)
Blanching	fish, fowl, innards, pig's feet	To remove unpleasant flavours.	Steamed Fish (133)
Repeated blanching in stock or water	shark's fins	To rid fins of fishy taste. Stock is preferred for adding flavour to fins.	Shark's Fins with Crab Sauce (125)
Rapid boiling in water or stock	fish head, marrow	To extract fat droplets.	Fish Head in Casserole (9)
Sautéeing or extraction using hot oil	ginger, spring onions (scallions), garlic, wild pepper, hot pepper	To bring out the characteristic flavours.	Economy Sauce (23)
Steaming	fish, fowl, belly pork, vegetables	To bring out and preserve the sweet (hsien) taste, to preserve the original essence.	Steamed Cucumbers (107)

Ingredients Added to Modify Flavour

INGREDIENT	ADDED TO	PURPOSE	ILLUSTRATIVE RECIPE
Sugar	fish, prawns (shrimps), vegetables, mushrooms, fowl	Restores or improves hsien flavour. Must be used in moderation, and never tasted as such.	Mushrooms in Broth (98)
Monosodium glutamate (MSG)	all ingredients except sweets and fruit	Intensifies flavour. Use sparingly as it leaves a characteristic after-taste.	Old and Fresh Eggs (123)
Vinegar	hot red peppers	Intensifies hot taste.	Spiced Tangerine Chicken (62)

Ingredients Added to Modify Flavour

INGREDIENT	ADDED TO	PURPOSE	ILLUSTRATIVE RECIPE
Ginger, spring onions (scallions), etc.	soups, stews, meat, seafood	Suppresses offensive flavours.	Duck Fried with Onions (106)
Wine or spirits (liquor)	seafood, fowl, meat	Suppresses rank flavours.	Carp in Lamb Broth (13)
Black pepper, wild pepper	tripe, seafood, pork, pig's knuckles, innards	Suppresses rank flavours.	Pig's Foot Jelly (103)
Sesame oil	seafood, especially prawns (shrimps) and crab	Added before cooking: removes fishy odour.	Mock Crab Roe (136)
Sesame oil	lamb, soups, sauces, jellyfish, marinated vegetables	Added after cooking: adds pleasant aromatic flavour if used in moderation.	Jellyfish (44)
Soy sauce	all meat, soups, sauces	Imparts meaty taste, colour and flavour.	Brown Stock Sauce (77)
Sesame seeds	seafood, sauces, pastry	Toast seeds in an ungreased pan and crush to bring out flavour.	Sesame Peanut Sauce (24)
Chicken, duck or pork fat	minced chicken or prawns (shrimps), meat balls	Imparts a definite flavour to bland ingredients.	Chicken-flavoured Cabbage (104)
Pickled black beans	seafood, meat, vegetables	Adds piquant flavour. Steam them in wine for 5 minutes. Chop finely.	Pan-roasted Peppers (67)
Brown bean sauce	meat	Imparts hsien taste.	Mock Fish (66)
Oyster sauce	meat, vegetables, seafood, innards	Imparts rich taste, hsien.	Sautéed Liver (110)

Common Practices for Control of Texture

METHOD	INGREDIENTS	PURPOSE	ILLUSTRATIVE RECIPE
Removal of tendons, membranes, ligaments and sheaths	fish, fowl, pork, beef	Homogeneity of texture.	Velvet Chicken I (29)
Removal of skin and bones	fowl	Where different textures interfere with each other.	Duck Steamed in Wine (128)
Trimming off fat	beef, pork	Principally to remove membranes under fat; to keep stock clear.	Beef Yuan Mei (7)
Cutting across the grain	beef, snails	Slices cut across are more tender.	Minute Beef (132)
Slicing with the grain	chicken, pork	To minimize shrinkage and preserve appearance.	Fried Slices (61)
Soaking in salt and wine	kidneys	Extracts juices which would otherwise form scum.	Blanched Kidneys (124)
Marinating in dry salt or sugar	fowl, meat, vegetables	Extracts water effectively.	Radish Flowers (28)
Adding dry salt	minced fish, prawns (shrimps) or chicken	Stiffens the paste, makes it crisp.	Basic Rule for Fish Balls (31)
Blanching in acidified water	tripe; poached fish, snails, chicken	Removes slime from tripe. Keeps pork tender. Keeps fish and snails tender.	Dipped Snails (93)
Soaking in lightly salted water (1¼ pints (3 cups) water plus ½ level teaspoon salt per pound)	prawns (shrimps), chicken, fish	Removes scum, makes meat tender, juicy. Do not use on pork or beef, as their flavours are destroyed by water.	Basic Rule for Prawns (25)
Salting and blanching	fowl, meat, tripe	Essential to maintain smoothness of juices.	Tungpo Pork (8)
Blanching	boned fowl	To set the shape of fowl.	Stuffed Duck (127)

Common Practices for Control of Texture

METHOD	INGREDIENTS	PURPOSE	ILLUSTRATIVE RECIPE
Blanching	*vegetables*	*To fix the colour and set the texture. Must be followed by rinsing in cold water and draining.*	*Spinach in Cream Stock (20)*
Air-drying	*fowl*	*Dries out skin, makes it crisp.*	*Peking Duck (57)*

Ingredients Added for Control of Texture

INGREDIENT	ADDED TO	PURPOSE	ILLUSTRATIVE RECIPE
Water	*minced meat, seafood, vegetables*	*To keep ingredients moist and light.*	*Pearly Meat Balls (76)*
Vinegar	*meat slivers, bamboo*	*Added to a sauté, keeps slivers tender.*	*Sautéed Pork (11)*
Salt, as brine	*meat, fowl*	*Extracts water, firms meat and fat.*	*Salt-cured Duck (119)*
Strong liquor	*fowl*	*Dries out skin.*	*Peking Duck (57)*
Cornflour (cornstarch)	*beef, pork, chicken*	*To bind juices of meat with seasonings.* It is essential to add liquid at last stage of cooking.	*Diced Chicken in Sauce (68)*
Cornflour and egg white (1 egg white plus 1 level tablespoon cornflour)	*seafood, chicken, lamb*	*To preserve the natural delicate texture. To form an impenetrable barrier between meat and hot oil.*	*Fish Fillets in Tart Sauce (59)*
Water-chestnut powder	*minced chicken, soups, sauces*	*Similar to cornflour but with smoother texture. Used as thickening.*	*Minced Chicken (70)*
Fat pork	*minced prawns (shrimps), pork*	*Keeps ingredients light.*	*Prawn (Shrimp) Balls (131)*

UTENSILS

The cleaver. There are two kinds of cleaver. The light cleaver slices, slivers and cuts through joints; its point picks up membranes covering meat so they can be stripped off. The heavy cleaver is used for chopping through bone and cooked meat, or for flattening uncooked meat. Chopping through bone with the light cleaver dulls its edge.

The important habits to develop in using the cleaver are rhythm and relaxation. With rhythm the slices become uniform and fall with geometrical precision, one after the other. The rhythm comes with relaxation of the hand and wrist, and rhythmic precision can be developed with practice. Concentrate not on the thinness or evenness of each slice or sliver, but on repetitive rhythmic motion. Do not consider each stroke an individual action—rather forget about it and move your wrist up and down. The slices will fall with astonishing ease and precision.

The cleavers are used with different motions according to the object being cut.

CLEAVER	INGREDIENT	MOTION	RESULT
light	*bamboo, vegetables*	*Straight up and down.*	*slices*
light	*root vegetables, bamboo*	*Straight up and down, but rotate root or shoot.*	*chunks*
light	*mushrooms, small pieces of meat*	*Bear down in and out.*	*slivers*
light	*pork, chicken*	*Bear down inwards.*	*slices*
light	*beef*	*Bear down outwards.*	*slices*
light	*skin and fat*	*Use sawing motion.*	*chunks*
light	*minced meat*	*Grasp handle and upper outer corner, chop straight up and down.*	*paste*
heavy	*raw meat with bone*	*Use short, powerful, sweeping arc.*	*pieces*
heavy	*cooked fowl*	*Use wide, rhythmic, sweeping arc.*	*pieces*

To make uniform slices, steady uncut portion with one hand and slice with cleaver in other hand. The cleaver descends at a uniform rate, but the ingredient fed to it is edged against it at a fast or slow rate, depending on the desired thickness. If the uncut portion is fed to the blade slowly, the slices are thin. If it is slipped under the blade quickly, the slices are thicker. The thickness of the slices depends on the touch of the fingers steadying the uncut portion. The slices fall parallel to one another. To make slivers, flatten the parallel slices with the palm or heel of the hand, and slice again in the same direction. To make dice, flatten the slivers with the hand, turn the board one-quarter of a circle and cut again.

The best description of the use of the cleaver is given by Chuangtse (4th century B.C.).

Prince Huei's cook was cutting up a bullock. Every blow of his hand, every heave of his shoulders, every tread of his foot, every thrust of his knee, every *whshh* of rent flesh, every *chhk* of the chopper, was in perfect rhythm—like the dance of the Mulberry Grove, like the harmonious chords of Ching Shou.

"Well done!" cried the Prince. "Yours is skill indeed!"

"Sire," replied the cook, laying down his chopper, "I have always devoted myself to Tao, which is higher than mere skill. When I first began to cut up bullocks, I saw before me whole bullocks. After three years' practice, I no longer saw whole animals. And now I work with my mind and not with my eye. My mind works without control of the senses. Falling back on eternal principles, I glide through such great joints or cavities as there may be, according to the natural constitution of the animal. I do not even touch the convolution of muscle and tendon, still less attempt to cut through large bones.

"A good cook changes his chopper once a year—because he cuts. An ordinary cook once a month—because he hacks. But I have had this chopper for nineteen years, and although I have cut up many thousand bullocks, its edge is as if fresh from the whetstone. For at the joints there are always interstices, and the edge of the chopper being without thickness, it remains only to insert that which is without thickness into such an interstice. Indeed there is plenty of room for the blade to move about. It is thus that I have kept my chopper for nineteen years as though fresh from the whetstone.

"Nevertheless, when I come upon a knotty part which is difficult to tackle, I am all caution. Fixing my eye on it, I stay my hand, and gently apply my blade, until with a *hwah* the part yields like earth crumbling to the ground. Then I take out my chopper, stand up, and look around with an air of triumph. Then, wiping my chopper, I put it carefully away."

"Bravo!" cried the Prince. "From the words of this cook I have learnt how to take care of my life."

The wo. The circular, round-bottomed frying pan is commonly called a wok, the Cantonese pronunciation having been wrongly rendered into English. The wo has several advantages over a flat frying pan. The heat is diffused over a wide area. Very little oil is required for a sauté or for deep-frying. A single egg or a large volume of leafy vegetables, a few slivers of meat or a whole fowl are cooked in the same size of utensil. The curved sides reduce spattering, and cradle the fish and fowl while they cook. While the wo is convenient and useful, it is not essential to any of the recipes described in this book.

A new wo may have a tendency to stick. Treat it as you would a cast-iron frying pan. Heat it gently with a small quantity of oil spread all over the inside surface. Remove the oil and wipe the surface dry, but do not wash it. It is not desirable to clean the inside surface with abrasives or strong detergents, as a seasoned surface is preferred.

When preparing the wo for sautéeing or frying, first heat the wo without oil, then add oil. As a result the metal is always hotter than the oil, and the ingredients do not stick to the surface. This practice is known as "hot pan, warm oil".

Above, the *ho*, a cauldron used in ancient times; below, the *ting,* a tripod used as a cooking vessel. When the *ting* was placed within the *ho*, the combination became a double-saucepan (double-boiler).

The steamer. A steamer is not readily replaced by any other utensil in the kitchen. A whole meal may be cooked in it with the use of a single burner. It keeps food warm without drying it out and takes up very little room.

Dishes which go into the steamer must be covered with cellophane, aluminium foil or an overlapping plate.

Cooked rice and noodles may be placed on racks lined with cheesecloth.

Yeast rolls or buns, cut into shapes and placed on squares of waxed paper or foil set well apart on the racks, undergo their second rising there, to be steamed when they have reached the required size.

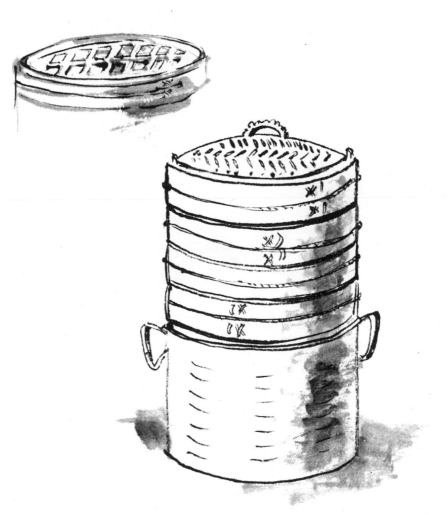

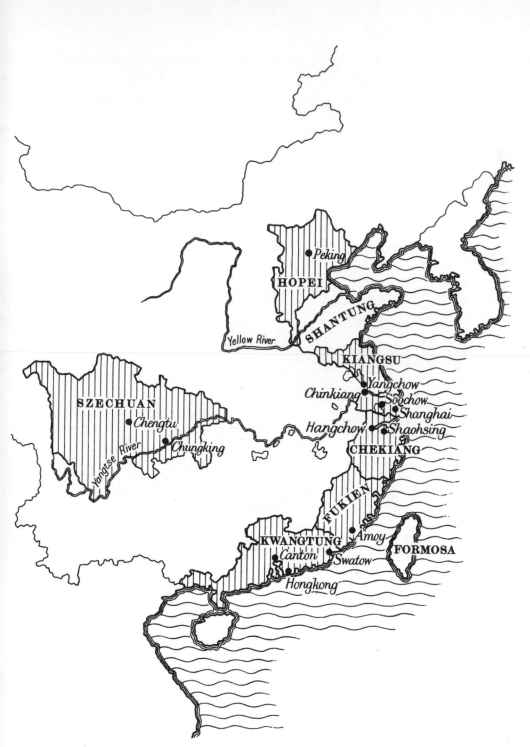

Gastronomic Map of China, showing regional specialities. Note how the geography of the region influences the cuisine.

SZECHUAN
sesame dumplings
spiced tangerine chicken
sweet potatoes, corn
hot red peppers
sour and hot soup
wild pepper
bamboo dry sauté

HOPEI
Chiaotse
Paotse
millet
almond tea
roasted potatoes
cabbage
lamb cooked in sauce
black plum juice
carp
Peking duck

KWANGTUNG
roast meats
winter melon soup
frog's legs
fried sparrows
chicken
"dipped" snails

KIANGSU·CHEKIANG
delicate noodles
dainty hot pastries
mullet, bream, shad
live prawns (shrimps)
vinegar

smoked duck's tongues
crabs and wine
brown stock sauce
fuzzy beans
juicy buns

FUKIEN
shredded pork
Popia, thin crêpes
squid, fried oysters
clear soups
crystallized melon
peanuts

1. Ancient Cuisine

餲 : *the fragrance of food.*

SHUOWEN

THE PEOPLE of ancient times sat on mats (not on chairs), ate from low tables, plucked on string instruments, drove elaborately carved chariots, hunted, sang, shot deer with bow and arrow, made bronzes cast from baked clay moulds, divined the future from cracks in heated tortoise shell, wrote poetry. "At fifty, a man was supposed to begin to decay; at sixty, not to feel satisfied unless he had flesh to eat. At seventy, he was thought to require silk in order to keep him warm; at eighty, to need someone [to sleep] with him to keep him warm; and at ninety, not to feel warm even with that." (*Neitseh, Li Ki*) What did they eat?

One has some idea of what cooking in ancient times was like. Through the centuries the classic texts, themselves often cryptic, were annotated by scholars, the fine print of the commentaries exceeding the length of the texts themselves. The commentaries were further annotated. Each sentence of the original text comes through to us with a sound both amplified and jammed by successive interpretations. Perhaps the message has been a little garbled, but it is better than no word at all. The following description of ancient cuisine is mainly reconstructed from the old texts: (1) *I-li* (儀 禮), the historical records of the Chou dynasty (1122–225 B.C.) for the description of sacrifices. (2) *Li Ki*, a collection of manuscripts from various periods, date uncertain but certainly not later than end of Chou dynasty (2nd century B.C.). The *Neitseh* (內 則) or "Regulations of the Household" contained therein is particularly interesting with respect to daily cooking in ancient times. (3) *Shuowen* (說 文), a collection of 9,000 archaic words dated A.D. 191. Scholars have used the dictionary to prove the existence of ancient objects or ideas; by the same token (though with less reason) they have taken the absence of words in *Shuowen* to prove that such objects, practices or ideas did not exist in the period prior to A.D. 191. (4) The *Shih*

Ching (詩 經), the *Book of Poetry* or *Book of Songs*, of which Confucius (6th century B.C.) was the editor.

The ancient cuisine was not distinguishably "Chinese". One has the feeling that it was just emerging from primitive cooking, for though there are three archaic words for steam (烝 烰 煦), and words for grilling (broiling), roasting, smoking and fermentation, there are no words for sautéeing, for blanching, or any of the more refined methods of cooking. There is a word for the fragrance of food (飶) and its smell (饙), and also words for putrid (餒), food that has "turned" (餲) and food that is not sufficiently cooked (饐). Minced meat and fermented relishes were known, but the remote flavour of antiquity is always present in the descriptions of sacrifices and in the practice of *mao pao* (毛 包), "scorched" pig roasted without evisceration. This is apparently still done today by some savage tribes of the South Pacific. The appreciation of fat, which we have already remarked on as being distinctly Chinese, was present, but no subtleties of textural variation are noted. The blending of flavours was achieved in a remarkable way, as will be discussed later.

Ancient cooking utensils were sturdy and ingenious, made of metal, clay or bamboo. A *bain-marie*, probably better than any modern vessel, was composed of a tripod (*ting* 鼎) placed within a round-bottomed pot (*ho* 鑊) containing boiling water. Boiling water surged about the legs of the tripod, and the steam passed over and around the vessel. A rather complicated recipe made use of this utensil. A suckling pig stuffed with dates, wrapped with hemp and motherwort (a kind of mint), was smeared with clay and baked. The baked clay broke off cleanly, having hardened about the hemp and herb. Then the crackling, which was clean and free of clay, was smeared with rice flour, and the whole pig was deep-fried, making it crisp and fragrant. The fried pig was placed in the *ting* with herbs related to mint, and steamed for three days and nights, "taking care that water did not enter the inner vessel". One imagines that the pig would have been fragrant with dates and mint, and that the tender pork fat would have melted to give a clear layer of delicate oil. This was prepared for older people, who in ancient times were given delicacies of very fat substances to eat, such as fat ladled over rice, and dog liver grilled in dog fat (*Neitseh*).

Millet or rice was steamed in a *ching* (甑), the process being interrupted by a cold-water rinse, so that each grain was separate.

The rice steamer consisted of an earthenware vessel with seven holes in its bottom, lined with bamboo matting.

The fish, hard to fit into any ordinary vessel, was steamed in a section of bamboo tubing, the natural partitions of its hollow stalk forming a convenient *poissonier*.

Some of the cooking utensils must have been large enough to contain whole quarters of pig and beef, as we deduce from the passage in *I-li*, on sacrifices made in honour of a high official.

"The minister placed the right shoulder, but not the rump, in the cauldron, also the shin and shank of the front legs, the rack, the loin and sirloin and the ribs, three intestines, three stomachs and one lung." An offering to an even higher official differed by the addition of two more lungs to what must have been a very large pot. The enormous bronze pots now standing in museums probably made excellent cooking utensils. These sacrifices were, of course, used later as food, for "when a gentleman makes a present of remains of a sacrifice, he must first taste it himself" (Confucius).

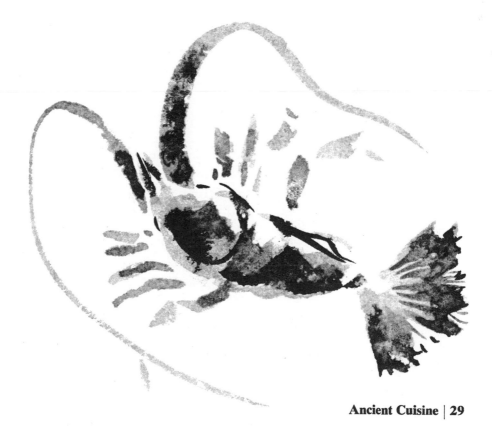

With reverent air, in dress correct,
With sheep and oxen pure, select,
When autumn comes, and winter cold,
Our temple services we hold,
    And offer sacrifice.
The victims slain some haste to flay;
Some boil the flesh; on stands some lay
The pieces boiled, which some dispose
In order due, exact and close,
    According to their size.
The while, the priest, inside the gate,
Lest elsewhere welcome be too late,
    Our sires asks to descend.
Complete and brilliant are our rites;
They grandly come, as he invites.
Though hid from us in shadowy veil,
Our offerings with delight they hail,
    And to our prayers attend . . . .

Before the fires some reverent stand;
Some take the mighty trays in hand;
Those with the roasted flesh they fill,
Those with the livers broiled. Then still
And reverent, the queen presides,
And every smaller dish provides,
    The pious feast to grace.
The guests and visitors draw near.
Divined for, now they all appear,
    And take an honoured place.
                    The Book of Poetry (SHIH CHING)

The savage air of ancient cookery came not only from the mode of preparation, but from the choice of ingredients. A good part of the food, as we shall see later, came from hunting and foraging. Domestic animals were valued, for the point was made that the sacrifices to officials and to one's ancestors were made from domesticated animals including sheep, oxen, pigs, fowl, horses and dogs. Yet in the ordinary food, elk, deer and muntjak, quail and pheasant, boar and wolf are frequently mentioned.

We bend our bows; our shafts we grasp;
There lies the huge behemoth low,
And boars are pierced—spoil for the guests,
At court, when wine-cups overflow.
                    The Book of Poetry (SHIH CHING)

The elderly were served the more tender meats, such as beef, marinated overnight in good wine, and meat balls made of beef, mutton and pork with six parts of cooked rice, fried first and then served in soup (*Neitseh, Li Ki*).

A number of vegetables and fruits were probably picked off the land. The royal fern (*Osmunda regalis*), smartweed (*Polygonum*) and a leafy variety of *Sonchus* were vegetables used as stuffing or flavouring. The first two named grow wild in marshy places. Spices used were ginger, cinnamon, a variety of hyssop, cardamom, onions, chives and mugwort (related to tarragon). Jams and jellies were made from peaches, quinces, plums and haws (fruit of the hawthorn), the last-named having a beautiful red colour. Bamboo shoots are mentioned in *The Book of Poetry*.

IN HONOUR OF THE MARQUIS OF HAN

The court sends forth its many lords,
To taste the cheer the king affords,
An hundred vases stand around,
All with the choicest spirits crowned.
The mats roast turtle and fresh fish
Present, and many a lordly dish.
And bamboo sprouts, and tender shoots,
And sauces fine, and fragrant fruits,
With their rich perfume fill the air.
Oh! but it was a banquet rare!
                    The Book of Poetry (SHIH CHING)

There were three ways of preserving meat. Of these, *fu* (salt-cured meat) was most adaptable. It was served simply with a complementary relish, made into soup, or fried and served with millet or rice. As an alternative, the meat was not salted but pounded with ginger and cinnamon and grilled. The third method was to make a relish by fermentation. Boned fish or meat was sliced, dried and chopped, mixed with salt, millet and yeast, and steeped in wine. It was packed in an earthenware jar, sealed and left for a hundred days. Venison relish was made with the bones. Wasps, deer, rabbit and goose meat were also used for this type of relish. Note that this method of making preserves is similar to that used in modern times, described in Chapter 6, for making fish relish. *Fu* bears a striking resemblance to the *bah-koa* of Fukien, paper-thin slices of meat cured by grilling, painted with soy sauce, sugar and spices. *Bah-koa* is a good present for people going on long voyages, as it keeps for months while retaining "the flavour of home". The main difference is that these pickles, relishes and cured meats are now relegated to an inferior level, *amuse-gueules*, where they were once the main courses. This is quite plain in the make-up of a banquet table of ancient times, consisting of twenty dishes in five rows (*Neitseh, Li Ki*).

beef broth	mutton broth	pork broth	roast beef
relish	beef *fu*	relish	minced beef
roast lamb	lamb *fu*	relish	roast pork
relish	pork *fu*	mustard sauce	fish forcemeat
pheasant	quail	hare	partridge

Ancient cuisine was to develop into something opulent, elegant and varied. But how was this to be achieved on a steady diet of pickles and preserved meats? Two devices brought variety into the food. Meat was fried in the fat of a different animal: lamb with beef fat, fish fried with goat fat and pheasant *fu* fried with dog fat. Since fat tends to have the characteristic *hsiang* (aroma) if not the *hsien* (flavour) of each ingredient, a contrast in flavours was achieved. More elegant food consisted of meat served with contrasting relishes, a salty *fu* with fish relish, spicy meat with a salty pickle of ant larvae. *Fu* soup was served with hare relish, other meats with pickled fruits or jellies.

All of these were washed down with wine, which in ancient times was commonly drunk raw and sweet. The sudden arrival of a guest "left no time to make wine". This process usually took overnight. "New wine makes one sick," wrote Su Tungpo several centuries later. But it was potent. There were five words, meaning (1) giddy (醺), (2) drunk but not confused (酲), (3) drunk and belligerent (酌 or 酇), (4) drunk and merry (酣), (5) sick from drink (to have a hangover) (酲). The common drink was *liao*, ladled into cups to avoid stirring up the dregs, or filtered through grass. Wheat, millet and rice were all used to make wines which were mixed with each other, diluted with water or fortified with aged wine. Prolonging the fermentation resulted in a clearer wine, due to the shrinking of the dregs, a sign of quality, judging by the occasions on which it was used.

"Heave ho," cry the wood cutters.
I have strained my wine so clear,
I have got a fatted lamb
To which I invite all [my uncles].
Even if they choose not to come
They cannot say I have neglected them.

Spick and span I have sprinkled and swept,
I have set out the meats, the eight dishes of grain.
I have got a fatted ox,
To which I invite all my uncles,
And even if they choose not to come
They cannot hold me to blame.

They are cutting wood on the bank.
Of strained wine I have good store;
The dishes and trays are all in rows.
Elder brothers and younger brothers, do
*   not stay afar!*
If people lose the virtue that is in them,
It is a dry throat that has led them astray.

When we have got wine we strain it, we!
When we have none we buy it, we!
Bang, bang the drum, do we!
Nimbly step the dance, do we!
And take this opportunity
Of drinking clear wine.

The Book of Songs (SHIH CHING)

One can distinguish between drinking on formal occasions, in the company of (distinguished) relatives and officials (*yao* 飫), which took place in the daytime, and the informal drinking taking place at night (*yu* 醧). During a formal dinner one kept the shoes on but off they came when the occasion was relaxed.

The refinement of taste in food came about gradually as the result of a more firmly established agriculture, which provided fresh food in abundance at least in certain seasons. The play of textures, so important in modern cooking, could not readily be carried out with meats stiff with salt or turned into tasty but amorphous preserves. The character of the cuisine was set in its direction by the time of Confucius. "For him the rice could never be white enough and minced meat could never be chopped finely enough. When it was not cooked right, he would not eat. When the food was not in season, he would not eat. When the meat was not cut correctly, he would not eat. When the food was not served with its proper sauce, he would not eat." The national preoccupation had early beginnings.

When critics became articulate, the food improved. In the poem of Ch'ü Yuan (3rd century B.C.), food becomes a worldly joy, and this excerpt from *The Great Summons* describes a feast which can almost be appreciated today. Ch'ü Yuan was on the verge of suicide for political reasons, and wrote *The Great Summons* to persuade himself to cling to life. He did drown himself, however, and his death is marked by a holiday (see Chapter 8).

> *O Soul come back to joys beyond all telling!*
> *Where thirty cubits high at harvest-time*
> *The corn is stacked;*
> *Where pies are cooked of millet and bearded maize.*
> *Guests watch the steaming bowls*
> *And sniff the pungency of peppered herbs.*
> *The cunning cook adds slices of bird-flesh,*
> *Pigeon and yellow-heron and black crane.*
> *They taste the badger-stew.*
> *O Soul come back to feed on foods you love!*
>
> *Next are brought*
> *Fresh turtle, and sweet chicken cooked with cheese*
> *Pressed by the men of Ch'ü.*
> *And flesh of whelps floating in liver-sauce*
> *With salad of minced radishes in brine;*
> *All served with that hot spice of southernwood*
> *The land of Wu supplies.*
> *O Soul come back to choose the meats you love!*
>
> *Roasted daw, steamed widgeon and grilled quail—*
> *On every fowl they fare.*
> *Boiled perch and sparrow broth—in each preserved*
> *The separate flavour that is most its own.*
> *O Soul come back to where such dainties wait!*

The dishes described can just barely be recognized as Chinese food, whereas the earlier concoctions cannot be so described. The use of spices, whelps (probably dog) and game recalls the feasts of ancient times. What is new is the mode of preparation. Slices of fowl are added at the last moment, lest they become overcooked and tough (compare to the addition of chicken in Chicken Congee, 2). The excellence of the boiled fish and sparrow broth lies in each having "the flavour that is most its own". Formerly, these were mainly recognized in the pungent fats of animals. It remains a delicate task to cook fish while preserving the *hsien* (sweet flavour), and to make game taste of itself and not seasoning. The antique flavour was still in the air, but the savouring of food had become more sophisticated.

Modern cuisine reflects the taste of a sophisticated leisured class, and did not appear in its present form (Chapter 7) until that wealthy class came into existence. In late Han (A.D. 2nd century) the splendour of the court shone. Inlay, lacquer and silk contributed to their art. During this luxurious period, and through the later dynasties of Sui and Tang, a profound change must have taken place. "Nowadays, people tend to eat too much. Besides feeding themselves they like to look at a lot of food. How can it please them to lounge about all day for the sake of some delicacies, soiling their mouths with roasts and smoked meats?" (A.D. 4th century) The next clues appear several hundred years later when Chinese cuisine emerged as a distinct personality, different from the semi-barbaric cookery of ancient China, with all the refinements fully developed. It could not under any circumstances be confused with Western, savage or tribal cookery. It was civilized.

The poet Tu Fu (712–70) spoke of the Empress Yang Kweifei's sisters at court.

> *The duchesses, smooth of face,*
> *In figure and feature firm and round,*
> *Dressed in pearl-beaded panelled gowns*
> *Parade their beauty.*
>
> *Glittering, tinkling, bobbing*
> *Drops of silver, spikes of horn, peacock feathers*
> *Quivered among flowers of silk, leaves of jewel.*
> *So they dressed their sleek heads.*
>
> *They are at ease in the Inner Court.*
> *With ivory sticks gold-tipped,*
> *Pick at the fish on a crystal plate, at camel hump.*
> *When bored they drink.*
>
> *In endless courses serve the Royal Table,*
> *With food like loops and skeins of silk entangled.*
> *Eunuchs stand at the palace gate:*
> *Piebald horses, reined, fret and wait.*
>
> from *The Parade of the Beauties*

Ancient Cuisine | 35

The luxury-loving Empress was blamed for the downfall of the Tang dynasty. She loved fresh lichees, which were shipped to her by a kind of pony express from the South to Changan, the capital of Tang in central China. She paid dearly for her extravagances, being forced to hang herself during a revolution. There is also a dish named after her (Kweifei Chicken). The plump, white, voluptuous Empress loved to drink, and the dish consists of a plump white chicken marinated in a great deal of alcohol, fried, stewed with wine and then sauced with more wine. What woman wants to be so represented? A subtle insult. We say that this suggestion of an imperial dinner resembles modern Chinese cuisine because of its exquisite fineness of preparation and the novelty of the texture-food, camel hump, which is still occasionally served. A fragment of a manuscript also suggests the ultra-refinement of court cuisine:

I was looking in an old trunk and came upon some menus served to the Crown Prince, in the notebook of a palace cook. Some of the choices were:

> *Kidneys, blanched and cooked with wine and vinegar*
> *Quail, sautéed with bamboo shoots*
> *Grilled pigeon, garnished*
> *Fried snake relish*
> *Fried mixed relish*
> *Forcemeat of lake fish*
> *Sautéed frog's legs*
> *Toasted minced kidney*
> *Braised sheat-fish*
> *Crab legs with venison*
> *Live river prawns*
> *Grilled fish*
> *Pig's knuckle slices, crisped, with wine and vinegar*
> *Toasted roe with fried kidneys*
> *Brains vinaigrette*
> *Consommé*
> *Fish maw in bouillon*
> *Huai whitefish steamed in wine*
>
> YUSHIHPI (玉 食 批)
> *probably Sung dynasty (960–1279)*

The refinement is excessive, bordering upon decadence. Note the eating of parts—kidneys, pig's knuckle, brains; the use of the texture-food, fish maw. The use of crab *legs*, not the most meaty but the most delicate of crab meat, restores to venison its sweet taste (*hsien*). In modern Chekiang-Kiangsu cooking, crab is used for the same purpose. Modern cuisine is built upon extracting from each ingredient its best quality, while all other qualities may be altered at the cook's will.

Savages eat all parts of animals too, but only civilized man will write about it or *choose* to eat parts. Gastronomy is a matter of words and taste as well as food. There is a difference between the savage gnawing at a bone, and the civilized eating of tiny parts. "To gnaw on bones" (*keng kutou*) denotes not hunger but sophistication, rather like the chewing of words in a few lines of a poem. The almost illiterate mull over words as if they were great curiosities, but so do the most literate. So it is with food. To the trained palate the flavour of food comes in bits and pieces, like words in a sentence. The flavour of food should not be apparent immediately but come to you in a matter of moments. The enjoyment of food requires time.

There arose the tradition of eating as a pastime. The olives, nuts and other sweetmeats we savoured were sampled to make the afternoons go. A dish of watermelon seeds meant an afternoon well spent (or perhaps lost?). "I chew at the thing all day, trying to get at the morsels around the joints," wrote Su Tungpo (1036–1101). When he was exiled to South China, he took only the spine of the lamb slaughtered every day, not wishing to compete with the rich families for the choicer parts. "I boil it in wine and sprinkle a little salt over it before grilling it. You have eaten food cooked by official cooks for the last three years, and I do not think you [his brother] have ever touched a bone. Do you think you can still enjoy this kind of flavour? I am delighted with it. It is like picking the meat from crabs' claws."

In the eleventh century, gastronomy was already the business of artists, scholars, purists, vulgarians and snobs, and even the kitchen servants tried to be gourmets. "Alas! the earth's gifts are balanced by the sorrows of this world. It is not only the rich who throw food away. Only the cheeks of the lamb head are used, and only the jowls of the fish, only the legs of the crab, and for wonton only its claws. The rest is discarded with the comment that it is not fit for the rich man's table. If someone picks up the food he is called a dog." (Yushihpi)

Haute cuisine had undergone a profound change, but the daily food remained somewhat like ancient cooking. The cuisine accumulated but never discarded, so that at the present time it resembles an old house full of things new to some but quite well remembered by others. Nothing is startling, nothing is surprising. We have accumulated all the knowledge of those who have gone before, and put it to use. We are reminded of this by an old cookbook, probably dated Sung (10th–13th centuries), written by a Madame Wu. This may be the earliest Chinese cookbook giving proportions in the recipes.

NOTES FROM MADAME WU'S COOKBOOK

Grilled Fish: Clean fresh fish and grill them over ashes until dry, then store them. Or remove the head and tails and grill them, dripping oil over them. Pack them in an earthenware jar and seal them with mud.

Preserved Meat: Slice freshly roasted pork or lamb and pound each slice two or three times with the back of the knife. Cut it into smaller pieces and drop them into boiling water. Immediately fish them out and dry the meat well with a towel. For each pound use 1 dish of good vinegar, 4 mace salt, pepper, oil and finely pounded cardamom. Also may be used for sacrifices.

How to Preserve Meat in Summer: Rub pan-dried salt into the meat. Place it in the bottom of a crock, weight it with a large stone, and leave it overnight. Hang it up to dry in a cool airy place and it will not spoil.

Pressed Knuckles and Head: Cook a pig's head and knuckles until very soft, bone them and wrap them in a clean cloth, and weight the parcel with a large stone. The moisture will run out overnight. The residue is very tasty.

Pickled Prawns (Shrimps): Do not wash the prawns. Use large prawns. Trim off the tail and feelers. For each pound use 5 mace salt and let them stand for half a day. Drain them and place them in an earthenware jar and on top of each layer place 30 grains wild pepper to make the flavour interesting. Then add 3 oz. salt for each pound, dissolved in good wine, and pour it over the prawns. Seal the jar with mud. In spring and autumn it will become tasty in 5 to 7 days. In winter it takes 10 days.

Shortbread: Mix 4 oz. butter, 1 to 2 oz. honey and 1 lb. flour. Make these into cakes and bake them on top of the stove.

Miscellaneous: If wine turns sour, place a little bag of charred peas within the jar.

Rub a drop or two of oil into the fish while washing it. The fish will not spatter when you cook it, and does not have an unpleasant smell.

When cooking various preserved meats, cover the pot closely and add one or two mulberry stones, which make the meat tender and fragrant.

In the summer, meat cooked with only vinegar will keep for 10 days.

The Chinese cuisine in its sprawling diversity had come into its own by the tenth or eleventh century, composed of the exquisite delicacy and artifices of the luxurious cuisine, the homely simple food of the peasants, the sophisticated texture-foods, the appreciation of parts, and the idea of eating for amusement. All subsequent periods did not affect it very much. Indeed, they had the effect of strengthening its characteristics. There developed a gastronomy consciously "Chinese" as opposed to Mongolian or Manchurian which grew and flourished during the periods of rule under these two foreign dynasties.

The Mongolians who founded the Yuan dynasty (1279–1356) came to China from the dusty and windy desert. They had lived in tents and dressed in furs, and their tastes were quite different, for they lived on milk, butter and lamb, an almost European diet. According to an extremely long and interesting cookbook of that dynasty, *Yinshan Chengyao* (飲 膳 正 要), written by the Imperial Physician, their cookery was not at all Chinese. They made a variety of jams from quince, peach and pomegranate and lemon, using refined white sugar. This is not known in Chinese cuisine. Foxglove yielded a distilled liquor; pine nuts, pine sap and aspen flavoured the wines, and they made rosewater, and almond oil. Butter was used extensively either in crude or clarified form. They drank clarified butter mixed with warm wine, and fried butter, tea and milk together. Another toddy was made from marrow pudding.

Mongolian Hot Toddy: To make marrow pudding, mix together 5 oz. turmeric [?] essence, 3 oz. foxglove essence, 1 oz. asparagus essence and 2 oz. ox marrow. Blend together with a silver spoon. Let it set. Dissolve a spoonful in warm wine. It fortifies the marrow, strengthens the muscles, builds up the blood and makes for long life.

The Mongolians also made wonton, but the dough was made from bean paste, not wheat flour. The filling was made with minced lamb and dried tangerine peel, the wonton served in lamb broth. This is similar to the lamb *chiaotse* of Peking, mentioned in recipe 54. The Mongolian cookbook emphasizes the totally different style of cooking which the Mongolians practised. It was semi-barbaric, and their delicacies appear extremely laboured.

Mongolian Meat Cakes: Stew lamb with beans. Strain it. Mince lamb very finely, with lamb heart, liver, lung, stomach, fresh ginger, cucumber pickle, 10 gourds, yams, cheese, 10 eggs. Fry the cakes with sesame paste. Season with salt, vinegar, onion.

Mongolian Chicken: Cook the following together in good stock: 10 chickens, 1 lamb stomach, 1 lamb lung, sliced ginger, 10 gourds, 20 eggs made into thin cakes and cut into flower pattern, gardenia seeds for yellow colouring, crushed coriander and almond paste. Season with onion and vinegar.

The refined Chinese cook of the thirteenth century would probably not accept this crude method of cooking whole lamb (compare with the American clambake). "Dig a pit 3 feet deep, line it with stones, and heat stones till red hot. Place a whole unskinned lamb in pit on iron rack with fragrant leaves, cover with willow branches and seal with mud."

The development of Chinese gastronomy went on uninterrupted by the presence of these Mongols, who despite their military power and vitality were never able to alter Chinese taste. The great stream of Chinese gastronomy surged about, seeking out hidden pockets where it had not yet penetrated. These side-streams met to form branches of the river. There was a mingling of different sources, all taking their energy from the great stream. They produced turbulence where they met, and the energy from these eddies pushed forward the flow of the great stream.

For example, the rich man came to eat the poorest peasants' food. This meant simply that the rich man would occasionally have meals identical to those of the peasant. It was delicious, and it provided more variety. Pickles and peanuts, fermented bean curd and congee, and little fried fish with soy sauce, were served with no excuses. Thus the rich had the best of all worlds. Rustic simplicity is most enjoyed by aristocrats, and opulence appreciated most by the poor. Today the most important officials still beg to be excused from the sumptuous banquets to have "a little meal at home" of gruel and bean curd. This has a twofold meaning. First of all, they really cannot stand the endless sequence of courses at the feasts, and secondly, they achieve a little touch of elegance by wanting to get away from it all. Herein lies the dual nature of Chinese taste.

Men's hearts love gold and jade;
Men's mouths covet wine and flesh.
Not so the old man of the stream;
He drinks from his gourd and asks nothing more.
South of the stream he cuts firewood and grass;
North of the stream he has built wall and roof.
Yearly he sows a single acre of land;
In spring he drives two yellow calves.
In these things he finds great repose;
Beyond these he has no wish or care.
By chance I met him walking by the water side;
He took me home and lodged me in his thatched hut.
When I parted from him, to seek market and Court,
This old man asked my rank and pay.
Doubting my tale, he laughed loud and long:
"Privy Councillors do not sleep in barns."

PO CHU-I (A.D. 820)

Is it surprising that the symbols of rustic life were celebrated in art and poetry, when society was complex, and a man was burdened by the glories and weights of name and obligation and position? When gastronomy became an interest of artists and scholars they emphasized those elements suggesting the simple life. In some, this was a little overdone.

Li Liweng ("The Fisherman", 1611–1676) was an exponent of rustic elegance in cooking. His taste ran to those objects associated in art with the recluse, the scholar. "The voice is superior to the flute, and better than the stringed instrument, for it comes closer to nature." He liked bland but exotic things. He professed to shun garlic, onion and chives for juniper berries. Not many people have tasted juniper berries. They suggest eccentric refinement, whereas the garlic and onion exude heavy, lingering, common odours. He never used garlic, never used onion, and cooked with only the tips of chives, not their stalks, which are more scented.

"Guests should be served something special. I often suggest to the little woman that she gather the dew which collects on flowers. When the rice is just cooked, pour a little of the dew on it, and let it stand, covered, for a while. The guests thought that I had served some special grain, but it was only ordinary rice. I kept this a secret for a long time. The dew on wild roses, cassia and citron flowers is best, as these fragrances are not easily distinguished from that of rice. The dew collected from garden roses is too easily identified."

Ancient Cuisine | 41

Li's comments on food are interesting because of the omissions. He scrupulously avoided all objects gross and common, preferring those associated with the gentleman scholar—bamboo, crab, mushroom and fish steamed in a pewter vessel. He was very particular about the cooking of congee and rice, the former much used by the poorest people. In a way, this enhanced the impression of rare sophistication. There may have been something of the *poseur* in Li.

It is true that one is reminded of a charming setting when eating bamboo, and thinks of a grove, green, isolated and calm.

PLANTING BAMBOOS

Unrewarded, my will to serve the State;
At my closed door autumn grasses grow.
What could I do to ease a rustic heart?—
I planted bamboos, more than a hundred shoots.
When I see their beauty, as they grow by the
  stream-side,
I feel again as though I lived in the hills.
And many a time on public holidays
Round their railing I walk till night comes.
Do not say that their roots are still weak,
Do not say that their shade is still small;
Already I feel that both in garden and house
Day by day a fresher air moves.
But most I love, lying near the window-side,
To hear in their branches the sound of the
  autumn wind.

PO CHU-I

Nor can one taste the mushroom without appreciating those out-of-the-way corners where they silently grow. The poetic connotations are real, and account for a good deal of their importance in the cuisine. "I would rather forgo meat than bamboo. Without meat one grows thin, without bamboo one becomes common. There is a cure for leanness but none for vulgarity," wrote Su Tungpo.

Of the "vulgarity" we have some idea. It is not so much vulgarity as lack of control, a desire for all the best all together. "I once went to a merchant's house," wrote the great gourmet Yuan Mei (1716-1799). "There were three separate tables, sixteen kinds of pastries and a total of forty-odd dishes. The host was very pleased with himself. When I returned home I cooked congee to ease my hunger." The common taste was for opulence, display, variety, exotic and expensive ingredients. A host would urge his chef to make the most expensive, most novel dish to serve his guests. The scope of Chinese gastronomy was expanded by these climbers and snobs who had little taste, but an interest in gastronomy, the sign of culture. This is another example of how the arts are supported by common rich men. The absurdities of the cuisine developed in an atmosphere of great culture and wealth.

Yuan Mei lived in the Ching dynasty. The ruling house was Manchu, not Chinese. It was the period of polychrome vases, ornately carved screens and cold, marble-inlaid chairs. The food equivalent of this style was produced in the kitchens. The cuisine of that time reflected very precisely the mixed intricate and opulent tastes of the period. "Nowadays, at the start of a feast, the menu is about a hundred feet long and there are many dishes and bowls on the table. This is merely display, not gastronomy. Official circles favour the 16-8-4 [probably 16 hors d'oeuvre, 8 entrées, 4 important dishes] or the Great Chinese Banquet, the Eight Little Dishes or Ten Great Specialities, and other vulgarities. Foul practices and bad cooking are only fit for marking the arrival of a relative or an official."

The Great Chinese Banquet was recently repeated in Hong Kong. In the eighteenth century it was already considered showy and vulgar, since this banquet was really a series of feasts lasting about two days.

THE GREAT CHINESE BANQUET

Bird's Nest Soup
  Slices of Unicorn
    Cassia Flowers on a Moonlit Boat
      Roast Whole Suckling Pig
        Deer Heart Garnished with Plums
          Lady's Grace

Fish Maw with Six Spices
  Deer Tail with Clams and Duck
    Dragon Liver and Phoenix Marrow (chicken liver and
        brains)
      Chicken Testicles
        Whole Squabs, Garnished
          Seal
            Clam Cakes

Felicitous Harmony (assorted hors d'oeuvre)
Bear's Paw and Partridge
Imperfect Pearls
Squab As You Like It
Sparrow's Tongues
Whole Roasted Raccoon
Honours and Rewards

Phoenix Bursting through the Clouds (cold plate)
Delicacies from Sung River
Jade on a Blue Field
Sautéed Shark's Fins
A Pair of Nanking Ducks
Sparrows and Pine Nuts
Deep-Fried Lobster Balls
Frogs

etc.

The world of gastronomy was created by the vulgar and the rich, as well as the clever cooks and persons of good taste. Adventures lie not only in the exploration of the beautiful places, but also in the raucous streets where people mill about, some casting looks around to see if others approve of them. The flavour of the cuisine was also to be found in its faults and excesses. Eating is the pursuit of flavour, and the real connoisseur can relish even bad taste in food, for bad food often has a history or a genealogy to it. One has only contempt for those persons of shallow knowledge who know only the names of good wines and elegant dishes. Good taste should be the result of personal selection, and one really cannot make a choice without a certain amount of general knowledge. Therefore it is quite important to taste everything. If a person remembers the taste of everything he has ever eaten, he may eventually become a gourmet. This quality is fundamental, for a person's awareness results first in judgment, then in choice, then in taste.

The taste of Yuan Mei was distinguished by clarity of flavour and presentation. Against the background of opulence he simplified the dishes. "I see a dish before I taste it, whether it be as clear as autumn skies or cloudy as amber. Its fragrance reaches my nostrils, but only my palate can appreciate the subtleties. Odours can be simulated, and looks are not so important. What matters is the unique taste of each thing." His taste so guided the conduct of his cuisine that the recipes are almost classics. His prawns, beef and pork each tasted of their own flavour.

"Do not fuss with the natural state of the food just to show that you are a clever cook. Bird's nest is beautiful—why shape it into balls? Bêche-de-mer should not be made into a jelly or paste. Li Liweng's magnolia pudding was created by artifice." He resented the corruption of Chinese food by Manchu cooks. "Manchu cooking is composed mainly of stews and roasts, and Chinese cooking consists of broths and soups. When Manchus invited Chinese or vice versa, we each served what we did best, so we did not imitate each other and lose our originality. Now people have forgotten this and try to toady to each other. Manchus serve Chinese dinners and Chinese serve Manchu food. If you sketch according to instruction, the drawing may have a name but does not come alive. A badly drawn tiger may look like a species of dog."

His own collection of recipes was original, often humorous and elegant.

Turtle on the Half Shell (Recipe of Lieut.-Col. Yang, Shantung): Remove the head and tail. Braise the meat with seasonings and cover it with its shell. Place one before each guest. How they will fear that it will get up on its legs and walk away! I thought this recipe worth passing on.

In the tradition of Chinese gourmets, he loved to munch and chew on odd bits. These were sometimes obtained at great expense.

Criss Cross Pork: Make this only from pigs raised at home. After slaughtering the pig, boil it until it is 80 per cent cooked. Turn off the heat and let it stand in the water for a while. Then remove the pork and slice those parts of the pig which moved the most (joints of neck, shoulder, leg, knee and foot). Slice them very thinly. When you serve it, the pork should be just lukewarm, neither hot nor cold. Poor scholars would rather invite guests to eat bird's nest than this dish of pork, for it must be served in quantity. It should be cut with a small sharp knife so that the fat, lean, soft and cartilaginous, and the chewy make a mosaic, each running criss cross to the other. Confucius did not eat meat unless it was cut straight. He would not have liked this.

He had a great curiosity about food, and collected recipes from his acquaintances. "In the twenty-third year of Chien-lung, Mr. Chin and I were in Kwangtung. We dined on fried bean curd with Mr. Cheng at his house. On either side, the cake was golden and smooth. The sauce tasted of snails, but not a snail was to be seen. On the following day I questioned Mr. Cheng, and he said, 'Oh, I can make it. I used chicken and sparrow brains instead of bean curd, which cost ten times as much and did not taste so good. Unfortunately, my sister died at that time and I had to return, and did not ask Cheng for the recipe. The following year Cheng died. To this day I regret it. I am waiting till I meet him again."

By the eighteenth century Chinese gastronomy had already developed its glories and its pitfalls, had encompassed the tastes of the food snob, the gourmet, the peasant and the artist. It is very much like that now. Nothing old had been discarded or forgotten. It was an unusual curiosity which led the Chinese to search everywhere and try all combinations in search of new tastes. Cooks and gourmets pursuing their vocations went far and deep. Some of them appeared to forget what they were looking for and got lost. One suspects they may have enjoyed the strange places in which they were left stranded. Others had technical skills, created new flavours or synthesized new textures. Yet others examined the sea and the woods and occasionally found minuscule edible fungi, or a novel part of a fish which was declared edible. Local produce, the personal quirks of some cooks, and the temper of Northerners and Southerners, the people living inland or by the sea, were all reflected in the gastronomy of China. The result is such a vast body of skills and styles in food that it encompasses major variations on certain basic themes, even contradictions in technique from region to region. It is composed of flavours that speak out loudly, but also contains dishes that are silent, subtle contests in flavour; or puzzles for gourmets.

From the Chinese point of view, the enjoyment of food is a facet of the art of living. The gourmet has practised his vocation almost everywhere. These are the scenes through which he moved: the hills and fields, terraced and green, at the side of which stood a shabby farmhouse where a simple meal was being prepared; craggy mountains marked by a steep path, beside which sedan chair-bearers paused, drinking strong bitter tea; a charming courtyard, in which a scholar was ladling rain water for tea; countrywomen at New Year's time, shaping glutinous rice balls between their palms; the crab feasts by moonlight; the temples and the monks and vegetarian food, and the mingled essences of the teeming streets. These were the scenes of life itself, in which eating was one of the more dependable pleasures.

2. Flavour

Nowadays, common cooks will put chickens, geese, ducks and pork all in one pot, so that all taste the same. I am afraid that their ghosts must be filing their complaints in the city of the dead.

YUAN MEI

COOKING IS the art of capturing flavours. But we must decide which flavours. Classic cuisine is always distinguished by the use of natural ingredients which leave an aftertaste. Lower orders of cooking rely much more on seasoning, while the cheapest kind of cooking is just a mixture of seasonings. A true flavour can be savoured and mulled over. Because it is composed of natural ingredients, whose make-up is too complex to re-create, all we can do is learn how to handle it. Counterfeit flavours are mixtures of seasoning. A mixture of six seasonings has so many tastes, no more. It arrives suddenly, shows its origins too clearly, and leaves abruptly. One cannot praise these superficial and transient flavours, though they appear so often.

This chapter is divided into three parts. First, we will discuss the plain flavours of rice, chicken, beef, pork, fish and bamboo, giving for each a recipe in which some problems arising in the cooking of the substance are overcome. We have carefully chosen the recipe which, to us, represents the best flavour of the substance.

Second, we discuss a uniquely Chinese technique, the blending of complementary flavours, with four illustrative recipes.

Third, we discuss the created flavours—an expensive stock made from three kinds of meat and two cheap sauces for noodles. The stock makes use of the deep flavour of natural ingredients, which is extracted by the cook and can be savoured slowly. The two amusing sauces, used in low-grade restaurants of the "quick lunch" variety, or at stalls, show what can be done with only seasonings.

PLAIN FLAVOURS

滋
味

The Flavour of Rice: Boiled Rice; Chicken Congee

The true flavours are the ones which cannot be counterfeited. No cook has ever been foolish enough to re-create the flavour of rice. For this reason, if anyone ever doubts the real flavour of things, let him eat plain rice. "A gourmet will eat plain rice and not ask for other food."

Rice has its *hsien* (sweet natural taste). The *hsien* is concealed in the grains, and meted out bit by bit in the aftertaste. The dual nature of the taste of rice (immediate and aftertaste) is what makes it impossible to duplicate. It is also difficult to describe; one can only call attention to it. Yuan Mei spoke of the "juices" of rice. These can be tasted if one chews plain, well-cooked rice. Water dilutes the "juices", soaking removes them; thus, in the cooking of rice no excess water can be tolerated.

The essences of rice are in the cooking water. If the rice is lacking in flavour, it is because the water has not been measured out correctly. Add so much rice to so much water, as the doctor brews medicine. Measure out the water to the exact spoonful. You would not think it would make so much difference.

LI LIWENG

*1. Boiled Rice (白 飯)

Use exactly equal volumes of rice and water (2 cups rice plus 2 cups water = about 6 cups rice, cooked). Wash the rice and rake it with the fingers. Rinse it well and drain thoroughly. Add measured amount of water. Place it in a pot with a close-fitting lid. Bring it to the boil over high heat, and immediately stir once to loosen the grains from the bottom. Replace the lid, reduce the heat to very low, and do not open the pot again for 15 to 20 minutes, until all the water is absorbed. Each grain must be separate, white and tender.

The fine lines of gastronomy are never so clearly drawn as in the cooking of rice, and congee, a rice gruel. Congee is made with short-grain river rice, while boiled rice is made with long-grain rice. Congee must be slightly glutinous, rice grainy. In congee "rice and water should be interlocked, as if it were one soft, rich mixture". The *hsien* should be distributed throughout the gruel. There is little distinction between the solid and liquid portions of congee. "Congee which is all water is not right, nor should it appear all rice." "Congee should never be pasty, nor should clear water overlie the grains beneath."

Country people love to eat rice, and the rich love congee. Doctors recommend it to convalescents as it is very digestible. Women on diets eat it because it is quite filling but has little substance. Scholars in particular like to talk about it. It has rustic connotations. Congee and pickled vegetables belong in the little hut in the mountains of the landscape painting, all in keeping with the air of sophisticated withdrawal from society. A sixteenth-century artist (Kao Lien) said, "Make a soft rice and finish it in chicken, meat or prawn (shrimp) broth. Add diced cooked meat, chopped very finely, and bamboo, mushrooms or pine nuts, cut very finely. At the last moment, stir in pickled vegetables." Note the use of bamboo, mushrooms and pine nuts, favourite subjects of painters. One suspects that it was due in some part to affected simplicity as well as gastronomy that plain food found its way to the rich man's table.

*2. Chicken Congee (鸡 粥)

4 oz. (½ cup) river rice	1 chicken breast
Scant 2½ pints (6 cups) chicken stock	¼ level teaspoon salt
	2 tablespoons water

Wash river rice. Bring it to the boil in chicken stock; then reduce heat to very low and simmer for 2 hours.

Meanwhile, skin and bone the chicken breast and slice it with the grain. Flatten the slices with a few whacks of the side of the cleaver. Add salt and water.

When the congee is ready to serve, turn off the heat. Stir the chicken slices, then stir them into the congee and let it stand for 3 to 4 minutes. Serve in bowls.

Water may be substituted for chicken stock to make plain congee. The Cantonese embed sliced preserved eggs in congee, or stir slices of fresh fish into it. The heat of the gruel is sufficient to cook thin slices of chicken or fish. A little congee liquid may be added to sautéed vegetables to improve their flavour.

Quite apart from the artistic connotations of congee its popularity is really physiological. Anyone who has had to sit through three or four banquets in succession knows that the exalted appreciation of fine food can be traded for animal comfort. Lavish banquets satisfy the eyes, nose and palate, but starve the rest of the system. For the sake of the stomach and intestines eat congee.

The Best Flavour of Chicken:
Plain Chicken, with three sauces: Sesame Soy Sauce;
Oyster Sauce; Fresh Ginger Sauce

Cooking chicken is such a delicate operation that it requires a great deal of thought. At its best, the *hsien* (sweet flavour) is tasted not only in the skin, but also in the meat and marrow. The fat should be fragrant but firm, the meat tender and juicy, the bones succulent. This stage comes at a precise point between the inedible, metallic taste of raw chicken and fibrous dryness. How does one capture it? In the following recipe, these measures are taken:

Seal the skin to keep the juices in. The Cantonese method outlined below requires plunging the chicken into boiling stock, to firm the skin instantaneously.

Poach but never boil chicken. The white meat of chicken is easily overcooked. It becomes fibrous when the meat shrinks, contracts and separates from the juices. This must not be allowed to happen. Keep the heat of the chicken below boiling point at all times. The chicken which has been plunged into boiling stock is allowed to cool down to room temperature while immersed in the stock. *During the slow cooling down of the stock, the chicken becomes cooked.*

Time precisely. Since the chicken is cooked by the heat of the surrounding liquid only, the volume of liquid should be exactly such that, when both reach room temperature, the meat is just tender, but the marrow still a little raw. One prolongs cooking time by increasing the volume of liquid. If larger chickens are used, increase the volume of stock.

Supporting ingredients. Ginger and spring onions (scallions) are added to the liquid to suppress the rank flavours. These are essential ingredients. Chicken stock is preferable to water, as the latter dilutes the flavour. The chicken is served cold, chopped up, with any one of several sauces. If a thick-skinned, plump, tender chicken is prepared in this fashion, no sauce is really necessary.

*3. Plain Chicken (白 切 鷄)

2½ pints (6 cups) water
2½ pints (6 cups) canned chicken
   consommé
2 spring onions (scallions)

3 slices ginger or 1 level
   teaspoon ginger powder
One 3-lb. chicken, trussed
Oil

Bring water and chicken consommé to the boil with spring onions and ginger or ginger powder. Immerse the chicken breast side down, so that the thickest part is in the centre of the pot. Bring it quickly to the boil again and immediately cover the pot; turn off the heat and remove the pot from the heat. Let it cool, covered, to room temperature. This takes 5 to 6 hours, or it may be left overnight.

*   *   *

Remove the chicken from the pot, discard the string, and drain it well. Rub it lightly with oil. If possible, chill the chicken so that the juices set. Chop it up into small pieces. It is best to chop it just before serving, so that the juices stay in the meat.
    Serve the chicken cold, with one of the following sauces.

*4. Sesame Soy Sauce (醬 油 調 蔴 油)

5 tablespoons soy sauce
1 tablespoon sesame oil

½ level teaspoon MSG

Stir ingredients together and pour over the chopped chicken.

*5. Oyster Sauce (蠔 油 汁)

4 tablespoons oyster sauce
3 tablespoons chicken stock

2½ level teaspoons sugar

Stir until sugar is dissolved, and pour over chicken.

*6. Fresh Ginger Sauce (生 薑 汁)

2 level tablespoons chopped spring
   onions (scallions)
2 level tablespoons peeled and
   very finely slivered or minced
   fresh ginger

1 level teaspoon salt
4 tablespoons oil

Do not attempt this recipe unless the ginger is very young and tender and free of fibres.
    Place spring onions, ginger and salt in a heatproof 1-pint jug or Pyrex container. Heat oil almost to smoking point and pour it over the mixture in a thin stream. Stir the sauce and let it stand for at least 15 minutes. Spoon mixture over cold chopped chicken.

The Unmistakable Flavour of Beef: Beef Yuan Mei

While the best flavour of chicken lies in its fat, the best flavour of beef lies in the meat, particularly in the juices. For this reason, the flavour of beef is readily appreciated in rare steak or in stews. In rare meat the juices have not yet solidified, and in stews they are again liquefied. In the overdone steak or the underdone stew the juices are trapped in solids and the meat appears to have no flavour.

The two difficulties in cooking beef are blood and texture. Blood makes stews cloudy, forms scum, and is generally unpleasant to look at. One must suppress its rank and unpalatable taste, and somehow cope with its solids. The Cantonese make a rich, homely beef stew or soup with flank steak and onions (*ngao-nam ngao-yok tong*) which is frankly thick and cloudy with coagulated beef juices. The flavour is excellent, but the appearance untidy. In the following recipe, wine suppresses the rank taste of blood and also keeps the juices from coagulating in the broth. The proportion of alcohol in the mixture (about 12 per cent) probably effects this by preventing the blood from running out of most of the meat. In the course of cooking most of the alcohol evaporates, a supporting ingredient which removes itself after the job is done. The finished product does not taste of alcohol.

The problem of texture is met by choosing the proper cut of meat, and by the method of trimming it. The front legs of the steer are sinewy and less meaty than the hind legs. The meat on the hind legs is tender, but too lean for this type of recipe. Shin of beef (shank) is best. The bone, whitish membranes and solid fat must be trimmed off before stewing. This is essential to the final quality of the stew, which is perfectly clear, free of fat and has the colour of brandy. The flavour is unmistakably that of beef, *hsien* (sweet and natural) and *nung* (rich). It is quite unnecessary to add salt.

7. Beef Yuan Mei (清煨牛肉)

3 lb. boned shin (shank) of beef in   12 fluid oz. (1½ cups) pale dry
* one piece   sherry*

Carefully trim off all fat and membranes from the beef, so that it is homogeneous in texture except for the sinews running through it. Cut beef into large chunks. Stew it in a tightly covered pot with sherry made up to 1 pint (2½ cups) with water, for 3½ hours, or until very tender.

"Do not add other ingredients with the intention of enhancing flavour."

In Western cooking the two problems of blood and texture are neatly circumvented by serving tender cuts of beef almost raw. In rare steak blood forms part of the juices—raw, rank and barbaric to Chinese taste.

The Fragrance of Pork: Tungpo Pork

At one time the butcher shops of Soochow were variously called Genuine Straw Mat, Original Straw Mat, Old Straw Mat, etc., just because there is a story about an Immortal in disguise who flung a bit of mat into a pot of belly pork to give it a special fragrance. The fragrance is easy enough to produce. What is important is that it stands out in a clear field. Instead of being heavy, the pork should appear light; clean instead of messy; smooth instead of lumpy. The flavour of pork is effusive. While the cooking of chicken and beef means the careful carving out of its best flavour from the raw material, the flavours of pork must be restrained. At its best, pork is tender, sweet, fragrant, tasty, rich without being oily (in other words, *nun, hsien, hsiang, nung, yu-er-pu-ni*).

A geometrically precise square of belly pork is stewed and then steamed in a little sauce, so that it is served with an absolutely clear layer of melted fat overlying a smooth brown sauce. The surface is a rich brown colour, the fat smooth and custard-like, the meat brown and tender. The square of fat was named after Su Tungpo, the poet, for unknown reasons. Perhaps it is just because he would have liked it. The square of fat is regarded with much passion, tenderness and expectation. Second-rate versions of it appear everywhere, differing from the following version by their failure to clear the field for the delicacy of the pork fat which, if prepared accordingly, tastes fresh and clean like fresh (sweet) butter. In order to keep the flavour clear, the meat is first salted to remove the bloody juices, blanched to remove the scum, then stewed very slowly, and finally steamed for hours to tenderize the fat slowly. Inferior versions of this are made by stewing pork for a few hours without steaming it (Belly Pork in Brown Stock Sauce, 78). The result is lumpy fat. If the salt rub and blanching are omitted the juice becomes messy and lumpy. The simplicity of appearance, smoothness and clarity of flavour have to be wrested from the manifold flavours of pork.

Tungpo Pork is customarily served at the end of a meal with

bowls of rice. People sigh, shout and groan with happiness when they see it. This is one of the pinnacles of gastronomy, and sums up the appreciation of fat in Chinese cuisine.

8. Tungpo Pork (東 坡 肉)

1¼ lb. belly pork in one piece　　*1 tablespoon wine*
2 level tablespoons salt　　*2 spring onions (scallions)*
2 tablespoons soy sauce　　*2 slices ginger*

Trim pork into a precise square. Wash it and wipe it dry with a towel. Rub it with salt and let it stand for about 2 hours. Discard the blood-tinged liquid.

Bring 5 pints (12 cups) water to the boil and blanch the meat in it. Rinse it free of scum and repeat the blanching with a fresh portion of boiling water. Place the pork skin side up in a pot with a tight-fitting lid, adding soy sauce, wine, spring onions, ginger and 2 tablespoons water. Bring to the boil, then reduce the heat to very low and simmer for 2 hours, adding a little more water if necessary. Keep the amount of liquid as small as possible, and do not keep uncovering the pot to see how the pork is progressing. Let it stew in its own juices.

Discard the spring onions and ginger. Place the square skin side down on a dish of soup plate dimensions; add the juices and cover it very closely with foil, cellophane or an overlapping plate. Steam it for 4 hours, until the fat is tender and can be cut with a spoon. Invert the square so that the fat is uppermost, and pour the juices around it carefully.

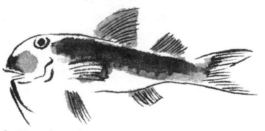

Trapping the Flavour of Fish: Fish Head in Casserole

Of all parts of the fish, the brain and the skin are tastiest. This is because they contain the most fat. The pursuit of the flavour of fish developed into the cooking of only fish heads, the large brainy heads of bream and mullet (fresh-water fish) being particularly suited to this practice. The taste of *bouillabaisse* in large part comes from the absurd, big-headed Mediterranean fish. In preparing fish head, observe the following rules.

Use freshly killed fish. The Romans made sure that the fish were freshly killed by having it done before their eyes. When the fish grew plump in the Yellow River, it was the custom to visit the riverside restaurants, and have it brought to the table live and wriggling, to be stunned and brought straight to the kitchen. This point cannot be over-emphasized.

Do not overcook fish. The freshest fish loses its sweetness if overcooked by even a few minutes.

Boil the fish head rapidly with stock to extract oils. They are volatile, easily destroyed. The oils will fuse with the stock if vigorously boiled together. The flavour of the fish will then be trapped with the stock. The same method is used to extract oil from marrow bones (Cream Stock, 16). Instead of floating as a separate layer on top, the oil becomes incorporated into the soup in the form of fine droplets. In the following recipe the flavours are collected by the addition of bean curd, so that they can be chewed.

The fish head is customarily cooked in a *shakuo*, a covered casserole.

9. *Fish Head in Casserole* (砂 鍋 魚 頭)

One 1½-lb. fish head	¼ level teaspoon salt
1 spring onion (scallion)	½ level teaspoon sugar
2 slices ginger	A few grains of wild pepper or
¼ teaspoon vinegar	peppercorns
1 tablespoon light soy sauce	6 oz. or 1½ cakes bean curd, cubed
¾ pint (1¾ cups) stock	(1 cup cubed)
¼ pint (½ cup) wine	¼ level teaspoon black pepper

Remove the gills from the fish head and scrub it free of blood. Place it in a flameproof casserole and add the spring onion, ginger, vinegar, soy sauce, stock, wine, salt, sugar and a few grains of wild pepper or peppercorns. Bring it quickly to the boil and keep it boiling for about 15 minutes. Add bean curd cubes and simmer for 5 to 10 minutes longer. Add black pepper just before serving.

When guests are late, other delicacies may wait, but the fish should be kept alive, and killed only after the guests have arrived. In the short while that it takes to kill and cook the fish, the fish is at its best. If it is cooked first, then its best "fish flavour" is gone, swimming about in the air with no one to appreciate it.   LI LIWENG

When I went to East Kwangtung, I tasted the eel soup at Mr. Yang's. It was delicious. I learned that the reason was simply this. It was freshly killed, freshly cooked, served immediately and tasted at once, all without delay.   YUAN MEI

The gastronome is perhaps a kind of fool, getting excited about things of no importance. Why not just eat and be done with it? Life would be so simple if we tasted nothing. But this is impossible. Tastes good and bad are long-drawn-out things, like sights and sounds. How can one taste vegetables and not find them sweet, bland, acerbic, thin or acrid? Simply cooked vegetables come only as a relief, like a drink of water. But, as someone said, there are twenty kinds of water.

Sights and sounds have depth, and so should taste. It is not enough to eat sweets as children do, to be swallowed and forgotten. The palate likes convoluted tastes, one leading to another in unexpected paths. In short, the flavour should be *nung*, rich. This does not usually exist in nature (though ripe bananas are *nung*) and the natural taste must be rounded out by supporting seasoning to give it the necessary depth of flavour. The object of the seasoning is not to mask the natural taste, but to enhance it. The flavour should be very distinct, not necessarily simple.

The method described below is the "dry sauté", which may be applied to vegetables, fish, mushrooms and meat. The seasoning is dissolved in liquid, and during the sautéeing the water is evaporated away. Having nowhere to go as the water evaporates, the seasoning enters the bamboo. This is a trick for putting seasoning in ingredients without being obvious about it. The dish is served without sauce.

*10. Sautéed Bamboo Shoots (乾 炒 冬 笋)

12 oz. bamboo shoots, slivered
  (3 cups slivers)
2 tablespoons oil
1½ teaspoons light soy sauce
5 tablespoons stock

½ level teaspoon salt
2 tablespoons wine
½ level teaspoon MSG
½ level teaspoon sugar

Sauté slivered bamboo in oil and soy sauce until all the liquid has evaporated. Meanwhile, mix together the remaining ingredients and stir until dissolved. Add to the bamboo and sauté until all the liquid has evaporated; then reduce the heat to low, cover the pan, and after 2 or 3 minutes serve it, stirring once or twice.

COMPLEMENTARY FLAVOURS

The principle of complementary flavours is a fundamental one, very difficult to put into practice or to innovate upon. Too many encounters with bad cooking may give one the impression that in Chinese cooking all ingredients may be mixed indiscriminately. They sometimes are, but the resulting confusion was not meant to be. The matching of flavours follows a set pattern and is formal, not casual, though people differ on how flavours should be matched. Cantonese cooks like to mix contrasting colours and unrelated textures. Their dishes are rather garish according to Peking taste, which prefers the matching of like to like. Some wish the flavour of each ingredient to be preserved, but the *pièce de résistance* of Amoy cooking (*Popia*, 81) depends on the fusion of flavours. Often the contrasts are very subtle, but they are perfectly definite. In other cases the contrasts are sharp. The bitter is matched with the sweet, the bland with the piquant, the acrid with the unctuous. The putting together of the different flavours (*tiaowei*) is itself an art. It is rather like creating chords in music, harmony through precise differences.

Mixed Sautés: Sautéed Pork; Bamboo with Pickled Mustard Green

The one form which is common to all of the regional cuisines is the mixed sauté. This is a standard form, readily adaptable to a number of common ingredients. In order to achieve complementarity of flavours, each ingredient should taste of itself, but be so blended with the other ingredients that all flavours are tasted simultaneously. Consider also the following points.

Cutting of ingredients is important for achieving the proper effect. Slices are matched with slices, slivers with slivers, dice with dice, chunks with chunks. This makes the dish easy to eat (*shuang-kou*).

Quantities of each ingredient are balanced. Generally, about equal volumes of all ingredients are used.

Heat during sautéeing. There are two ways of sautéeing meat, over high or moderately low heat. With *high heat*, the meat is seared and juices sealed in. The meat is more tender and tasty, but the other ingredients do not taste as good. If meat is sautéed over *moderately low heat*, the juices tend to run out, and are taken up by the other ingredients. The flavour of the dish as a whole is much better, but the meat tends to become a little tough.

Texture. This depends on cutting, heat and the addition or omission of cornflour (cornstarch). Always remember to trim meat free of sinews, membranes, etc., slice pork and chicken *with* the grain, beef *against* the grain. Dusting of meat with cornflour keeps it juicy, but prevents juices from entering other ingredients. Marbled meat is more tender than very lean meat, well-hung meat better than freshly butchered meat.

*11. Sautéed Pork (炒 豬 肉 絲)

1 lb. pork	1 teaspoon soy sauce
Choice of vegetables (see method)	½ level teaspoon sugar
3 tablespoons oil	½ level teaspoon salt
1 teaspoon vinegar	

Trim the pork and sliver it with the grain. Sliver one or two of the following vegetables to make an equal volume of vegetable: bamboo, Spanish (yellow) onion, celery, mushrooms, pickled vegetables, chives, asparagus.

Heat oil in a wo. Add the pork and sauté until blanched. Sprinkle with vinegar and let it evaporate. Add soy sauce and sugar, and sauté for a few minutes longer. Finally, add the vegetables, sprinkling them with salt, and continue to cook, mixing constantly with a scooping motion, so that the ingredients are pushed up the sides of the wo and fall down again to the centre. The cooking time varies according to the size of the pork slivers and the tenderness of the vegetables.

This is a classic combination of simple country flavours.

*12. Bamboo with Pickled Mustard Green (鹹 菜 炒 笋)

About 9 oz. pickled mustard green or Plain Pickled Vegetables (117), chopped	7 teaspoons oil
	½ level teaspoon sugar
	¼ level teaspoon MSG
About 6 oz. bamboo shoots, chopped	3 tablespoons stock

Sauté vegetables in a wo together with the remaining ingredients until the stock is all absorbed. Reduce the heat to very low, cover the wo and allow the flavours to blend for about 5 minutes, stirring once or twice. This may be kept warm over low heat without loss of flavour.

Strange Bedfellows: Carp in Lamb Broth;
Fried Prawns (Shrimps) and Turnips

We elucidate the common principle by exaggeration. The flavour of lamb is very sweet, though rank. The rankness is suppressed by cooking with wine. Carp is the richest and meatiest of all fish, and requires the support of a meat broth. The fish and lamb broth are eaten together, with a spoon. Each tastes of itself, but at the point where they meet there is no difference. The effect is very complex, novel and amusing. The emasculated delicacy of this recipe is typical of Soochow gastronomy, discussed at length in Chapter 4. The word *hsien* (sweet, 鮮) is composed of the fish (魚) and the lamb (羊). They have met.

13. Carp in Lamb Broth (羊 肉 湯 川 鯉 魚)

LAMB BROTH
2 lb. stewing lamb (about 1 lb. meat
　and 1 lb. bone)
½ lb. (white) onions
1 pint (2½ cups) water
¼ pint (½ cup) pale dry sherry
1 teaspoon light soy sauce
¾ level teaspoon salt
½ level teaspoon sugar

CARP
One 3-lb. carp
5 pints (12 cups) water
2 teaspoons vinegar

To prepare the lamb broth: Simmer all the ingredients together for 3 hours. Discard the solids and let the liquid cool. When set (jelled), remove the solid white fat on top and make the volume up to about 12 fluid oz. (1½ cups) with water. Reserve.

To prepare the carp: Carefully remove all the blood and rinse the fish very well. Cut off the head and tail, using the middle section only (about 1½ lb.). Wrap the section in cheesecloth. Bring water to boiling point and add vinegar. Lower the carp into the liquid and keep it at just below boiling point. Poach the fish for about 12 minutes, turning it once. Let it cool, then separate it into two or more pieces, removing the spinal bone.

Bring lamb broth to boiling point. Place the pieces of carp in it, heat through and serve at once.

The matching of flavours goes beyond the contrast of the sweet with the sour, or some other obvious combination. At its best, the putting together of ingredients becomes a composition. Flavours have weight, and the compositions must be balanced. Most people think that in the following recipe there are only two main ingredients, prawns (shrimps) and turnips. Actually there are three, and the third one is salt. This is a balance of flavours poised on three points. As one bites into it, the sweet juices of prawn and turnip run together. Note that these flavours would fly off in different directions, were it not for the salt. "Of all savoury foods salt is the most important," says an old text. This is a very amusing combination for those who can taste. The prawns should be small and tender, with thin shells. The turnips must be young and juicy.

*14. and 15. Fried Prawns (Shrimps) and Turnips
(鹹 酥 蝦 拌 蘿 蔔)

MARINATED TURNIPS
1/4 lb. turnips
1 ice cube or 2 teaspoons iced water
1/2 teaspoon vinegar
1 level teaspoon sugar
1/4 level teaspoon salt

FRIED PRAWNS
1/2 lb. prawns
Fat for deep-frying
Salt

To prepare the turnips: Peel and slice them paper-thin with a cleaver or with strokes of the peeler. The slices must be so thin as to be pliable. Marinate them with the remaining ingredients for 2 hours, then squeeze them dry.

To prepare the prawns: Trim off the legs and feelers of the prawns and dry them individually. Fry them in deep fat until golden and drain well. Sprinkle the fried prawns liberally with salt while still hot.

Just before serving, mix the prawns lightly with the turnip slices.

Flavours do not support each other unless at one moment they seem to fuse together. The delicious point comes when the carp and lamb broth are tasted together, when the juices of pork and bamboo mix, or when the tongue momentarily mistakes the *hsien* of turnip for the *hsien* of prawn. Eating is a game, a kind of amusement for adults, and these are its most diverting moments. The idea of complementary flavours was only brought in to bring variety to the art of eating.

新
味

CREATED FLAVOURS

Making up flavours for things which have no taste has resulted in this particular group of recipes. Curiously, these have arisen from the very rich and the very poor. When you are very poor, you have nothing to cook with, no ingredients save seasoning. If you are very rich, your taste runs to the flavourless delicacies, and the cook must spend a day or two working up a stock to supply the missing part. In either case one is required to make something out of nothing.

A Rich and Subtle Flavour:
Cream Stock, including accessory recipes
for fish maw, bêche-de-mer, shark's fins, spinach
and cabbage in Cream Stock

The expensive solution to the problem is to make Cream Stock. The recipe is laborious but well worth the time. This versatile stock enriches a number of different ingredients, and is by far the smoothest and most subtle of soups ever tasted. It is satiny, the shine coming from minute droplets of fat. The flavour cannot be simulated. Extraneous seasoning is unnecessary, except for a little salt at the end of the operation. Some prefer it without salt, leaving in the single flaw to show up its near-perfection. A sip of the finished product tells the cook that it was worth all the effort. The procedure consists of the following steps.

Breaking of the bones. The essence of the soup is the marrow. Encased in bone, the flavour will never come out unless the bones are broken. Rib, thigh and drumstick bones are richest in marrow. Use the dull edge of a heavy cleaver to break the bones approximately every 2 inches.

Slashing the meat. This permits the juices of the meat and marrow to enter the stock. Slash meat through to the bone with the sharp edge of a light cleaver.

Removal of scum. Essential to the smoothness of the stock. After water is brought to boiling point, keep it at a gentle boil, and proceed to remove the scum which collects as foam.

Rinsing. The rinsing water is measured and reserved. The meat juices coagulate upon boiling and clog the meat, preventing other juices from coming into the stock. Rinsing and rubbing the meat in cold water unclogs it and releases those juices. This procedure permits a second portion of the juices to form and run out. Note that the flavour of pork comes out before all the others in the rinse water.

Simmering. The flavour of the soup comes from the meat juices, extracted by simmering. The meats are discarded without regret, as they are completely tasteless by this time.

Removal of floating fat. The richness of the soup comes from the suspended fat. The excess is removed as it floats to the top.

Rapid boiling. This is what gives the stock its creamy quality. The bones are boiled rapidly in order to extract the marrow and to form the emulsion of the sweet juices of the bones and the stock. The stock is not milky, but golden and rich and turbid, so that it is called the cream of everything that went into it. During the rapid boiling, water which has evaporated is replaced with the rinse water.

Finishing the stock. The few cups of stock are filtered through cheesecloth. The bones are re-extracted once only with a small portion of water to save what remains in the residue, and finally both portions are combined.

Use of stock. The stock sets upon cooling, and can be kept for a few days in the refrigerator. It is better to use it the day after its preparation, as the rich sweet taste gradually disappears.

16. Cream Stock (奶 湯)

1¼ lb. duck (quarter of a duck)	*¾ lb. pork fillet (tenderloin)*
One 4-lb. chicken	*3 spring onions (scallions)*
½ lb. pork rib bones	*4 slices ginger*

Separate all the joints of the duck and chicken, so that they will not stick up when boiled. Break wing, leg and drumstick bones. Break rib bones of the pork. Slash the meat around these bones to expose them. Place the duck, chicken, pork rib bones and pork fillet in a large pot with 2½ pints (6 cups) water, spring onions and ginger. Bring to the boil and skim off the scum as it rises to the surface. Simmer for 15 minutes, removing the foam as it appears.

Place 2½ pints (6 cups) cold water in another large pot or bowl. Remove the stock from the heat, and place a few pieces of the meat and bones at a time in the cold rinse water. Rub the meat and bones with the fingers, dislodging the coagulated juices. Continue until all the meat and bones have been rinsed. *Do not discard the rinse water: reserve it.*

Return the pieces of meat and bone to the first pot, bring to the boil and reduce the heat. Simmer for 1½ hours. Meanwhile, bring the rinse water slowly to the boil, skimming off the scum, and let it cool.

Remove the meat and bones from the simmered stock and let them cool. Remove most of the meat from the bones and discard it. Remove the fat from the stock, and return the bones to it. Bring the stock to a rolling boil and keep it boiling for the next 2½ hours, with the lid on to reduce evaporation. Add portions of the rinse water every half-hour.

Place a layer of cheesecloth over a sieve, and ladle the stock through it. The volume will be about ¾ pint (2 cups). Add about ¾ pint (2 cups) cold water to the bones, bring it to the boil, and filter the liquid through the cheesecloth. Combine the two portions of stock. Let it cool, and carefully remove the thin layer of fat on top when the stock has set.

Makes about 1½ pints (1 quart) stock.

In the following recipes using Cream Stock, no seasoning other than a little salt is required. Use this at your discretion, but try to keep the taste bland, so that the subtle flavours of the stock may be tasted.

17. Fish Maw in Cream Stock (奶 湯 魚 肚)

1 oz. dried fish maw, softened, and cut into ½-inch chunks (42)
12 Fish Balls (31) or 6 Pearly Meat Balls (76)
¾ pint (2 cups) Cream Stock (above)

Prepare the fish maw, and fish balls or meat balls, as directed.

Bring Cream Stock to the boil and add the fish maw, and meat balls if used. Simmer for 30 minutes. If fish balls are added, poach them for 3 minutes in the stock just before serving. Serve immediately; otherwise the fish balls will not be crisp.

18. Bêche-de-mer in Cream Stock (奶 湯 海 參)

½ lb. dried bêche-de-mer, softened and cut into ½-inch chunks (41)
Generous 1½ pints (4 cups) Cream Stock (16)

Prepare bêche-de-mer as directed and stew it in Cream Stock for about 2½ hours, until tender but resilient.

19. Shark's Fins in Cream Stock (奶 湯 魚 翅)

½ lb. dried shark's fins, prepared
  as directed (43)
About 1¼ pints (3 cups) Cream
  Stock (16)

Prepare the shark's fins as directed. Steam them in sufficient Cream Stock to cover for 1½ to 2 hours, depending on the texture of the fins. The final texture should be tender and slightly crunchy, but not elastic.

The recipe for Cream Stock came from the northern province of Shantung, which supplied the ingredients for the magnificent cuisine of Peking, in its neighbouring province. It was famous for its spinach and cabbage, so tasty that they were occasionally given the best treatment. The *hsien* of the vegetables was borne up by the rich stock, an example of matching complementary flavours. The proportions of solid to liquid are somewhat different for the following two dishes. They belong to the form "half-soups", *tang-tsai* (湯 菜), in which the solids are taken with the juices or broth in about equal proportions. (Other examples of *tang-tsai* are Happy Family (100), Carp in Lamb Broth (13), or bouillabaisse.)

20. Spinach in Cream Stock (奶 湯 菠 菜)

½ lb. spinach
5 pints (12 cups) water
1 pint (2½ cups) Cream Stock (16)

Blanch spinach in water until the leaves turn dark green. Drain immediately and rinse under the cold tap until thoroughly cooled. Wring out the leaves very thoroughly. You may cut them into wide ribbons (about ½ inch wide). Wring them out again. This keeps the colour green even when the spinach is cooked again. Heat the Cream Stock. Add the spinach and heat through.

21. Cabbage in Cream Stock (奶 湯 白 菜)

½ lb. Chinese cabbage
¾ pint (2 cups) Cream Stock (16)

Scrub the Chinese cabbage very thoroughly and cut it into ½-inch sections. Simmer it in Cream Stock until just soft and tender, about 30 minutes.

Complexity of Flavour by Use of Seasonings:
Economy Sauce, Sesame Peanut Sauce, including
directions for the Preparation of Noodles to be Served Cold

The poor man had no chickens, ducks or pork to cook with, and could not afford to make Cream Stock. With a few pence worth of ingredients he did the best he could, and in a way it was just as much appreciated. In a slapdash fashion he was doing exactly the same as the trained cook, attempting to give a little flavour to some rather tasteless ingredients. The trick is to stir seasonings together, so that they can be tasted individually, and thus create a little excitement for the palate. Because the flavour of the following seasonings is never complete, a taste creates the appetite for more. Soon, a whole bowl of noodles has gone down, and another meal is taken care of. The man who has to work and earn a living and do all sorts of mundane things is much better off without too sensitive a palate. A great bowl of noodles full of mixed flavours, too hot, too sour, too aromatic, too salty, too spicy, just fills him up so that the job can be done. These cold noodles are especially liked in summer. Some people prefer them to Cream Stock.

*22. Preparation of Noodles to be Served Cold
(冷 拌 麵)

¾ lb. dry noodles or 1 lb. fresh   5 pints (12 cups) water
   noodles   1 tablespoon oil

You can use dry or fresh noodles.
   Boil them in water until just tender. Drain the noodles in a colander, rinse them under the cold tap until cooled, and shake off excess water. Dribble oil over the noodles and blend with chopsticks.

To the cold noodles add one of the following sauces.

*23. Economy Sauce (經 濟 麵)

3 spring onions (scallions), very
  finely chopped
2 teaspoons Red Pepper Oil (63)
2 teaspoons sesame oil
2 tablespoons vinegar
4 level teaspoons sugar
1½ level teaspoons salt

½ level teaspoon white or black
  pepper
½ level teaspoon crushed wild
  pepper
2 level teaspoons MSG
4 tablespoons oil

Mix all the ingredients except the 4 tablespoons oil in a heatproof jug
(4-cup Pyrex measure).

Heat the oil until almost smoking. Pour it in a thin stream over the
mixture, and stir immediately. Let it stand for about 15 minutes, then
pour neatly over the cold noodles.

The hot oil extracts all the flavours of the spices without burning
them. In the following recipe, the predominant flavour is that of
sesame, which does not appear unless the seeds are slowly toasted
in a heavy ungreased frying pan and then crushed.

24. Sesame Peanut Sauce (芝 蔴 花 生 醬)

2 level tablespoons (or more)
  sesame seed
1 lb. bean sprouts
1 level tablespoon peeled and
  slivered fresh ginger
Oil
¾ level teaspoon sugar
1 tablespoon sesame oil

4 level teaspoons peanut butter
4 tablespoons water
2 tablespoons soy sauce
2 teaspoons vinegar
½ teaspoon Red Pepper Oil (63)
2 level teaspoons sugar
2 level teaspoons MSG
½ level teaspoon black pepper

Toast the sesame seeds by spreading them out in a very thin layer over
the bottom of an ungreased frying pan and slowly heating them until
toasted. When the colour is light brown, remove the seeds from the heat,
cool them and crush lightly until the flavour comes out. These may be
kept in a closed jar until required.

Blanch bean sprouts in 5 pints (12 cups) boiling water for about 30
seconds. Drain them very thoroughly in a colander. Marinate the ginger
for a few hours with 1 teaspoon oil and ¾ level teaspoon sugar.

Mix 1 tablespoon oil with the sesame oil, peanut butter and 2 level
tablespoons sesame seed, toasted and crushed as above, until thoroughly
blended. Then add the remaining ingredients and stir until homogeneous.

Place the cold noodles on a large platter, pour the sauce over them and
mix lightly with chopsticks. Then place the bean sprouts over the noodles
and sprinkle with marinated ginger.

3. Texture

*Eggs beaten once are stiff, beaten a thousand times are soft. Kidneys
cooked for an hour are tough; after a day they become tender.*

YUAN MEI

THE MERIT of each dish lies two-thirds in its flavour and one-third
in its texture. The latter is an inescapable quality of the food,
whether good or bad. So it must be controlled. The texture of each
ingredient is sensed by the tongue, the teeth and the throat. It
depends on the cutting of the ingredients, the addition or omission
of salt and water, and the method of cooking.

The texture is always a perfectly definite quality, which is in a
way harder to control than the flavour, because once set it cannot
be corrected. You cannot unboil an egg. That is why the perfect
soft-boiled egg is rarely to be had. A great deal of art and experience
goes into its making.

Textures can be combined like flavours. In the same ingredient
it is possible to find the tender (*nun*) and the crisp (*tsuei*). The other
textures are: gelatinous, smooth, melting; spongy, juicy; resilient,
crunchy; gliding, *velouté*; chewy, deliberately fibrous; light, fluffy;
homogeneous, smooth, non-fibrous.

In this chapter we shall discuss the deliberate alteration or
conservation of the texture of various ingredients—prawns
(shrimps), fish, chicken and duck. The second part of this chapter
is devoted to the texture-foods, a unique feature of Chinese cuisine
whose existence is in itself a sign of its high sophistication.

火
候

CONTROL OF TEXTURE

The principal ingredients which affect the texture of prawns,
chicken, fish and vegetables are salt and water. Their textures are

altered or maintained according to the proper use of salt and water, without any change in flavour. On the other hand, pork and beef can never be soaked in water without losing flavour.

Water makes substances swell. Prawns, fish, chicken and vegetables placed in plain or lightly salted water take up water. This is extremely desirable in some instances to make up for the water lost during cooking. Prawns become plump almost visibly when placed in water, and when these are cooked, they actually become crunchy. Fish and chicken swell slightly, and remain tender when they are subsequently sautéed. Vegetables regain their original crispness, fill out and straighten. Wilted parsley quickly regains its decorative effect if placed in a glass of water like a bunch of cut flowers.

Dry salt or sugar makes vegetables wilt by causing them to lose water. As a result, they become pliable and petal-like when cut into flower-shapes. (The gain or loss of water by the methods just described occurs by osmosis.) To put it crudely, water goes in or out depending on whether there is relatively more water outside the ingredient or inside it. This can take place when the ingredient is cut or sliced, but not after it has been minced.

The effects of water and salt on fish or meat pastes are quite different. Water makes these pastes softer and capable of being even more finely divided. Salt stiffens the pastes so that the fluffy texture can set and become crisp or tender, as the case may be. It is entirely comparable to the addition of salt to beaten egg whites.

How to Keep the Texture of Prawns (Shrimps) Crisp:
Basic Rule for Prawns, including three variations utilizing
the basic recipe; Whole Prawns; Whole Prawns Sautéed
with Tea Leaves; Diced Prawns with Croûtons

This excellent recipe is capable of almost endless variation.

25. Basic Rule for Prawns (Shrimps) (嫩 炸 蝦)

1 lb. prawns
1¼ pints (3 cups) water
Salt
2 egg whites

2 level tablespoons plus 2 level
teaspoons cornflour (cornstarch)
1¼ pints (3 cups) oil

Shell, wash and de-vein the prawns. Place them in water to which you have added ½ level teaspoon salt, and let them soak for 30 minutes. Turn the prawns into a colander or sieve, rinse them very thoroughly, and let them drain for at least 10 minutes, or pat them dry with a towel. Leave them whole, or dice them, according to the recipes below. Place prawns in a bowl, and mix in the egg whites, cornflour and ½ level teaspoon salt. Let them stand in this mixture in the refrigerator, covered, for 3 to 24 hours, the longer the better.

*　　*　　*

Stir the prawn mixture with chopsticks. Heat a wo for a minute, then add the oil. When the oil is hot but not smoking, add half the prawn mixture (½ lb.), stirring once immediately with chopsticks. Remove the prawns after 20 to 30 seconds, when they have turned white and pink, and drain them well. Repeat with the remaining prawn mixture and serve immediately, or reserve them. These keep well if covered and stored in the refrigerator, to be reheated briefly before serving.

Whole Prawns

1 lb. prawns, prepared as above　　*½ level teaspoon salt*
8 fluid oz. (1 cup) chicken stock　*½ level teaspoon MSG*
1½ level teaspoons cornflour
* (cornstarch)*

This is the best way of all.

After preparing the prawns as directed above, drain them very thoroughly, turn them out on to a flat plate and serve immediately.

Or have ready in a separate deep frying pan, mixed and simmering, a sauce made up of the chicken stock, cornflour, salt and MSG. After frying the prawns, transfer them directly into the sauce without draining them completely. Stir very lightly and briefly with a wooden spoon, and serve immediately.

*26. Whole Prawns (Shrimps) Sautéed with Tea Leaves (龍 井 茶 炒 蝦)

1 lb. whole prawns, prepared as
    directed (25)
2 level tablespoons Lungching or
    other Chinese tea

¼ level teaspoon sugar
¼ level teaspoon salt
2 teaspoons pale dry sherry

This is very elegant, with an unusual flavour.

Place the tea in a heatproof measuring cup. Fill the cup to the 8 fluid oz. mark with boiling water, cover it and let it steep for at least 15 minutes. Pour off the liquid, reserving the leaves. Place the whole cooked prawns in a frying pan without additional oil, and add the tea leaves. Sprinkle with sugar, salt and sherry, and mix very lightly, as little as possible. After the alcohol has evaporated, serve immediately.

*27. Diced Prawns (Shrimps) with Croûtons (麵 包 炒 蝦)

1 slice white bread
Fat for deep-frying
2 tablespoons chicken fat or oil
    (chicken fat preferred)
2 level teaspoons cornflour
    (cornstarch)
4 fluid oz. (½ cup) water

6 fluid oz. (¾ cup) milk
1 level tablespoon very finely
    chopped spring onions (scallions)
¼ level teaspoon salt
½ level teaspoon MSG
1 lb. diced prawns, prepared as
    directed (25)

One of the few Chinese recipes calling for bread and milk. Very good. Be sure the croûtons are well drained.

Cut the bread into small cubes. Deep-fry them in fat until lightly browned, and drain them very thoroughly on paper towels, spreading them 1 cube thick.

Stir together the remaining ingredients, except the prawns, in a separate pan over low heat. When the sauce is smooth and bubbling, add the diced cooked prawns and heat through. Add the croûtons and stir once or twice. Serve immediately.

Wilting of Vegetables by Means of Salt and Sugar: Radish Flowers

When marinating raw vegetables, add water or an ice cube to the marinade if you wish them to remain crisp. (Compare with Marinated Turnips, 15.) Omit water entirely and add dry salt and sugar if you wish the vegetables to become limp and pliable. This makes a beautiful garnish, with many tiny soft petals resembling those of chrysanthemums.

*28. Radish Flowers (冷 拌 紅 蘿 蔔)

About 6 oz. (1¼ cups) prepared   1 level tablespoon sugar
*   radishes (see method)   1 level teaspoon salt*

Scrub radishes, and pick out only the perfect ones. Remove their tops and root tips. Make downward slashes about three-quarters of the way to the bottom, about one-sixteenth of an inch apart. Turn the radish around one-quarter of a circle and repeat the slashing, making a grid pattern.

Place the radishes in a jar with an airtight cover together with sugar and salt. Screw the cover on tightly and shake the jar to distribute the sugar and salt. Place in the refrigerator for 3 to 24 hours, shaking the jar once or twice.

*   *   *

Discard the juice. Serve the radishes plain or as a garnish. Press down on each radish slightly, so that the red "petals" part to reveal the white within.

The Texture of Chicken:
Velvet Chicken I and Velvet Chicken II—textures
synthesized from the breast meat, including also a note
on the poaching of chicken legs

Every time one is served tough chicken one is reminded of the fact that meat is just muscle. The breast of chicken is composed of two muscles, one overlying the other. The outer muscle is large and its fibres radiate from a single ligament embedded down the centre at slightly different angles from each other; for this reason it is quite tough. The inner muscle is small and choice, called the sprout (*ya*, 芽) because of its shape. In the sprout all the fibres run parallel to one another, ending in a silky ligament at the tip. Some people use the sprout exclusively, but this is very extravagant. Overcooking causes the fibres to lose water, and to contract and toughen. Accordingly, chicken has to be prepared so that it either imbibes water or its fibre structure is completely destroyed. These are the reasons for the rather laborious recipes for chicken breast.

Velvet Chicken I is the standard form which belongs to classic cuisine. It has a texture resembling a custard or soft-boiled egg, rather than that of ordinary chicken. Because this is very difficult to achieve with a paste of chicken and egg white, it is a kind of *tour de force*. The special character of chicken is almost completely lost in the re-creation of texture, and it somewhat resembles the smile of the Cheshire cat after it had disappeared. It is also rather like a soufflé—flavour coupled with a significant lack of substance—and should float down the throat like pieces of white cloud, the overall effect being *gliding*.

Connoisseurs can still identify the chicken in Velvet Chicken II. The fibre structure is still more or less intact, but softened by the water it has absorbed, and held together and shielded from direct heat by a thin coating.

In slicing or mincing chicken breast remember always to remove the almost invisible membranes encasing each muscle. It is these nearly invisible structures which give chicken breast bad texture. Pick at the surface with the point of the cleaver to lift the membrane and then strip it off.

29. Velvet Chicken I (芙 蓉 鷄 片 (甲))

1 pair of chicken breasts (about 1 lb. including skin and bone)	Oil
	1 tablespoon chicken fat
2 teaspoons iced water	1 level tablespoon cornflour (cornstarch)
6 egg whites	
2 level teaspoons water-chestnut powder	½ pint (1¼ cups) chicken stock
	2 level tablespoons water chestnuts, blanched snow peas or chopped ham (optional)
½ level teaspoon salt	
¼ level teaspoon MSG	

In order to achieve the proper texture, smooth and soft as custard, (1) the paste must be homogeneous, fibre-free; (2) egg whites are worked in avoiding formation of bubbles; (3) water-chestnut flour is used in preference to cornflour (cornstarch), making the paste smoother; (4) oil must be at low temperature, just sufficient to set the little pieces. You might use up the yolks left over by making Mock Crab Roe (136).

Skin and bone the chicken breasts, and remove the outer membranes. Using the point of a cleaver or a chopstick, scrape the meat into a paste, working always in the direction of the fibres. The silky white ligaments provide a firm grip on the muscle as you do this. Chop the paste very finely with a cleaver for about 3 minutes, repeatedly drawing the edge of the cleaver over the paste towards the board, to show up the very fine, fibrous membranes which are caught in the paste. Add the iced water in the course of chopping and drawing the paste.

Collect the paste in a bowl. Work in the egg whites, water-chestnut powder, salt and MSG with the fingers (to avoid the formation of bubbles). Continue to work the whole mixture until very smooth and homogeneous like double (heavy) cream.

In a shallow frying pan heat sufficient oil to give a ½-inch layer. When it has reached about 160°–170°F., stir it to even out the temperature. The paste is dropped into the warm (not hot) oil by means of a spatula or in half-teaspoonfuls, to make flat, almond-shaped pieces. A slight nudge under the set paste dislodges it. Remove the paste after a further 10 seconds' heating. The pieces must be snowy white and free of bubbles. If they turn slightly brown or are pocked, let the oil cool a little before proceeding. This part may be made in advance, and the pieces reheated in sauce.

*   *   *

Stir together 1 tablespoon oil, the chicken fat, cornflour and chicken stock over medium heat until smooth and bubbling. Reduce the heat. Stir in the chicken pieces very slowly. At this point, you may add water chestnuts, blanched snow peas or chopped ham, if desired. Serve immediately when heated through, taking care not to boil or overheat the chicken.

The addition of extraneous ingredients to this dish interferes with the appreciation of its texture. An interesting alternative method of preparing it is to pass the raw egg white/chicken paste through a very coarse sieve or through a slotted spoon into the warm oil. The pieces set as pea-sized drops. This looks very pretty when mixed with green peas of the same size. It deviates from the classic form, which is a mound of almond-shaped pieces covered by a steaming, rich, smooth sauce, garnished with a few white slices of bamboo or water chestnut.

Velvet Chicken II is also a deviation from the classic recipe, but is presented without apologies. It has been said that one feels very civilized while eating it. Surely this is worth a few hours' work.

30. Velvet Chicken II (芙 蓉 鷄 片 (乙))

2 pairs chicken breasts (about
   2 lb. including skin and bone)
1½ pints (4 cups) water
Salt
2 egg whites
2 tablespoons pale dry sherry
2 level tablespoons cornflour
   (cornstarch)
1 level teaspoon sugar
1 level teaspoon MSG
¼ level teaspoon white pepper
5 oz. (1 cup) snow peas
8 large dried Chinese mushrooms
Oil

SAUCE
1 tablespoon oil
1 tablespoon chicken fat
1 level tablespoon cornflour
½ pint (1¼ cups) chicken stock

Skin the chicken breasts and remove the bones and external membranes. Freeze the meat, and slice it with the grain into pieces the size of a florin (quarter), about ⅛ inch thick. Soak the slices in water to which you have added 1 level teaspoon salt. They will swell, and become tender. Turn the slices into a colander or sieve, and rinse them well, washing away the slime. Allow to drain for about 10 minutes. Place half of the chicken slices flat on a chopping board and pound then with the dull side of a cleaver. The purpose of this is to separate the fibres, not to cut them. Pound the slices until shredded, about 5 minutes. Do the same with the remaining portion of chicken.

Mix both portions and blend them thoroughly with the egg whites, sherry, cornflour, sugar, MSG, white pepper and ½ level teaspoon salt.

Wash, string and blanch the snow peas by pouring boiling water over them for 30 seconds. Slice them across diagonally if they are too large.

Soak the Chinese mushrooms in hot water to cover. When softened, trim off the stems and cut each mushroom in half. Reserve the water. Sauté mushrooms in 2 teaspoons oil and ¼ level teaspoon salt, then add the mushroom soaking water and evaporate it away. Reserve the mushrooms.

Prepare the sauce and leave it in a wo or frying pan.

*   *   *

Have ready a large, coarse-meshed sieve placed over a bowl.

In a second wo heat a generous ½ pint (1½ cups) oil. Stir the chicken mixture with chopsticks, add half of it to the hot oil, and stir immediately with chopsticks. It will blanch and float almost at once. Transfer the pieces to the sieve to allow them to drain. Meanwhile, fry the remaining portion of chicken and set it aside to drain. Bring the sauce in the first wo to the boil, add the mushrooms and snow peas, and finally the chicken. Heat through and serve immediately.

On the poaching of chicken legs: The dark meat of chicken becomes very tender, gliding and palatable when poached in *acidified* stock. Do not overcook the meat. Cut chicken legs into sections, and each section into two or three pieces. You may slip out the bones if desired. Make Cheap Stock (89), adding ½ teaspoon vinegar per 1½ pints (3½ cups) boiling stock. Drop the chicken into the boiling stock, and poach it for about 15 to 20 minutes, until the meat begins to contract. Drain the chicken, discarding the poaching water, which is inexpensive and contains scum. Serve the chicken with any one of the three sauces given with Plain Chicken (3).

How to Make Fish Crunchy:
Basic Rule for Fish Balls, with three ways of serving them;
Fish Balls in Soup; Fish Balls with Pickled Vegetables;
Fish Balls and Noodles

The monotonous, flaky texture of fish can be made at once crunchy, crisp, resilient and tender. The following rule is interesting to observe as the texture of the raw fish alters visibly. First, the fish is made into a smooth paste, with water added, then salt worked in. Next the paste is shaped into balls and poached. If the paste is not finely enough divided, the balls are lumpy. If too much water is added, the texture is too loose and fails to be crunchy. If not enough salt is added, the ball falls apart and becomes mealy. If fish balls are boiled instead of being poached, they become spongy. All of these things are to be avoided.

Work slowly and patiently, and measure accurately. The final texture is tighter and crisper than that of *quenelles de brochet*.

The pike, a fresh-water fish, is used because of its large, fleshy proportions and few bones. Scrape the fishmeat from the skin and bones, avoiding fibres and membranes. Even so, a few are drawn in and must be removed in the course of chopping and drawing the paste. When the flakes have been chopped to a fine meal, draw the paste over the board with the cleaver. The purpose is to crush the paste and to bring out the fibrous and stringy membranes trapped within. Pick these out by hand or with the point of the cleaver. The mealy paste is converted to a sticky, shiny gum by the addition of salt. This fascinating change occurs almost instantaneously, and is responsible for the main texture change from insipid to crunchy. Balls squeezed out between the circle formed by index finger and thumb are dropped into ice-cold water. Note how contact with water hardens the surface of the ball. Slowly, the ice-cold water is brought to the boil, and then held just below boiling point. Poached balls are made ahead, to be reheated gently, never boiled. They are extremely versatile, and amusing to make.

31. Basic Rule for Fish Balls (魚 丸)

A 2½-lb. pike (approx. 1¼ lb.
  scraped fish)
6 tablespoons iced water
2 level teaspoons salt
1 level teaspoon MSG
6½ pints (16 cups) iced water or
  water and ice cubes

Cut off the head of the pike and discard it. Split the pike in half by cutting along its back. With the skin side down, the white and yellow lining of its belly is exposed. Remove it. Remove all the bones. Carefully scrape the fish with the point of the cleaver, so that membranes, fibres and skin are left behind. Collect all the fishmeat in this fashion. Discard the skin. Chop the fishmeat for 5 minutes, removing any fibres or stringy membranes as they appear. During this operation, add 6 tablespoons iced water, one tablespoon at a time.

When the fish paste is sufficiently homogeneous to form smooth ribbons when squeezed between the fingers, proceed to work it with the cleaver like mortar with a trowel. Collect the fish paste in a flat mound at one end of the chopping board, place the cleaver ½ inch from its nearest edge, and draw it down towards the board. You will see some fibres, which must be picked out. Continue in this fashion until all the paste is transferred to the other end of the board, then work it in the other direction, and continue to do this until no more fibres appear.

Place the paste in a bowl. Work in salt and MSG with the fingers. The paste will become stiff and sticky. Continue to work it for a few more minutes until it is shiny. Cover the bowl and place it in the refrigerator for 1 hour.

Meanwhile, place the iced water, or water and ice cubes, in a pot. To form fish balls, take a handful of fish paste in your palm, and form a circle about ½ inch in diameter with the crook of the index finger and thumb. As the paste is forced through, enlarge and finally narrow the circle to nothing. Touch the tip of a teaspoon to the base of the ball, and tip the ball into the iced water. Continue until all the paste is used up. To cook the balls, slowly bring the water to the boil, then reduce the heat and poach the balls for 7 to 10 minutes. Remove the balls and cool them. They may be stored in the refrigerator for a few days. Makes 32 one-inch balls.

32. Fish Balls in Soup (魚 丸 湯)

1 recipe Spare Ribs Soup (112)
12 Fish Balls (above)

Bring the soup to the boil. Reduce heat to simmering point. Add the fish balls and poach them for 3 minutes. Serve immediately.

33. Fish Balls with Pickled Vegetables (泡菜炒魚丸)

12 Fish Balls (31)
Approx. 6 oz. (1½ cups) Plain
  Pickled Vegetables (half recipe
  117)

4 teaspoons oil
¼ level teaspoon sugar
¼ level teaspoon MSG

Cut the fish balls into ¼-inch slices. Chop the vegetables and sauté them with oil, sugar and MSG, adding the fish slices later.

34. Fish Balls and Noodles (魚 丸 湯 麵)

¾ lb. dry noodles, prepared as
  directed (22)
1½ pints (4 cups) chicken stock
  or Cheap Stock (89)

12 Fish Balls (31)
Soy sauce
Vinegar

Prepare noodles as directed but do not add oil. Heat stock to boiling point, add the noodles and heat through. Then add fish balls and heat for a few minutes. Season to taste with soy sauce and vinegar.

A Variation of the Texture of Duck : Crisp Spiced Duck

The preoccupation with texture is real and not casual. They say that crazy people take one idea and pursue it to the bitter end. A talented and crazy cook must have been the first to make Crisp Spiced Duck, for the skin is crisp and brittle, the meat crisp and tasty, and the bones crisp and melting. The whole duck is crisp and crunchy, aromatic and full of flavour throughout.

In order to make this successfully you must: (1) Use a duckling, so that the bones are tender and edible. (2) Break almost every bone in its body to allow the marrow to run out and the marinade to seep inside the bones. (3) Force the duck apart, tearing the skin, flesh and bones away from each other (but keeping the duck whole) so that the marinade can penetrate every fibre. (4) Fry the duck slowly and evenly, until it is a *dull* brown colour.

The duck is served whole, and cut at the table. It should look slightly flattened, deep, dark, dull brown, like a badly carved wooden duck. Taken piping hot on a warm soft bun, it is a feast.

35. Crisp Spiced Duck (香 酥 鴨)

A 4- to 4½-lb. duckling
1 level teaspoon salt
¼ level teaspoon wild pepper
3 tablespoons soy sauce
1½ level teaspoons sugar

½ level teaspoon MSG
2 tablespoons pale dry sherry
1 spring onion (scallion), cut into
  sections
About ¾ pint (2 cups) oil

Clean the duckling and wipe it dry. Break the drumstick bones at the shin, and push them in to shorten the legs. Break the drumstick, thigh, wing, rib and back bones, using the dull edge of a heavy cleaver or a hammer. The duck should appear somewhat flattened when you have done this. Cut along the ridge of the breast bone with scissors to free the meat. Bear down on the breast. Turn duck on breast and press on it, so that the flesh will separate from the bones.

Rub the duck inside and out with salt and wild pepper, and marinate it for 8 hours or overnight in a mixture of soy sauce, sugar, MSG, sherry and spring onion. Place the duck in a crock with the marinade. Seal the vessel tightly and place the crock in boiling water for 2 hours. Remove the duck and let it drain on a rack.

*   *   *

In a wo, heat sufficient oil to cover one half of the duck. Fry it slowly for about 50 minutes, turning twice, to allow the duck oil to be fried out and the bones to become brittle. The frying is continued until the skin is dull, not shiny, when lifted out of the oil. Serve with Ribbon Rolls (52) and Wild Pepper Mix (36).

*36. Wild Pepper Mix (花 椒 鹹)

5 level tablespoons salt
4 level teaspoons black pepper

1 level teaspoon wild pepper,
  crushed

Stir the salt and peppers together in a small pan over low heat until very dry and aromatic. Cool and store it in a tightly closed container.

Textural Variations of Bean Curd: Vegetarian Ham

Many people treat bean curd with contempt because it is so cheap, and after all, it *is* made of beans, and it *is* a curd. Could anything be more unappetizing? They cannot believe that insipid curd can be interesting.

The curd in its natural form is very much like custard (Bean Curd and Spare Ribs Soup, 112). But it can be made crisp (Fried Bean Curd, 45); juicy and spongy (Spongy Bean Curd, 102); like noodles, firm and tasty (Bean Curd Slivers, 71), or, dried in sheets and cooked with sauce, into Vegetarian Ham. Buddhists are vegetarians, consequently a small pocket of gastronomy has developed, fascinating in its attempt to create the ordinary flavours and appearance of fish and meat by use of vegetarian ingredients. For the fancy which caused Central Europeans to make marzipan pigs and babies of embryonic size and pinkness had its Chinese counterpart. One feels one could not converse with such people. Their thinking must be totally different, and it is best to stay some distance from them. The Buddhists, whether monks or ordinary people, mingled freely with the non-vegetarians, and because the manners of Chinese society are all-embracing and diffuse, felt obliged to provide food which looked and almost tasted like meat. This was a sign of hospitality. Their cuisine was based on nuts, spices, vegetables, sauces, sesame, peanut and vegetable oils, and bean curd. The last was the factotum, now appearing as duck, then as chicken, then as fish. Its very lack of personality made it an excellent actor.

This school of cooking arose mainly in the temples, where one could simultaneously enjoy the arts of gastronomy, tourism and appreciation of landscapes—the last-named, like a rich lode to be mined, always there for those with the eyes to see. One would arrive at the temple in late afternoon after a day's uncomfortable ride in a sedan chair. Somehow, the rods would always hit one's legs at the wrong point, or the hammock-like seat would make the back stiff. One had broken the ride with walks, to give the bearers a rest, and also to stretch the muscles, picking one's way among bare rocks whose sides were covered with moss and lichen. Unaccustomed to this exercise, as were our friends, we approached the monastery already disorientated by this mild adventure. The view from the sedan chair was at an impossible angle, green and wet mirrored rice fields giving way to paths of bamboo, covering us with filtered green sunlight so we scarcely knew which was up or down; and then pine trees, growing in profusion where no one had planted them. Then the scenery grew bare, and we saw before us those very same cliffs, bare, but in places covered with dark green, that generations of painters had tried to capture. This was not a landscape to be painted in oils, but in water-colours, where the clouds could easily melt into the mountains, and the pines into the clouds. It struck us that painters did not have particularly good imaginations, and painted only what they saw. If you look at a painting, think that perhaps somewhere the original exists, just as it is. Then we arrived at the monastery, and the world was again upon us. For we were treated to exactly those phrases of polite greeting that we had desperately tried to get away from. But the monastery, grouped within enclosing walls, had a certain charm in the dimming sunlight, and the stillness of the mountains came upon us. The mists appeared to come and go. Would we have supper in the chilly courtyard? We preferred it in the huge empty dining hall, where dozens of plaster idols stared at us in characteristic poses, ranked like choristers in a church. A dining room such as this had its charm, its peeling plaster walls celebrated in poetry as "the broken-down monastery". We were seated on stools in the vast dining hall, with the monks acting as hosts. Their manners would have qualified them for officialdom, were they not already placed in their own hierarchy. This was not the night to break illusions. We had a magnificent meal, then retired to the simple rooms. The night air seeped in, making the covers damp and sleep difficult. In such circumstances, could not one solve a gastronomic puzzle?

> *"duck"* = *fried dried bean curd*
> *"crab"* = *sautéed fresh walnuts with sauce*
> *"chicken"* = *sautéed cabbage*
> *"fish"* = *bean curd and potatoes*
> *"fried eel"* = *turnips, mushrooms and bamboo*
> *"prawns"* = *potatoes*

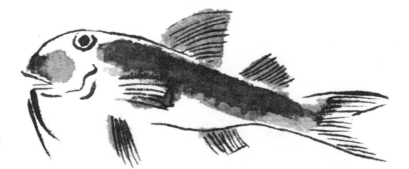

37. Vegetarian Ham (素 火 腿)

2 oz. (3 sheets) dried bean curd
3 tablespoons soy sauce
2 tablespoons water
1 level teaspoon sugar
½ level teaspoon MSG

1 level teaspoon fennel
½ star anise
2 cloves, crushed
½ level teaspoon wild pepper, crushed

Soak the bean curd in water for about ½ hour until soft. Mix together the remaining ingredients, and marinate the bean curd in this mixture for about 2 hours.

Select the largest and smoothest sheet and lay it on a flat surface. Place the remaining sheets on top of it evenly, so that when rolled up it will form a cylinder of regular dimensions. Roll it up *very* tightly. Place it on a single piece of cheesecloth or old sheet and roll it up, with the cloth overlapping at both ends. Tie the bundle at both ends like a toy firecracker, at the two points where the bean curd ends. Steam the roll for about 1 hour. Cool the roll and unwrap it. Slice the roll into ¼-inch slices and serve cold.

Such an expedition as we have described was for men, but women also enjoyed Buddhist cuisine. Wealthy ladies would make a pilgrimage to the temples in the city, ordering in advance a vegetarian lunch. In the earlier part of this century this was one of the few occasions on which women could go out by themselves. The school of cooking which originated in the temple kitchens expanded, and was taken up by the Yangchow cooks, specializing in delicate pastries and noodles. The challenge of simulating textures and appearance was irresistible. They were, in fact, able to reproduce even the intricate diamond pattern of duck skin, by lightly scoring smooth bean curd and filling in the cuts with a soy sauce mixture. Vegetarianism, which had originated for ethical reasons, finally became the gastronome's business, and fell into the fine hands of the pastry cook.

No idea in Chinese cuisine remained pure, but was pulled in different directions by a multitude of different minds. It became common in the best and the worst sense of the word. Therefore, when one speaks of court cuisine or the street vendor's concoctions, it is only to define their origins and milieu. You may be sure that at some point the labourer and the official tasted one another's food.

THE TEXTURE-FOODS

珍饈

The most important are *Bird's Nest, Tree Fungus, Bêche-de-Mer, Fish Maw, Shark's Fins,* and *Jellyfish.*

This extraordinary group of ingredients has only two things in common: unusual textures and insipid flavours. These are absurdities, not for general daily use, but prominent in banquets and feasts. In order to become even palatable, they are completely dependent on the flavour of other ingredients. Yet they stand close to the heart of Chinese gastronomy. These are the gastronome's pets, the cook's burden, the host's pride and the guest's joy. Perhaps in their ultimate artificiality they are the most sophisticated of food. This is the end product of the appreciation of texture.

The six texture-foods most prized are:

tree fungus (silver): crunchy, resilient, gelatinous
bêche-de-mer: smooth, unctuous, resilient
jellyfish: crunchy, elastic
bird's nest: soft, resilient, crunchy
fish maw: spongy, tender, resilient
shark's fins: smooth, melting, resilient

With the exception of black fungus and jellyfish, these are all expensive and quite rare in origin, if not in use. Popular taste seizes upon the rare until it becomes all too common. The host puts it on the menu, knowing that it is expensive and *because* it is expensive. The guests know it is expensive, and are delighted to taste it.

The texture-foods are the gourmets' pets because the matching of flavour to texture is an exercise in taste. It may appear that all six items are somewhat similar, but they have acquired very different characters in different settings. In classic cooking bird's nest and silver fungus belong to the "clear and light", while the fins, bêche-de-mer and fish maw are heavy, the black fungus neutral. Jellyfish cannot be changed, or it disappears into nothing; therefore it is always served cold, in curls like the locks of a lady's coiffure. Occasionally, it is used to simulate bird's nest, as fried pork fat membrane is made to substitute for fish maw, but both of these practices are despicable. For though artifice may be the sign of sophistication, one should still distinguish between the really artistic "nothing" and its fake copy.

It is utterly hopeless to attempt the cooking of these texture-foods unless one is prepared to spend time and expense in preparing the sauces and stocks which accompany them. Otherwise, one would as soon eat the paper this is printed on. The complementary sauces and stocks must be made out of the best ingredients, otherwise the diner would prefer a plain bun and sausage at the street stall, rather than pay for his food with time wasted at a bad banquet. For the cook, the work in preparing the food would be utterly lost. Why then these absurdities?

The reason lies in the exercise of skill. Both the making of these dishes and their appreciation take a certain amount of education. The key quality in these dishes is a certain rightness of the texture, for each substance a different quality. This texture must be wedded to another attribute, such as richness or clarity of flavour.

The Texture of Body and Delicacy: Bird's Nest,
its preparation; including a recipe for Sweet Bird's
Nest, and notes on other ways of serving Bird's Nest

Bird's nest is the secretion of the swift, used in building its nest prior to egg-laying. In its original form, the twigs and down are still embedded in it. Although this is the most difficult to prepare, it is also the most expensive and best, because it clearly is the genuine article. Inferior grades of bird's nest are loose, and have already had the impurities picked out. The nests are found in caves and cliffs of the South Pacific. This delicacy is served hot or cold, sweet or salty, but never plain. The proper texture is a combination of *body and delicacy*.

38. Preparation of Bird's Nest (燕 窩)

2 oz. dry bird's nest   *2½ pints (6 cups) water*

Soak the bird's nest in cold water. It will double in volume when softened. Rinse it very well with cold water, and pick out the down. Shake off excess water.

39. Sweet Bird's Nest (甜 燕 窩 湯)

2 oz. dry bird's nest, softened as   *6 oz. candy sugar (rock candy)*
* above*   *Just over 1½ pints (4 cups) water*

Stew or *steam* (preferably) the softened bird's nest, sugar and water together for 1 hour. Serve this chilled or tepid.

As bird's nest is inordinately expensive, you may cut down the amount used by mixing in, in place of 2 oz. bird's nest, ½ oz. dry bird's nest, softened as above, and ½ oz. agar-agar. Hold the agar-agar under the cold tap for a few minutes until it swells, then chop it into very thin pieces, like bird's nest. Stew the bird's nest in syrup as directed, and when it has cooled, add the chopped, softened agar-agar. Never heat agar-agar unless you want to make a jelly. See Bird's Nest with Bean Sprouts (129).

A certain prefect once served large bowls of plain boiled bird's nest. It was completely tasteless. Others praised it, but I said with a smile, "I just came to eat bird's nest, not to get it wholesale." We were each served several ounces of it, to do us honour. Had he given us each a bowlful of pearls, we would have valued them as much, and found them quite as inedible.

Mushroom slivers, very finely cut bamboo and shad maw [see below] may be used, or a tender pheasant. I tasted an excellent bird's nest soup made with winter melon in East Kwangtung. Two substances, clear and tender, matched to each other, cooked simply in chicken and mushroom broth. The bird's nest acquired the colour of jade—it was not pure white.

YUAN MEI

A Crunchy Fungus: Preparation of Tree
Fungus, with notes on the uses of black and silver fungus

The edible tree fungus is white (silver) or black. The ancient Romans, according to Apicius, also ate tree fungus. Silver fungus is much more expensive than black and is prepared in exactly the same fashion as bird's nest, after the preliminary softening described below. In those recipes it may be substituted in part or wholly for bird's nest. The two substances are always cooked in fat-free stock or in a light syrup.

Black fungus is more common, never served as a sweet, but used in rich stocks, clear soups, stews and sautés. Both types of fungus are quickly prepared. The texture is *crunchy*.

*40. Preparation of Tree Fungus (銀 耳，木 耳)

¼ oz. (¼ cup) dry tree fungus   *About ¾ pint (2 cups) water*

The main impurity is sand, which settles to the bottom of the water used
for soaking.

Soak the dry tree fungus in water. As it softens, it swells. Work the
fungus with the fingers to loosen the impurities. In about 30 minutes
the fungus will have reached its maximum size (three times the original
volume). Lift it out, rinse it well and shake off excess water.

Silver fungus: See recipes under Bird's Nest. *Black fungus:* Bêche-de-Mer
Gourmet (130), Sautéed Pork (11), Chicken 4-4-4-4 (105), *and* Sautéed
Prawns (Shrimps) (25).

*Tender Resilience: Preparation of Bêche-de-mer,
including suggestions for its use*

Bêche-de-mer (sea slug): A hollow, boneless body from the South
Seas, native of the coral reefs. The bêche-de-mer is bought dried,
like a rock. It has to be soaked for days to swell up, next it must be
cleaned out thoroughly and boiled several times. Then it should
be stewed. The final texture is *tender resilience*. This is the gourmet's
point of view. For the cook, what mixed feelings! For the preparation of bêche-de-mer is part agony and part cynicism and part
enjoyment. Should one really spend such effort on nothing? When
alive, the bêche-de-mer was a low animal, feeding on clams, and
other creatures—as one soon discovers upon cleaning out its
digestive system. The whole animal is almost nothing but a digestive
tract. Did it know what it was doing? In a way the cook comes to
think that it could not have wished for a better fate than to be
cooked and served with such loving care and expense. Other
animals have died with less to-do. The form of the bêche-de-mer
seems to have been designed for the plate, rather than the plate
for the food (artichokes, clams, oysters). Occasionally, a cook will
come to love its placid and smooth form.

41. Preparation of Bêche-de-mer (海参)

½ lb. dried bêche-de-mer
3 pints (7 cups) meat consommé
  (half canned, half water)

Rinse off the bêche-de-mer and place it in water to cover in a bowl large enough to allow room for expansion. Change the water once a day for three days or more. On about the third day it is soft enough to clean. Split it down its length with a cleaver and, holding it in a bowl of cold water or under the cold tap, pull, brush and scrape it inside and out. Remove all the long fibrils and the sand.

Use diluted consommé to soften the bêche-de-mer further. Bring half the diluted consommé to the boil, and boil the bêche-de-mer for 10 minutes. Discard the liquid, cool the pieces in water, and rinse out the pot. Bring the remaining consommé to the boil. Meanwhile, scrape off the lining of the inside of the animal. This tears off easily. Scrub the pieces inside and out with cold water. Place them in the boiling consommé and cook again for 5 to 10 minutes. Discard the consommé.

Make sure the pieces are clean. Slice them in ½-inch chunks and place them in cold water until ready to use. There will be 1 lb. prepared bêche-de-mer. See Bêche-de-mer Gourmet (130) and Bêche-de-mer in Cream Stock (18).

It is without taste, contains some sand, has a fishy smell, and is quite difficult to make properly. The Chien family prepares it cold for summer with mustard green, also cutting it into slivers to be done in chicken stock. It is excellent. The Chiang family uses dried bean curd, chicken legs and mushrooms to cook bêche-de-mer. This is also very good.

YUAN MEI

A Puffed, Spongy Texture: Preparation of Fish Maw

Fish maw is the air bladder of the fish, a large, gas-filled sac which helps the fish to alter the density of its body in relation to the surrounding water pressure. It undergoes great changes in volume as the fish swims up and down. It is obtained as a stiff, cream-coloured, dry leaf (which becomes puffed when fried), or as a stiff, voluminous, puffy sponge, light as air. Fish maw is always put in rich juices or soup, so it becomes *spongy and juicy*.

42. Preparation of Fish Maw (魚 肚)

1 oz. puffed fish maw   *Water*

Dried puffed fish maw is soaked in water to soften it. Soak the fish maw in a quantity of cold water, weighting the maw down with a small plate, and occasionally squeezing the bubbles out of it. After 1 to 2 hours it is sufficiently softened.

Bring 3 pints (8 cups) water to the boil, and place the maw in it. Boil for 5 to 10 minutes, then drain and rinse the maw and chop in into ½-inch chunks. This is now ready for use. See Fish Maw in Cream Stock (17) and Happy Family (100).

The Firm, Smooth Texture: Preparation of Shark's Fins, including notes on various methods of presentation

These are simply the fins, stripped of skin, then repeatedly boiled to loosen the mucilaginous material, which is then scraped off. So, although the fins are dried when sold, they have already been cooked several times, and must be soaked and cooked again to make them edible. Shark's fins come in several grades and prices. The better and more expensive fins are gelatinous, thick fins, still attached to the base (comb fins). The cheaper variety are thinner, and are sold loose. Fins must be cooked in water or stock to soften them, and to remove the fishy smell. The ideal texture is *smooth resilience*.

43. Preparation of Shark's Fins (魚 翅)

4 oz. shark's fins   *About ½ pint (1 cup) best stock*
2 Spanish (yellow) onions   *1 tablespoon pale dry sherry*

Comb fins should be wrapped in cheesecloth to preserve their appearance. Place the shark's fins in 2½ pints (6 cups) cold water. Change the water three or four times over a period of 24 hours. The fins will soften. Heat 4 pints (10 cups) water to boiling point together with the onions. Add the fins and boil them for 10 minutes. Remove the onions. Drain the fins, rinsing them well with cold water. If a fishy odour lingers, repeat the boiling with onion water.

Loose fins are packed tightly in a bowl. Cheesecloth is removed from comb fins and the comb arranged in the bottom of the bowl, so that when inverted the fins form a hemisphere of almost parallel lines. Add sufficient stock to cover the fins, and 1 tablespoon sherry. Cover the bowl closely and steam it for 1½ to 2 hours, depending on the size and type of fins. The fins are now ready to use in any one of the following ways. See also Shark's Fins in Cream Stock (19).

Some people like to serve shark's fins in an earthenware casserole (*shakuo*), which looks rather elegant. Others stuff a whole, boned, blanched duck (126) with loose fins, and steam it with a little stock, spring onions (scallions), ginger and salt for about 2 hours, so that the duck and the fins both become very soft. The oil is skimmed off and seasoning corrected. Serve this whole. Shark's fins are very good when prepared as above (43), and then scrambled with egg yolks, eggs, and a generous amount of oil. The eggs should not be entirely set. This makes an elegant little dish. For great banquets, crab meat and crab roe are added to the eggs, making the sauce even more magnificent. See Shark's Fins with Crab Sauce (125).

Another way is to combine loose fins with very thin slivers of turnip in chicken stock, so that no one will know which is which. If you add ham, use less turnip. Blanch turnips twice to rid them of their smell. All ingredients should be blended into a rich and smooth whole.

If shark's fins remain unyielding [tough] it is a fiasco. The Wu family uses only the upper half of the fins. This is rather chic.

YUAN MEI

Quivering Crunchy Curls: Jellyfish, prepared in the customary manner

When alive, this organism must have been quite large, for as a pressed sheet, the form in which it is bought, it measures over 15 inches in diameter, and is an almost perfect circle. When soaked in water, it is somewhat softened. Its ideal texture is *tender, crunchy and elastic*, the result of being cut into strips and scalded, so that it forms curls. It is a very popular hors d'oeuvre, despite always being served in the same fashion.

44. Jellyfish (海 蜇)

½ lb. (2 rounds) jellyfish
2 tablespoons sesame oil
4 teaspoons soy sauce

¼ teaspoon vinegar
½ level teaspoon sugar

Soak the jellyfish in several pints of water, changing the water two or three times over a period of 16 to 24 hours, to rid the jellyfish of its fishy smell and sand. Cut it into thin strips, ¼ inch by 1½ inches, and place the strips in a heatproof bowl. Scald with boiling water for about 10 seconds. Drain immediately and shake off excess water. Let the strips cool. Drain off excess water again. Using chopsticks, mix in the sesame oil, soy sauce, vinegar and sugar.

4. Regional Cooking

Ch'ih : *Peking and Szechuan*
Ch'a : *Chekiang and Kiangsu*
Chiah : *Fukien*
Sik   : *Kwangtung*

Variations on the word eat

THE REGIONAL CUISINES of China are as different as its dialects. The dialect and the cuisine were bonds which tied a person to his place of origin. When moved elsewhere, the same ways might be thought provincial, or uncouth, subject to misunderstanding, suspicion and plain indifference. Eating and talking were national pastimes, but actually each one of us was the centre of the conversation, each meal a focus of interest. We were not easily swayed nor convinced by foreign tastes. Yet when the best was called for, classic cooking, which was independent of region, was invariably presented, so that like speaking in Mandarin, we always met strangers or distinguished guests on the best ground.

In this chapter we shall consider the five gastronomic regions of China. There are three great schools, those of Peking, Szechuan and Chekiang-Kiangsu (these two neighbouring provinces at the mouth of the Yangtse comprising a region). We shall also discuss the lesser cuisine of Fukien (the province from which our family came) and the methods practised in Kwangtung. The last two are the lesser cuisines because of their narrower range.

PEKING

京菜

From the Vendors: Fried Bean Curd
From the Low-grade Restaurants:
Minced Pork Sauce (for noodles); Basic Yeast Dough,
with five variations; Crescents (Chiaotse)

The day could begin with sweet almond tea and it could end with dry hard biscuits; these were sold by street vendors until about four in the morning. Since the tea vendors went to work at about that time, there was really no interval between day and night when "a little something" could not be had. Other vendors sold persimmons, frozen hard in the intense cold of winter. These were thawed in a bowl of water, and people enjoyed them just as much as the fresh turnips, carrots and water chestnuts which were eaten like fruit. It was a casual parade of vendors that passed through the alleys of Peking, each with his cry or sound at his particular hour. These sounds were made with wooden sticks or bells or small brass gongs, and each vendor making his precarious living formed a part of a now vanished way of life, unaware that decades later his particular sound or cry could evoke such nostalgia. It was a good time for many people, comfort and service were real and cheap. Vendors of steamed bread (*mantou* or Plain Buns, 48) appeared at breakfast time, and in the afternoon the watermelon-seed vendor trotted by. One could easily spend a whole afternoon gossiping and cracking the seeds between the teeth. We were like squirrels cracking nuts. Our tongues and hands were kept busy.

   The wonton and fried bean curd vendors passed by late at night, stoves suspended on the ends of poles, now and then hailed by a servant emerging from a rich man's home to get a snack for his master. More often, they were stopped by other night workers. The night labourers and rickshaw-pullers, whose gruelling efforts made them sweat and pant even in winter, paused in their work, ate silently, and continued their labour.

It is interesting that in classic cuisine chicken is made to taste like bean curd, and in vegetarian cooking bean curd is sometimes made to look like chicken. But in the commonest and crudest, cheapest kind of cooking, all that bean curd can be is itself. The sauce is salty, sour, hot and aromatic.

*45. Fried Bean Curd (炸 豆 腐)

2 cakes (8 oz.) bean curd
Fat for frying
5 tablespoons soy sauce
3 tablespoons vinegar

1 teaspoon Red Pepper Oil (63)
2 level tablespoons chopped
   Chinese parsley or fresh
   coriander

Split each cake of bean curd in two by slicing it horizontally with a cleaver. Cut each square corner to corner to make 8 triangles. Pat the slices dry and fry them until golden brown in fat. Serve them hot or lukewarm with a sauce made of the remaining ingredients.

The flavour of Peking was in the cheap restaurants, where tiers of *paotse*, buns stuffed with pork and pork fat, cooked in a cloud of steam. How good to come in from the freezing cold, and warm oneself, the hot bun warming the hands even before one bit into it. Or to look into a big bowl of steaming noodles, stir it up with sauce, hunch over it, and gulp it down in big mouthfuls. The coarse food was full of robust flavour, uncomplicated by niceties. Thick wheatcakes (*laoping*) were wrapped about raw spring onions (scallions) and raw garlic, eaten just like that. Do not confuse these with the translucent crêpes of Southern China, discussed later (82). Southerners complain that the Northern *laoping* are too thick, too coarse. But they must be like that, or they would not taste right. Li Liweng said: "Southerners cook noodles in a soup containing salt, vinegar, sauces and other ingredients. The soup is delicious, but the noodles are tasteless. But this is what they like. They might just as well be drinking soup."

Compare the following recipe with the complications of Carp and Noodles (74), discussed in the section on Chekiang-Kiangsu.

*46. Minced Pork Sauce (for Noodles) (炸 醬 麵)

1 lb. fresh noodles or ¾ lb. dry
   noodles
½ lb. pork
2 tablespoons oil
1 spring onion (scallion), chopped
2 tablespoons wine
4 tablespoons brown bean sauce
   (toupan chiang, 豆 拌 醬)

1 level teaspoon sugar
¼ pint (½ cup) water
Raw slivered garlic, raw sliced
   cucumbers or raw slivered
   spring onions

Prepare the noodles separately and keep them hot. Chop or dice the pork very finely, and sauté with oil, chopped spring onion, wine and brown bean sauce until the liquid evaporates and the oil separates out. Add sugar and water, and sauté again until the water evaporates and the oil separates.

Serve the noodles and sauce separately, with a separate dish of raw slivered garlic, raw sliced cucumbers or raw spring onions.

Millet and rice were delicacies. The main staples were noodles, wheat flour cakes and buns. Depending on the company and the occasion, the basic yeast dough was made into plain or fancy shapes.

*47. Basic Yeast Dough (發 麵)

2½ level teaspoons (1 package)
   dried yeast
4 tablespoons very warm water

2 level tablespoons plus 12 oz.
   (3½ cups) plain flour, sifted
8 fluid oz. cold water

Dissolve yeast in warm water. Let it stand for 5 minutes. Stir in 2 level tablespoons flour and let the mixture stand for 10 minutes. Measure the remaining flour into a large mixing bowl. Make a well in the centre and pour in the cold water. Work dough into a ball. Add foamy yeast mixture and work it in. Lightly flour a board and knead dough upon it for about 5 minutes, or until a smooth, stiff, *homogeneous* mass is obtained. Place dough in a large bowl, cover the bowl with a damp cloth, and let it rise in a warm place. The dough should not be over-warmed as the bubbles would become large, making the texture coarse. When dough is doubled in bulk, punch it down. Knead it for at least 5 minutes to give it body and make it homogeneous. This is important, otherwise dough will break and fillings spill out. Shape the dough as desired and steam it after a second rising.

This recipe makes 8 Plain Buns (48), or 16 Filled Buns (49), or 16 Pinwheels (51), or 16 Ribbon Rolls (52), or 24 Duck Buns (53) or 24 Pastry Peaches (134).

*48. Plain Buns (饅 頭)

Divide Basic Yeast Dough (above) into 8 equal portions, shaping each into a ball. Cut eight 2½-inch-square pieces of foil and arrange them on steamer racks. Place the dough balls on the squares of foil. After a second rising of about 30 minutes, steam the buns for about 25 minutes.

*49. Filled Buns (包 子)

Shape Basic Yeast Dough (47) into two rolls about 8 inches long, and cut each roll into eight sections. Roll out each section on a floured board into a circle about 4½ inches in diameter. Place filling in centre. Gather free edges together, pinching them together to seal buns. Place buns, sealed side down, on pieces of waxed paper or foil 2 inches square, spaced out on steamer racks. After a second rising of about 30 minutes, steam the buns for 20 minutes.

*50. Meat Filling for Buns (肉 包)

1 lb. lean pork, finely diced	*6 tablespoons wine*
¾ lb. fat pork, finely diced	*4 tablespoons soy sauce*
6 cloves garlic, very finely chopped	*¼ pint (⅔ cup) water*
or put through a garlic press	*1 level teaspoon sugar*

Simmer all the ingredients together for 1 hour and allow to cool thoroughly before filling the buns.

If desired, substitute 1 level tablespoon curry powder plus ½ level teaspoon salt plus 1 tablespoon soy sauce for the 4 tablespoons soy sauce to make curried meat filling.

*51. Pinwheels (花 卷)

Divide Basic Yeast Dough (47) into four equal pieces and roll each piece into a rectangle about 8 inches by 10 inches. Oil the top very lightly, and roll dough up like a carpet, from the narrower end. Slice the roll into four 2-inch sections. Make a deep slash across the centre of each section and bend back from slash, doubling it up to form a double pinwheel. Place 1½-inch by 2½-inch squares of paper or foil well apart on steamer racks. Place double pinwheels on each square, pressing down slightly to flatten them a little. Allow to rise for about ½ hour to desired size and steam for 20 minutes.

*52. Ribbon Rolls (銀絲卷)

Divide Basic Yeast Dough (47) into quarters and roll each quarter into a 10-inch square. Oil dough lightly on top. Cut each square into two rectangles 4½ inches and 5½ inches wide. Trim the long edges of each 4½-inch piece so it has two parallel sides. Roll up each 5½-inch piece tightly and unroll it, to oil its other side. Cut this rectangle lengthwise into the thinnest possible ribbons, gather them together in a bundle, and lay them down the middle of the 4½-inch piece. Roll the latter about the ribbons loosely. Overlap the edges and seal by pressing lightly. Trim both ends. Place the long rolls aside to rise. Meanwhile, arrange 1½-inch by 2½-inch pieces of paper or foil on steamer racks. When the long rolls have risen to desired size (about 30 minutes), cut each roll into four equal sections. Place rolls on the racks and steam for 20 minutes.

*53. Duck Buns (for Peking Duck, 57) (鴨包)

Divide Basic Yeast Dough (47) into quarters. Shape each quarter into a roll about 6 inches long, and cut it into six equal pieces. Roll each piece into a ball, and with a rolling pin roll it out into a long oval about 2½ inches wide and 3½ inches long. Lightly oil the top, and double it back so that the lower edge protrudes slightly. Place buns on 2-inch by 1½-inch squares of paper or foil, set well apart on steamer racks. Let them rise and then steam them for 15 minutes.

Each variety of Italian *pasta* has its Chinese counterpart. *Chiaotse* (Crescents) are like ravioli. Northerners make a whole meal of them, and like to boast that they can eat two or three dozen at a sitting. Crescents are pieces of dough filled with uncooked meat and vegetables. In Peking the fillings were made with lamb or pork. The crescents were either boiled or fried and steam-boiled. In Szechuan the crescents were made with pork and cabbage, served with three sauces mixed together (see 63–5). The Southern corruptions of this recipe differ by their smaller, more dainty size, and by the introduction of prawns (shrimps), bamboo and mushrooms to the filling. In our opinion they are *not* better than the original form.

*54. Basic Recipe for Crescents (Chiaotse) (餃 子)

DOUGH
1 lb. 2 oz. (5 cups) plain flour, sifted
12 fluid oz. (1½ cups) water

FILLING
1¾ lb. Chinese cabbage
3 pints (8 cups) boiling water
1 lb. lean pork, minced (ground) or very finely chopped
½ lb. fat pork, minced (ground) or very finely chopped
2 spring onions (scallions), very finely chopped
3 slices ginger, very finely chopped
3 level teaspoons salt
2 level teaspoons MSG
3 tablespoons soy sauce
1 level teaspoon sugar

To make the dough: Put flour in a large mixing bowl. Make a well in the centre and pour in water. Form dough into a ball, and knead it on a lightly floured board for about 10 minutes. This is necessary to obtain a strong, homogeneous dough. Shape the stiff dough into a ball and cut it into quarters. Shape each quarter into a cylindrical roll about 12 inches long. Cover the rolls with a damp cloth until they are cut. Cut each roll into fifteen sections. Dust them very lightly with flour to coat them evenly. Roll each section into a round about 3 to 3½ inches in diameter. A stroke or two of the rolling pin is sufficient to form these circles. Keep them separate.

To make the filling: Wash the cabbage and sliver or chop it very finely. Blanch it in boiling water and heat it for 3 minutes. Drain immediately in a colander. Rinse under the cold tap and drain thoroughly. Mix the cold, drained cabbage with the pork, spring onions, ginger, salt, MSG, soy sauce and sugar. Blend the ingredients together very thoroughly with the hands.

Place a round of dough in one palm, and 1 rounded teaspoon filling in its centre. The shape should be a rounded crescent with a ridge running along the top. Gather the edges of the circle together by pleating the far edges every ¾ inch, and pinching them with the near edge, which remains unpleated. Place the pieces apart from each other on a floured tray. They may be made well ahead of time and stored in a cool place. This recipe makes enough dough and filling for 60 pieces.

*55. Plain Boiled Crescents (水 餃)

Cook the crescents (above) in two batches, dropping them into 6½ pints (16 cups) boiling water for 10 minutes. They are served with soy sauce and vinegar.

*56. Crusty Fried Crescents (鍋 貼)

These delicious pastries are browned at the bottom and boiled on top. When done, invert the entire block of crescents on to a round plate, so that it is served bottom up.

Prepare crescents as directed (54). Pour 2 tablespoons of oil into a 10-inch frying pan and heat it almost to smoking point. Place the crescents one behind the other to form a closed circle and fill the centre of the circle with more crescents. A 10-inch frying pan accommodates about 15 crescents. Reduce heat to moderate and fry the crescents for 3 minutes, until the bottoms are lightly browned. Add ¼ pint (½ cup) water. Bring to the boil, cover the frying pan and lower the heat. Boil the crescents for 10 minutes, then evaporate the liquid by boiling uncovered for about 5 minutes. Serve with soy sauce and vinegar.

We have dwelt at length on the coarse and plain flavour of the lower-grade food, because it has to do with the greatness of Peking cuisine. The gastronomy of Peking is great because, at its most sophisticated, the superficial simplicity of the food is coupled with robust flavour. The higher class of cooking in Peking differed from coarse cooking by its control of texture, but at its best retained the bold simplicity of plain food. The enormous work which went into the elegant cooking of Peking may not be apparent to the uninitiated. It hid its cleverness of technique, and took its cues from the clear and good flavours of the plump fish of the Yellow River, the delicious spinach and cabbage growing on the broad, treeless flatlands of Shantung, and the fat ducks.

The flavour of Peking was to be found in the teahouses and restaurants where smoky pine fires gave the lamb a special flavour, and in the admittedly rancid fat in which sweet pastries were fried. It was in the cluster of people about the *huokuo*, a chafing dish in which raw vegetables and meat were dipped, or in *shua yang rou*, a similar dish made with lamb. Never mind that the lamb was rank and "foreign"-smelling, and that the fried sweets made one lethargic and heavy. Gastronomically, *huokuo* was often a disaster, despite the noises made about it. "I find all the hullaballoo a bore," wrote Yuan Mei. "Everything should be cooked properly at its right temperature, in stock simmering or brought to a rolling boil, timed to the exact moment. In the chafing dish everything is at the same temperature. The flavour disappears."

Peking was a city of officials, great families, workers; of Chinese and Mohammedans. The narrow alleyways broadened into avenues whose dimensions reflected the tone of imperial grandeur. Restaurants flourished when officials entertained, and the wealth of the capital encouraged the development of fine cooking. The banquets became lengthy and intricate poems. "As much care is spent over the choice of dishes as is devoted to the composition of a Cabinet." Some restaurants had claimed special distinction. The "Yueh Sheng Chai", we are told, started their stock-pot one or two hundred years ago, while the "Ming Yueh Chai" boasted that its stock had been in continuous use for sixty years. All this, despite political upheavals, rebellions and revolution. The sauces became rich, and the flavours were not to be duplicated. A speciality was *chiang yang rou*, lamb cooked in sauce.

From the Best Restaurants:
Peking Duck; Fish Fillets in Tart Sauce

The greatest dishes are complete in themselves, having every virtue of good food. Peking duck is one of the justifiably famous stars of the cuisine. Because the flavour is very simple and fragrant, even children and other people with undeveloped palates like it. Its appearance is simple, and its presentation always follows the same order: first the skin, then the meat, then the soup from the bones. The skin is crisp and fragrant, but not oily (*yu-er-pu-ni*). The meat is tender and juicy, the soup rich and sweet with cabbage. The making of it has become a small branch of Chinese gastronomy in itself. It is very difficult to think of a comparable dish in Western cooking. It most closely resembles a bacon, lettuce and tomato sandwich in its distinctions between textures and delicate flavours.

The skin is the most important part of the duck. In order for it to be crisp but not fat, it must be dry. (1) Air must be introduced between the skin and the flesh. In China, fowl are often eviscerated through a small opening under one of the wings, not through the rear end, as is the practice in Europe and America. Air is pumped into this small opening, so the duck balloons out. This permits faster drying of the skin. Since we cannot do this, alcohol is used to draw out the water. Sugar syrup is rubbed into the skin to make it brown later. (2) The duck is hung up to dry for at least 24 hours in a cold, stiff breeze. The purpose of this is to permit drying of the skin, which then pulls away from the meat. This dish is a result of the cool and crisp Peking weather, which allowed the duck to be hung in this way when raw. (3) During roasting, the duck is either hung up by its neck or placed on a rack, which permits the fat to drip off and the duck to brown evenly.

The meat is served sautéed with bean sprouts and hot red peppers for contrast in texture, then with a chorus of *Ah's* from the table, the glorious cabbage soup made from duck bones is brought in. The speedy appearance of duck soup resulted, of course, from the restaurant being at least one duck ahead. It requires prolonged boiling to extract the juices of marrow.

57. *Peking Duck* (掛 爐 鴨)

A 5-lb. duck
Salt
5 tablespoons gin or vodka
2 level tablespoons sugar
1 tablespoon water
Hoisin sauce (海 鮮 醬)
Spring Onion (Scallion) Brushes (88)
Duck Buns (53)

2 spring onions (scallions), very finely chopped
1 level teaspoon ginger slivers
1 level teaspoon dried hot red peppers
2 tablespoons oil
½ lb. bean sprouts or slivered bamboo shoots

Clean the duck and wipe it thoroughly dry. Rub its body cavity with 2 level teaspoons salt. Place the duck in a shallow dish. Pour the gin or vodka over it and rub the duck well. Let it stand for 3 to 4 hours, turning occasionally to coat the skin with the alcohol. Mix the sugar and water together and rub very evenly into the duck skin. Truss the duck and hang it up to dry in a cool, windy place for at least 24 hours. The duck must hang free so that all parts may be dried out. The skin will pull away from the flesh. Roast the duck in a 375°F. (Mark 4) oven for about 1¼ hours, placing the duck on a rack well above a pan of water which will catch the drippings. The skin will become a brown, brittle casing. The duck is served as three separate courses.

(1) *Skin.* The skin is removed in large pieces, cut into pieces about 1½ inches by 2½ inches, and served on a flat plate with no garnish. Some very thin slices of breast meat may be included. At the same time serve Hoisin sauce with spring onion brushes, and steaming hot duck buns. With a spring onion brush, paint the skin with sauce and place it between the folds of the bun.

(2) *Meat.* Carve the rest of the meat from the bones and cut it into slivers. Sauté spring onions, ginger and peppers in oil for a few minutes, then add the duck meat and ½ level teaspoon salt. Add the bean sprouts or slivered bamboo, sprinkle with another ½ level teaspoon salt, and sauté for a few minutes over high heat. Keep the bean sprouts crisp.

58. Duck Soup (鴨 湯)

Duck carcass (from above)
1¼ pints (3 cups) water
1 slice ginger
1 spring onion (scallion)

½ level teaspoon salt
1 lb. Chinese cabbage, cut into
   1-inch sections
½ level teaspoon sugar

This is the traditional end of a Peking duck. Break the wing, thigh and drumstick bones. Crush the ribs and spine. Add water, ginger and spring onion, and bring to a vigorous boil. Keep it at a vigorous boil for about 45 minutes, adding water as necessary to maintain the same level. Strain out the solids. Add salt, cabbage and sugar, and stew together for 30 to 40 minutes, until cabbage is very tender.

In the best of the cuisine, fairly elaborate methods of cooking were devised for certain ingredients. In order to keep the sweetness and lightness of fish, pieces of fillet were first passed through hot oil, and then passed through sauce. This method was called *chua chiang* (抓 搶), literally grab and snatch, or in this book, the "two passes" method (compare with Minute Beef, 132). The dish is all white, completely covered with a glistening sauce.

59. Fish Fillets in Tart Sauce (醋 溜 魚 片)

1 lb. fish fillets (sole, flounder or
*   pike)*
2 egg whites
3 level tablespoons cornflour
*   (cornstarch)*
½ level teaspoon salt
12 fluid oz. (1½ cups) chicken
*   stock*

2 level teaspoons sugar
1 teaspoon light soy sauce
¼ level teaspoon MSG
About 1 pint (2½ cups) oil
1 tablespoon vinegar

Slice the fish fillets with the grain into pieces ½ inch by 1 inch. Mix the slices with the egg whites, 2 level tablespoons cornflour and salt. This may be kept in the refrigerator for a few hours.

When ready to prepare the fish, mix the chicken stock, the remaining 1 level tablespoon cornflour, sugar, soy sauce and MSG together in a frying pan. Heat, stirring, until smooth and bubbling, then keep the sauce at simmering point. A small excess of sauce is made to permit easy coating of the slices.

Meanwhile, heat a wo without oil for a few minutes, then pour in the oil. When the oil is hot, stir in half the fish mixture, stir it once and lift it out with the aid of a slotted spoon after about 30 seconds. Transfer it directly to the simmering sauce. Continue immediately with the remaining half of the fish. Stir the fish in the sauce as little as possible, but make sure that all the pieces are coated, at the same time adding the vinegar. Serve immediately, with just sufficient sauce to give the fish a smooth and glistening appearance.

From the Mohammedans: Sautéed Lamb Slivers

In Peking, the Mohammedans specialized in cooking lamb, distasteful to many Chinese. Its tripe, head, giblets and shin were sliced very thinly, sprinkled with crushed wild pepper and salt, and served with wine. A sheep's horn served as salt-shaker.

"There are seventy-two ways of cooking lamb. Of these only eighteen or nineteen are palatable," wrote Yuan Mei, who owned a great garden in Nanking, presumed setting of *Red Chamber Dream*. Chinese cuisine accommodated the Mongolian taste for lamb, but never did it justice. Peking was the height of culture on the borders of the Mongolian desert, and curiously its strength came from the constant introduction of foreign elements, which made the Chinese wince and attempt to civilize them. In the Chekiang-Kiangsu region they were protected by geography from rough and foreign elements, so in its gastronomy at least that culture lacked grandeur and developed an ultra-refinement bordering on vulgarity. But in the mixing of Chinese with foreign culture the results were not always good. The following recipe is an attempt to cook lamb for those who dislike its characteristic taste, that is, a Chinese version of Mongolian lamb. Note (1) the use of the "two passes" method; (2) the slivering of all ingredients, typically Chinese; (3) the matching of flavours. The result cannot be called eating lamb (though it is quite palatable), as one who ventured into the Mongolian desert discovered.

*60. Sautéed Lamb Slivers (炒 羊 肉 絲)

½ lb. trimmed lamb (see method)	3 medium carrots
1 egg white	½ pint (1 cup) oil
4 level teaspoons cornflour (cornstarch)	1 level teaspoon salt
	1 level teaspoon sugar
2 large Spanish (yellow) onions	1 tablespoon sesame oil
½ lb. turnips	2 tablespoons wine

Trim off all membranes, fat and bone from sufficient lamb to make ½ lb. trimmed lamb. Cut into slivers and mix with the egg white and cornflour. Let the mixture stand while you sliver the onions, turnips and carrots.

Two wos are needed. Heat oil in the first wo. Fry onions in oil for about 1 minute, then transfer them to the second wo. Add turnips and carrots to the onions, and sauté for about 10 minutes with ½ level teaspoon salt and the sugar. When the vegetables are ready, reheat the remaining oil in the first wo. Stir in the lamb and fry it, stirring gently, for 30 to 60 seconds. Transfer lamb to second wo and mix lightly with chopsticks, adding sesame oil, wine and the remaining ½ teaspoon salt.

A Chinese reporter who visited Mongolia in the 1930's wrote:

As soon as we entered the softly lit tent [of a Mongolian chieftain], we were seated, and a whole white steaming lamb on a great, gold-inlaid, wooden platter was brought in, like a dinner for gods. The meat was delicate, the fat pungent and rich. This lamb resembled the lion by the bridge on the Thames. So beautiful did the lamb look that I expected to see cherubs hovering over it at any moment. My reveries were interrupted by my companion, who asked me to wash my hands. We sliced off pieces of lamb with a shiny knife and then picked them off the plates with our fingers. This was the famous "Grab Your Own Lamb" (手 抓 羊). The lamb had been half-steamed and smothered with juices and broth all about. Who would have thought that this most primitive of peoples would have such simple and elegant taste in food? We in China tend to cover the flavour with spices, or to lose it by boiling. Natural flavours are the best, and too much fuss over food is unnecessary. True, grabbing the pieces of lamb is primitive, but it tastes better that way. The lamb was prepared simply by cooking with some rock salt.

After dinner we entered another tent which had been prepared for us. Gold and silk glimmered softly in the interior. A jewelled lamp hung from the ceiling, throwing its light upon the yellow satin curtains. The floor was covered with multi-coloured carpets. Our beds were prepared for us. Fox and sable coverlets, lined with silks of many colours. On top was thrown a bear skin, over six feet from head to tail. The tent was also furnished with chairs, a table, tiger skin, a Western clock, a Kanghsi bowl with Hamil plums, almonds, grapes, and crisp pears from Suiyuan, apples, dates and so forth. We were served brick tea. Four court ladies came in bearing the chief's wife, who performed a dance for us to the sounds of string and brass. So exquisite were her movements and her face, that we sat spellbound, and we did not stir until she had been carried out again by her maids.

SZECHUAN

Entering the gorge, the river seemed blocked in front.
Then from the cliffs a cleft appeared like Buddha's niche.
The swirling waters began to leave their wide expanse,
And narrow themselves into a deep abyss.
The winds bellowed through the cliffs,
And the clouds spewed forth from the caves.
Overhanging cliffs whistled in the high winds,
And twining vines glistened in resplendent green.
Bamboo groves stood over rocks, dripping cold verdure,
And rhododendrons dotted the mountainside.
Falling cataracts spread a shower of snowy mist,
And strange rocks sped past like horses in fright.

SU TUNGPO

In the heart of China lies a triangle formed by three ranges of mountains. Along the foot of one runs the Yangtse River on its north-east course to the sea. In the centre of this triangle lies the fertile Chengtu plain, with its moist and mild climate, which could supply the whole province with food. This is a land of enormous cliffs, craggy mountains and startling scenery. Farmhouses were built at corners of wet green fields, and the smell of red peppers grew strong as you approached them. It was said that even monks were allowed to eat red peppers. Far from making them too excited, peppers just kept out the moisture of the climate. They were considered therapeutic, like the use of whisky in Scotland. Rice and bamboo thrived in the clammy weather, but fish were rather scarce. Geographically and historically, Szechuan was a little kingdom which developed in virtual isolation, immersed and imprisoned in its splendid scenery. Its dogs and horses (and, with apologies, its people) tended to be stunted and pugnacious, and its food resembled nothing else on earth.

The Manifold Flavour: Fried Slices
The Mala *Flavour (Aromatic Hotness):*
Spiced Tangerine Chicken

The cuisine of Szechuan is a brilliant freak which breaks all the rules and gets away with it. Their use of relishes and seasonings is another language. One is shocked by the first taste, then one begins to see that theirs is a different logic. The purpose of the hot red peppers is not to paralyse the tongue, but to stimulate the palate. The hotness is the key which opens up the spectrum of Szechuan flavours. The dryness of texture even becomes meaningful.

Under stimulation of hot peppers the palate becomes more sensitive and can accommodate a number of flavours at once. First comes the mellowness after the hot taste is passed, then the *manifold flavour* characteristic of Szechuan, in which the sour, salty, sweet, fragrant, bitter and hot can all be tasted at once. The immediate flavours are lost in the fiery hot taste of pepper, but they remain in the aftertaste, after the fire has died down. Szechuan cuisine is largely based upon seasonings and relishes, but so prepared that they arrive as a single, manifold flavour which the tongue teases into its separate components. The gourmet will realize this after tasting Fried Slices (61).

Mellowness and the manifold flavour are curiously related to the dry, chewy texture much emphasized in this cuisine. If a taste is hot, water just makes it worse. The mellowness comes only if the food is rather dry but oily. Secondly, the flavours are meant to be chewed, not swallowed. Thus, while Peking taste prefers the soft and gliding, Szechuan is for the strong and chewy. The former is prettier, but the latter has more character.

In order to make Fried Slices as it should be (1) the pork has to be sliced with the grain, evenly, so that even after it shrinks when fried, all the slices are uniform. All membranes, fat, etc., are trimmed off before slicing. The texture must be homogeneous because this is to be chewed. (2) The purpose of the egg white and cornflour (cornstarch) is to keep the pork juices in the meat. (3) Slices are first boiled to harden the meat. (4) They are then fried twice to remove the moisture almost completely. After the first frying, the slices cool and become juicy again. The second frying removes this portion of water, and after a certain point the slices almost suddenly turn a reddish-brown colour. This is fascinating to watch. (5) Stop frying the slices about 2 minutes after the colour has changed.

61. Fried Slices (水 煮 肉 片)

1 lb. loin of pork
2 egg whites
3 level tablespoons cornflour
   (cornstarch)
Salt
1¼ pints (3 cups) water
1 spring onion (scallion)
2 slices ginger
1 teaspoon soy sauce

¼ level teaspoon black pepper
MSG
½ level teaspoon sugar
1 to 2 level teaspoons red pepper,
   crushed
¼ level teaspoon wild pepper,
   crushed
1 tablespoon dark soy sauce
¾ pint (2 cups) oil

Trim the pork and slice it with the grain into pieces about ½ inch by 1¼ inches. Coat the slices in a mixture of egg whites, cornflour and 1 level teaspoon salt. Pour the water into a pan, add the spring onion, ginger, soy sauce, black pepper and ¼ level teaspoon MSG, and bring to the boil. Add the pork slices in portions and bring to a rapid boil, without stirring, to set the egg whites. Boil the slices for 3 minutes and drain them well. Sprinkle with ½ level teaspoon each salt and MSG, the sugar, red pepper, wild pepper and dark soy sauce. Mix the seasoning in well.

Heat oil in a wo, and slowly fry the slices for 12 to 15 minutes with a minimum of stirring. Remove the slices and let them drain in a large colander or close-meshed sieve. Let them cool for about 20 minutes, then fry again for 5 to 7 minutes, until all the slices are a reddish-brown colour, chewy but not crisp.

The manifold flavour is characteristic of Szechuan. Its famous soup, the Sour and Hot, is popular because it is simultaneously sour, hot, salty, sweet and aromatic. The second characteristic of Szechuan cooking is similar to the first, and is distinguished by aromatic hotness (*mala*, 麻 辣). In this type of seasoning, chopped spring onions (scallions) and wild pepper (*Xanthoxylum piperatum*, 庇 椒) are the dominating seasonings. But, of course, the *mala* dishes also have the manifold flavour.

The following recipe makes use of the aromatic dried peel of tiny tangerines, product of Szechuan. The excellent flavour of wild pepper is brought out by lightly crushing it.

62. Spiced Tangerine Chicken (陳 皮 鷄)

6 chicken legs (2½ to 3 lb.)
3 tablespoons wine
2 tablespoons soy sauce
Salt
1 spring onion (scallion), cut into
   1½-inch lengths
2 level tablespoons flour (optional)
Fat for deep-frying
2 tablespoons oil

1 level teaspoon red pepper,
   crushed
¼ level teaspoon wild pepper,
   crushed
1 piece tangerine rind, crushed
   (about 2 level teaspoons)
1 tablespoon vinegar
A few tablespoons chicken stock
½ level teaspoon MSG

Chop the chicken legs into 1½-inch sections. Marinate them for 2 to 4 hours in a mixture of wine, soy sauce, 1 level teaspoon salt and spring onion. Drain the chicken, reserving the marinade, and, if desired, flour the pieces lightly. Fry the chicken in deep fat for about 7 minutes, until browned, and reserve.

Put the oil in a deep frying pan and sauté the red pepper, wild pepper and tangerine rind for a few minutes. Then add the browned chicken and mix well. Add the vinegar and let it evaporate. This makes the chicken tender and the peppers hotter. Add the marinade, made up to just under ¼ pint (about ½ cup) with stock, and season chicken with ½ level teaspoon each salt and MSG. Evaporate the liquid over moderate heat for about 15 minutes, until all the liquid is gone.

Three Sauces from Szechuan:
Red Pepper Oil; Reduced Soy Sauce; Spring Onion
(Scallion) Paste; to Be Served with Boiled Crescents (54, 55)

Chengtu, the capital of Szechuan, is situated west of the basin. Its houses looked out on to broad streets down which narrow grooves had been made for the passage of wheelbarrows, and though the appearance of the city was unimpressive, commerce and govern-ment made it important. Its high-ceilinged, one-storied teahouses had the air of the larger cafés in Paris, in which gossip, trade, flattery, opportunity and rumour buzzed. Formal banquets contained none of the hot local flavours, adhering to classic form. The texture-foods were by and large imported, parts of salt-water fish from the distant South Seas. They brought evidence of faraway places. It is not surprising that they were considered delicacies in Szechuan, and in the chilly North, and even in the lower reaches of the Yangtse. On the other hand, travellers stopping in Chengtu felt they had to taste its special dumplings, made inside out, contrary to the normal manner. Balls of sesame seed filling were swirled about on a tray of flour, acquiring a very thin coating that somehow held together when they were boiled. The ravioli-like *chiaotse*, plain and straightforward as served in Peking, was given a local twist, unmistakably Szechuan.

Plain Boiled Crescents (55) are served with three sauces, which are mixed at table to individual taste. Raw garlic paste may be substituted for spring onion paste. The colours are beautiful and the mixture delicious.

*63. Red Pepper Oil (紅 油)

5 tablespoons oil
4 level teaspoons ground red
 pepper (powder)

Heat the oil until quite hot but not smoking. Turn the heat off and wait about 30 seconds. Add red pepper, stir immediately, and allow to stand until cool. Filter the mixture through one thickness of paper napkin.

64. Reduced Soy Sauce (複 製 醬 油)

5 oz. (¾ cup) dark brown sugar
8 fluid oz. (1 cup) soy sauce
1 segment of star anise
¼ level teaspoon cinnamon
⅛ level teaspoon cardamom

Mix the sugar, soy sauce and star anise together in a large pot. Bring to the boil, and keep it at a foaming boil until the volume is reduced by half. Cool the mixture and add cinnamon and cardamom.

65. Spring Onion (Scallion) Paste (葱 泥)

About 8 spring onions (scallions)
Iced water

Chop very finely or mince the spring onions, and, using a measuring cup, measure out just over 5 fluid oz. (⅔ cup). Add iced water or an ice cube plus water to bring the total volume up to 6 fluid oz. (¾ cup). Stir to make a paste. If this is to be stored in the refrigerator, seal it tightly, as it is pungent.

Two Recipes from Szechuan:
Mock Fish; Pan-roasted Peppers

The annual run of the shad upstream stopped east of Szechuan, where they spawned in lakes as large as small seas. Farther upstream, the waters became more turbulent. The rapids cut through gorges, making navigation upstream laborious, and the waters ran too swiftly to make lakes where fish could be raised. This may be the reason for a peculiar dish of pork known as Mock Fish, an attempt to reproduce the taste of a well-sauced fish. If you close your eyes you can almost believe it. The contrariness of Szechuan cooking lies in the fact that veal or beef may be substituted in the recipe below with little change in its taste. The taste of the original substances is all but lost in the sauce. No one seems to mind, because the use of seasonings is extraordinary.

*66. Mock Fish (魚 鮮 肉 絲)

¾ lb. pork
2 teaspoons wine
1 tablespoon soy sauce
1 level tablespoon cornflour
 (cornstarch)
Oil for deep-frying
4 teaspoons brown bean sauce
 (豆 拌 醬)
1 tablespoon water

1 tablespoon vinegar
1 level teaspoon sugar
½ level teaspoon red pepper,
 crushed
1 teaspoon pressed ginger juice
¼ teaspoon sesame oil
½ level teaspoon cornflour mixed
 with 4 tablespoons water

Sliver the pork very finely, and marinate it for 2 to 3 hours in a mixture of wine, soy sauce and cornflour. Deep-fry the slivers for about 2 minutes, until well browned. Set them aside to drain. In a bowl, mix together all the remaining ingredients except the cornflour and water mixture. Sauté the pork in the bean sauce mixture for a few minutes in a deep frying pan, until heated through. Then thicken the sauce with the cornflour and water, stirring gently to make it smooth.

The Szechuan palate demanded rich and convoluted flavours. These were easily supplied in the meat dishes, but other substances presented special problems. Bamboo grew in the moist climate, making the mountain-sides green. The taller bamboo grew shoots slenderly tapered, their slightly bitter taste offset by cooking with chicken skin in a rich stock. The dry sautés were popular; shark's fins, dried squid and fish besides bamboo were prepared in this fashion. The bamboo grew red, speckled with black and purple as well as green, both wild and cultivated. If you planted bamboo in the courtyard among the peach and cassia trees, it was only a few steps from there to the kitchen. At the time of the spring showers the variety known as "thunder bamboo" put forth its shoots. It was thinly sliced, and simply steamed on top of rice with a little salt, or boiled and seasoned with soy sauce. "Its flavour surpasses that of gourds, marrows (squashes) and cucumbers," wrote Li Liweng. It is almost like artichoke, at its best an exquisite mellowness and at its worst (canned!) only the texture remains.

It is well known that peppers wilt during cooking, but how many know that green peppers must be pan-roasted to bring out their real flavour? What is easily dismissed as merely crisp when nearly raw, suddenly turns out to be complex, rich and mellow.

67. Pan-roasted Peppers (爆 青 椒)

2 large green peppers	4 spring onions (scallions),
About 1 tablespoon fermented	chopped
black beans	1 teaspoon soy sauce
Pale dry sherry	¼ level teaspoon salt
1 tablespoon oil	1 teaspoon vinegar

Break the peppers into quarters, discarding the seeds. Steam or simmer the beans in sherry to cover. This causes the beans to swell and the flavour to come out. Chop the beans finely (the remainder may be kept in a sealed jar in the refrigerator). Mix 1 level tablespoon chopped beans with the oil, spring onions, soy sauce and salt, and reserve.

Heat a wo or frying pan until very hot, then lay the peppers on it, and press them flat against the surface until they have a few black streaks. Turn the pieces over, and when they are soft, a dull green colour and wilted, turn the heat off. Turn the peppers so that the inside surface faces upwards. Add the bean mixture and mix it in as the frying pan sizzles. Then add the vinegar. Serve the peppers at room temperature.

Variety by Means of Seasoning:
Diced Chicken in Sauce; Hot Red Pepper Chicken

The heavy emphasis on spices, sauces and relishes was in a way an escape from monotony. Pork and chicken were used exclusively in the relative absence of duck and beef and seafood. Two versions of chicken breast can be made to taste entirely different. In the first, chicken breast is soaked in water to make it tender. In the second, it is given a coating for the same purpose.

68. Diced Chicken in Sauce (醬 爆 鷄 丁)

2 pairs chicken breasts (about
   2 lb. including skin and bone)
Salt
4 level teaspoons cornflour
   (cornstarch)
8 oz. (about 1½ cups) bamboo
3 tablespoons Hoisin sauce
   (海 鮮 醬)

4 teaspoons brown bean sauce
   (豆 拌 醬)
1 teaspoon soy sauce
2 teaspoons vinegar
4 tablespoons oil
8 cloves garlic, peeled and crushed
¼ level teaspoon red pepper,
   crushed

Skin, bone and dice the chicken breasts. Soak the diced chicken for 20 minutes in 1½ pints (4 cups) water to which you have added 1 level teaspoon salt. Drain very thoroughly and coat the pieces with cornflour. Dice the bamboo. Mix together with Hoisin sauce, brown bean sauce, soy sauce and vinegar, and reserve.

Sauté chicken pieces in oil, together with garlic, red pepper and ½ level teaspoon salt. Stir in the reserved sauce mixture and mix thoroughly. After about 1 minute, add a scant ¼ pint (½ cup) water, and heat for 1 minute longer to thicken the sauce.

69. Hot Red Pepper Chicken (辣 子 鷄 丁)

6 to 8 dried whole red peppers
Oil
2 pairs chicken breasts (about 2 lb.
   including skin and bone)
1 egg white
Cornflour (cornstarch)

3 oz. (½ cup) blanched peanuts
Salt
½ level teaspoon sugar
½ level teaspoon MSG
1 teaspoon vinegar
1 teaspoon soy sauce

Simmer dried peppers in ¼ pint (½ cup) water and 1 tablespoon oil for about 10 minutes to soften them. These may be stored for later use.

Skin and bone the chicken breasts, and cut the meat into ½-inch squares. Coat them with the egg white and 4 level teaspoons cornflour. If possible, let this mixture stand for 1 to 3 hours.

In a wo, sauté the blanched peanuts and ½ level teaspoon salt in 1 tablespoon oil. Remove from the wo and reserve. Sauté the chicken and 2 level teaspoons softened red peppers, diced, in 3 tablespoons oil, together with sugar, MSG and ¼ level teaspoon salt. After a few minutes, add the vinegar and allow it to evaporate. Then mix in the peanuts, and thicken the sauce with 1 level teaspoon cornflour blended to a smooth paste with soy sauce and 5 tablespoons water.

CHEKIANG-KIANGSU

Soochow, the good place. At dawn
The bamboo is cut smooth as jade,
Hsien and nun *on an earthenware plate.*
Soochow, the good place. The arbutus,
Sweet like heavenly dew,
Filling my cheeks with juice.
Soochow, the good place. Big beans
Picked when the flowers bend low
And munched when tea is served.
Soochow, the good place—when the shad
Come by. River globefish
In spring we cook with ginger and chives.
Soochow, the good place. In summer
Plump fish dart about the river
Avoiding the fisherman's boat.
Purple crabs and red wine dregs
Make the autumn pass.
When waxy meats and sturgeon appear,
Carp and bream leap into the pot.

KU TIEH CHING
(19th century)

Cutting its way through the gorges, the Yangtse finally reaches the lowlands of Hupeh where, broadening into a web of rivers and lakes, it slows down and takes a more leisurely course to meet the sea a few miles north of Shanghai. The two coastal provinces of Chekiang and Kiangsu are marked with lakes, rivers and canals, all stemming from the great river. But now the scenery is on a small scale, the huge cliffs of Szechuan, appalling in their grandeur, give way to the mirror-smooth lake. The willow replaces the pine. The narrow streets of the towns bustled; all was small, crowded and close to the ground. The vertical lines of Szechuan were replaced by the horizontal curves of the hills, set low. The arched bridges of Soochow formed almost perfect circles with their reflections in the water, and boats passed under them as through a hoop. All was scaled to the size of man.

Here the gastronomes were most numerous. They were in the cities and towns and resorts where wealth had made people knowing. Shops and restaurants catered to the demands of gastronomy and snobbery. The changing seasons were gastronomic events. The tiny towns dotting the mouth of the Yangtse, like the

string of villages in Burgundy, were gastronomically important—
Chinkiang vinegar, Shaoshing wine, Yangchow noodles and
pastries. The yearly run of the shad brought out a happy harmony.
The shad went up past Chinkiang, where the vinegar, black and
brilliant, suited its flavour admirably. Those shad lucky enough
to pass the town without being served on a plate with the vinegar
continued to Wuhu, another centre of gastronomy about a hundred
miles upstream, where shad were steamed plainly or with soy sauce.
Shad were awaited still farther upstream, where at Anching they
crowded the river, watched by impatient restaurateurs. Their
patrons, somewhat less anxious, debated between the unscaled
shad with its sweet oils and the skinned shad, covered with a layer
of web fat and steamed with wine.

At other seasons, there were mullet, perch and a red-eyed fish
full of bones. "In Nanking they first dry it, then fry the fish. A
proverb goes, if you straighten out a hunchback's spine he will die,"
wrote Yuan Mei. "I suggest that you cut diagonally along the back
with a sharp knife so that the small bones are almost severed. Then
fry it, adding other ingredients. When you eat it you will hardly
notice the bones. This is the recipe of Mr. Tao of Wuhu." This
suggestion has had no effect, for the method is still to roast the fish
and then fry it so that the bones become brittle.

Directly east of the river are Hangchow, Soochow and Shanghai,
three points enclosing a famous lake. People broke the serene
beauty of the lake with their loud voices. Gastronomy was everyone's hobby, whether he be writer, artist, businessman, or without
profession. Few people could remain silent and knowing in the
atmosphere of competitive appreciation. They came to the lake for
the food and the scenery, both to be vociferously admired in the
somewhat vulgar dialect of the region. But who could placidly look
at willows skimming the surface of the lake without noticing the
bubbles made by the darting fish? This leads naturally to the problem of cooking fish. The head always takes longer than the body,
yet both are to be enjoyed. In some restaurants this problem was
overcome by surgery. The small lake fish were starved for one day
to clean out their systems, then split and slashed in such a way that
the head and the two sides of the body were spread out. The
thicknesses at various points were unequal, but such that the total
cooking time for all parts was the same, about 3 minutes.

The characteristic of this cuisine is exquisite delicacy, achieved by obviously elaborate preparation. All ingredients were available in this mild and fertile land, and they became all mixed up in the overworked dishes. Generally (in one person's opinion) the effect resembled the embroidered silk pictures of phoenixes and flowers, a lot of work in bad taste. The richness of the cuisine was such that ingredients were used to flavour each other. Prawns were used almost as seasoning, crab roe or milt as fat, pork for its sweet taste. Is this not the principle of complementary flavours? No. The object in putting one ingredient in with another is to show up its individuality, not to lose it. "Nanking people like to eat bêche-de-mer with turtle, and shark's fins with crab flakes and crab roe. I frown at this," wrote Yuan Mei.

The Cook's Fine Hand:
Minced Chicken; Bean Curd Slivers; Including Two Ways of Serving the Slivers: The Hill of Beans; Bean Slivers in Stock

The taste of this region was moulded by the gastronomes. As there was nothing they had not tasted, cooks were pressed into trying new combinations. Their handiwork in chopping and slivering was to be admired as an end in itself. Cleverness was noticed and appreciated. The cuisine of Chekiang and Kiangsu left nothing alone. Floral patterns in food, and the garish assortment of hors d'oeuvre which preceded the feasts were winners in the game of cooking and eating. In this section we give two examples of the handiwork of the region: Minced Chicken, which is interesting to those who like decorative cooking, and Bean Curd Slivers, which require a fine hand to cut and a fine palate to enjoy.

70. Minced Chicken (翡翠鷄片)

1 chicken breast (about ½ lb.
   including skin and bone)
1 teaspoon cold water
2 oz. (1 cup) prepared spinach
   leaves (see method)
1 egg white
1½ level teaspoons water-chestnut
   powder

Chicken or duck fat
⅛ level teaspoon ginger powder or
   pressed juice
Salt
4 tablespoons chicken stock
2 teaspoons pale dry sherry
¾ level teaspoon cornflour
   (cornstarch)

Skin and bone the chicken breast, and remove the membranes and sinews. With the point of a cleaver scrape the chicken into a paste. Mince or chop it very finely and add water. Be sure to remove any stringy membranes adhering to the paste, so that the texture will be smooth.

Strip spinach leaves from the stalk, discarding the latter, and weigh out 2 oz. (1 cup). Blanch spinach for 2 minutes and drain well. Rinse immediately with cold water and wring out the leaves. Mince or chop them very finely.

Blend the chicken paste and spinach with the egg white, water-chestnut powder, 1 teaspoon chicken or duck fat, ginger powder or pressed juice, and ⅛ level teaspoon salt. Grease a rice bowl with chicken or duck fat and pack the paste in very smoothly. Steam it for 25 minutes. Let it cool. Slice it across the centre, and round off the outside rim. Slice it very thinly and arrange the slices in a floral pattern on a plate.

Mix the chicken stock, sherry, cornflour and a little salt together in a small saucepan, and heat until the alcohol evaporates. Pour this over the chicken slices and cover the plate closely. Steam it for 10 minutes to heat through.

The zest for food left nothing untouched. Bean curd was pressed and cut "to fit the eye of a needle", requiring the services of an expert. Its mild and mellow taste, resembling that of raw almonds, could best be savoured by the lake, whose opalescent tones changed with the movement of the low-hanging clouds. Its suave delicacy is one of the best examples of ultra-refinement. The hours of work which went into its preparation were taken as a matter of fact, and one could enjoy this "little nothing" while sipping tea or wine.

71. Basic Rule for Bean Curd Slivers (乾 絲)

If pressed bean curd (豆 腐 乾) is available, start with Step 2. Otherwise, make pressed bean curd from the softer curd as directed.

1. Pressing. The purpose of weighting bean curd is to squeeze out the water, firming the curd to concentrate the flavour. Place a clean tea towel on a flat board and lay 1 lb. (4 cakes) bean curd on it at about 1-inch intervals. Place another clean tea towel on top and weight it with 6½ pints (12 cups) water in a flat-bottomed pot (total weight about 7 lb.). Dictionaries or encyclopedias may be substituted for the pot of water. Leave it overnight. The pressed curd is about ⅜ inch thick. Place it in simmering (*not boiling*) water for 2 minutes. Cool the cakes.

2. Slivering. This is not as difficult as it sounds, for the light cleaver held horizontally makes thin and even slices with ease. Guide the cleaver with one hand and steady it with the palm of the other. A ⅜-inch cake can be made into 10 or 12 squares; experts can make 15 or 16 slices. Arrange the slices in the original square and sliver them finely.

3. Scalding. Place the slivers in a large, heatproof bowl or enamel pot. Pour over them 3 pints (8 cups) boiling water and let it cool to room temperature. Repeat this process twice, allowing the scalding water to cool down to room temperature each time.

In this step the starch is removed. The first two rinses are cloudy and a pale yellow colour. The last portion of water is clean. Pour the third portion away and keep the slivers in cold water until ready to use.

72. The Hill of Beans (燙 乾 絲)

1 recipe Bean Curd Slivers (above)   *3 level teaspoons sugar*
3 tablespoons dark soy sauce   *1½ teaspoons sesame oil*

Pile the slivers in a high mound on a small plate, and scald them with a quantity of boiling water, tipping the plate to drain them. Stir the remaining ingredients together to dissolve the sugar. Pour over the bean slivers and mix in lightly with chopsticks, keeping the whole in a mound.

73. Bean Slivers in Stock (奶 湯 乾 絲)

Generous 1 pint (2⅔ cups) Cream
  Stock (16)
1 recipe Bean Curd Slivers (71)

Heat the stock. Add slivers and heat through, then serve immediately. Do not boil slivers.

Boatwoman's Recipe:
Carp and Noodles, including a menu for
a simple meal on a boat

The cuisine was also the product of the sauce-makers, the pâtissiers, the wineshop-keepers, teahouse-owners and restaurateurs. The wineshops did not serve food except in September and October, the crab season. At these times they were moved to cook perch with crab roe and noodles. Shanghai wineshops would provide the vinegar, ginger and soy sauce for crabs. Then one ordered great quantities of steamed crab from another shop, and gave oneself up entirely to eating. Crab called for wine, and wine called for more crab. So the words "drunk by moonlight, with goblets flying" written on the front of the shops were quite appropriate. When this season passed, the wineshops returned to their usual routine of serving "one-legged crabs" (bean sprouts), jellyfish and slivered turnips, and peanuts. In the city, the wineshops opened on to the street, while the tables for drinking were set behind it. One passed by an L-shaped, glass-topped counter, between jars of wine, and picked one's way back to the courtyard, going through a dark back room where jellyfish and peanuts were set out, ready to bring to the customers. The courtyard was open to the air, and much quieter than the street. In its centre was a large beehive of a copper pot, with various openings in which bottles of wine were set to warm. You could sit in the courtyard or upstairs, while the vendors circulated, selling duck's tongues and smoked chicken.

Boatwomen plying the canals took on visitors for the day, and held their own in cooking skills, with their bowls of steamed chicken soup, and fried fish, killed and cooked at the end of the boat. Passengers lounged in stockinged feet in the centre and front of the boat, taking their ease on the smooth, polished woodwork.

The sound of chopping fish comes from the bow,
And the fragrance of cooking rice issues from the stern.

SU TUNGPO

It is said that when once the Emperor came down the canal, an ambitious boatwoman cooked some noodles for him. This was the dish.

74. Carp and Noodles (鯉魚麵)

FRIED CARP
1 small carp (about 2½ lb.)
2 egg whites
8 level teaspoons cornflour
Fat for deep-frying

SAUCE
Carp head, skin and bones
1 tablespoon brown bean sauce
  (豆拌醬)
1 slice ginger
10 dried Chinese mushrooms
½ lb. prawns (shrimps)
1 egg white

Cornflour (cornstarch)
¼ level teaspoon salt
8 fluid oz. (1 cup) stock
1 teaspoon soy sauce
½ level teaspoon MSG
½ level teaspoon pepper

1 lb. bean sprouts
1 lb. fresh noodles or ¾ lb. dry
  noodles (former preferred)
½ pint (1 cup) oil
1 level tablespoon very finely
  chopped spring onions (scallions)
8 fluid oz. (1 cup) rich stock

Prepare the carp: Skin and bone it, reserving the head, skin and bones. Dice the fishmeat (about 1¼ lb.) and coat it with the egg whites and cornflour. Fry for about 2 minutes in deep hot fat and drain thoroughly.

Prepare the sauce: Simmer the head, skin and bones of the carp for about 20 minutes in a generous ½ pint (1½ cups) water, together with the bean sauce and ginger. Meanwhile, soak the mushrooms in water to cover. When softened, trim off the stems and dice the caps. Reserve the mushrooms and their soaking water. Wash, shell and dice the prawns, and coat them with egg white, 4 level teaspoons cornflour and salt. Reserve.

Strain the carp-bone stock, discarding all solids, and add stock, soy sauce, MSG, pepper and 1 level tablespoon cornflour. Heat the mixture, stirring, until smooth and bubbling, and add the diced prawns all at once. Bring up to boiling point again and add the diced mushrooms and mushroom water. Simmer the mixture for 30 minutes. Add the fried carp, and heat through. This completes the sauce.

Wash and drain the bean sprouts, and pick off the root tips. Cook the noodles in boiling water until barely tender. Drain them well, and fry slowly in oil in a wo, without stirring, until the bottom is toasted and a little crusty. Turn the noodles over to brown the rest. Drain them and remove oil from wo. Return noodles to wo, add the bean sprouts, and cook until just done, about 5 minutes. Add spring onions and stock.

Meanwhile, reheat the carp sauce. When both noodles and sauce are ready, place the noodles on a large curved dish and pour the carp sauce over them.

It is in extremely bad taste to serve elaborate food in a simple setting. To serve an Emperor or a common man on a little boat, make no fancy sauces, cook simply and well, and be quick about it.

Poached chicken legs, with plain soy sauce (see Chapter 3)
Fish Balls and Noodles (34)
A fresh green vegetable, sautéed
Duck in Brown Stock Sauce (78)

Pretty and Dainty: Juicy Buns; Pearly Meat Balls

The Chekiang-Kiangsu idea of eating was quite different. It was really a sampling of specialities made by experts. There was always plenty of service, and little boys could be made to go and fetch hot pastries for lunch, running all the way back before they cooled. This was comfort. Note how in a modern cafeteria the roles are reversed, and instead of the food coming to you, you must go and get it from hostile and surly attendants.

75. Juicy Buns (湯 包)

FILLING

½ lb. Chinese cabbage, very finely chopped

½ lb. belly pork, both fat and lean, minced (ground)

½ pint (1 cup) water

1 tablespoon light soy sauce finely chopped

1 level teaspoon very finely chopped ginger

½ level teaspoon salt

¼ level teaspoon sugar

¼ level teaspoon pepper

DOUGH

1¼ level teaspoons (½ package) dried yeast

2 tablespoons very warm water

1 level tablespoon plus 7 oz. (1⅞ cups) plain flour, sifted

4 fluid oz. (½ cup) cold water

5 tablespoons vinegar

3 tablespoons soy sauce

Very finely slivered ginger

Prepare the filling: Simmer all the ingredients together, covered, for 1 hour. The belly pork skin should be included in the stew and removed after cooking. Cool the mixture, and place it in the refrigerator. It will set like a jelly.

Prepare the dough: Follow the directions for Basic Yeast Dough (47), but using instead the proportions given above. After the first rising, knead the dough for about 5 minutes until very firm and homogeneous. Shape it into a long roll, cut it in half and cut each half into ten pieces. Roll each ball between the hands to round it. With a rolling pin, make a circle of 3-inch diameter.

Place a tablespoon of filling in its centre and seal the edges by pinching them together. There must be no breaks in the dough (impossible if dough has been well kneaded) or leaks (impossible if edges are firmly pinched together). Cut twenty 1½-inch squares of foil and place them on steamer racks. Place buns, sealed side down, on foil and let them rise until the contours are nicely rounded (about ½ hour). Steam the buns for 20 minutes, and serve hot, with separate dishes of vinegar mixed with soy sauce, and ginger. Makes 20 buns.

Juicy Buns were also called Little Buns (小籠包). The word "little" is much used in connection with food, particularly in this region. It has several connotations. (1) Tasting and sampling (degustation, 小吃); in consequence, dishes were small and varied rather than large and hearty. (2) Daintiness. This tendency resulted in the making of smaller and smaller pastries. Finally, Yangchow pastries each made one bite, though they came in different shapes, fillings and flavours. (3) The little eating place (小館子). When slumming, Shanghainese chose to frequent "the hole in the wall", preferably in an obscure street. It pleased them a great deal to find one where you could have a little bite, or taste the little sauté (小炒). In short, they liked amusing little things. It is typical of the region that rich, heavy pork and glutinous rice should be made into something dainty and attractive.

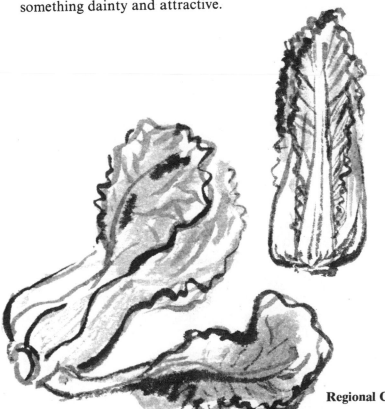

76. Pearly Meat Balls (珍珠肉丸)

2½ oz. (6 level tablespoons)
  glutinous rice
1 level teaspoon salt
¼ lb. fat pork, minced (ground)
¼ lb. lean pork, minced (ground)
1½ teaspoons wine
½ level teaspoon sugar

2 teaspoons light soy sauce
1 level tablespoon cornflour
  (cornstarch)
½ level teaspoon MSG
Oil
5 tablespoons soy sauce
3 tablespoons vinegar

Put the rice in a 2-pint measuring cup (4-cup Pyrex bowl), and fill it to the 24 fluid oz. (3-cup) mark with water. Let it stand for 45 minutes, then drain it. Mix rice with salt.

In a separate bowl, mix together the pork, wine, sugar, soy sauce, cornflour, MSG and 1 tablespoon water. Blend the meat thoroughly with seasoning and shape it into 1-inch balls. Roll the balls in the glutinous rice and place them on an oiled plate or dish. Cover it closely and steam it for 30 minutes. Serve with soy sauce and vinegar, mixed together in a separate dish.

The Rich Mysterious Flavour:
Brown Stock Sauce, including directions for cooking eggs,
bean curd, chicken parts, tripe, ribs of pork or beef, belly
pork, duck and chuck (flank) steak in the sauce

The characteristic look and taste of the food of this region, some-how indefinable because it was heterogeneous, was only in part due to the mixing of fresh ingredients in their fine minces. It came in two shades, light and dark. We have discussed the light and now come to the dark. It is due principally to soy sauce, but there is much more to it. Butchers' shops, like *charcuteries*, and restaurants had stock sauces in continuous use, which somehow acquired lives and personalities of their own, not to be traced to any single ingredient. Each thing cooked in it took away some of its flavour, but also contributed, so that with repeated exchanges, the stock sauce became so concentrated as to form a loud but ghostly chorus of flavours from all the animals which had passed through it. We have found that this recipe is remarkably useful in even a relatively small household, for the busy housewife need only immerse the ingredient in the simmering stock, and pay no attention to it until a set hour. Despite the sameness of the sauce, each ingredient still tastes of itself. This is because it is never overcooked.

The stock sauce is penetrating and it is desirable to use it only with fat ingredients. The exception to this rule is chuck (flank) steak, which becomes dry and chewy and is made into a confection. Fat meat such as duck, wings and ribs are excellent prepared in this fashion. The recipe may be halved, but the amount given is sufficient to cook a whole duck with very little trouble.

*77. Brown Stock Sauce (滷 汁)

24 fluid oz. (3 cups) chicken or meat stock
8 fluid oz. (1 cup) soy sauce
8 fluid oz. (1 cup) wine

5 oz. (¾ cup) brown sugar
1 or 2 star anise
4 to 6 whole cloves
1 piece ginger

Mix all the ingredients in a saucepan and bring to the boil. Allow to cool and store in the refrigerator. Use as needed when cooking ingredients listed in Uses of Brown Stock Sauce (78). Total volume: 2 pints (5 cups).

Keeping stock in condition: After each use the fat is skimmed off, and the volume made up to the original to keep the flavouring the same. More soy sauce, wine, sugar and spices are added as needed.

Salting and blanching meat: The rank taste of meat is removed by salting and blanching it before immersion in the boiling stock. This removes the scum and keeps the stock very clear. For each pound of meat, rub in 2 level tablespoons salt and leave for several hours or overnight in the refrigerator. Blanch the meat by placing it in boiling water 1½ pints (1 quart) water per pound, until scum appears. Rinse meat with cold water, rubbing it free of scum.

Uses of stock sauce: Both plain and elaborate food are prepared with it, served hot or cold, with or without sauce. Some ingredients, as indicated below, are added to boiling stock which is then allowed to cool down to room temperature. The gentle heat imparted by this process is sufficient to cook the food. The remaining ingredients, as indicated, are added to boiling stock sauce and then simmered in it.

Ingredient	How prepared	Stock sauce
12 eggs	hard-boiled, shelled	32 fl. oz. (4 cups)
10 cakes (1 lb. 4 oz.) bean curd	pressed (71)	32 fl. oz. (4 cups)
1 lb. chicken livers	trimmed of fat, cut into lobes	32 fl. oz. (4 cups)
1 lb. chicken giblets	trimmed of fat	20 fl. oz. (2½ cups)
2 lb. chicken wings	cut into sections	20 fl. oz. (2½ cups)
1 lb. pig tripe	washed with vinegar and blanched	20 fl. oz. (2½ cups)
1 lb. beef tripe	scrubbed thoroughly and blanched	16 fl. oz. (2 cups)
2 lb. spare ribs *or* short ribs of beef	salted, blanched, and cut into 2-inch lengths	24 fl. oz. (3 cups)
1 lb. belly pork	left in a large whole piece	to cover
A 5-lb. duck	salted and blanched	40 fl. oz. (5 cups)
1½ lb. chuck (flank) steak	trimmed of fat, salted and blanched	22 fl. oz. (2¾ cups)

[1] The ingredient is cooked during the slow cooling of the stock sauce. The period required for cooling is about 2½ hours for 10 fl. oz. (1¼ cups), and about 4 hours for 32 fl. oz. (4 cups).

[2] A very attractive assortment of hors d'œuvres may be made from reduced portions of these selections. Be exquisitely neat in making the slices and garnish the plate with Chinese parsley or Radish Flowers (28).

BROWN STOCK SAUCE

Mode of Cooking	*Ways served*
Time required to cool stock[1]	Hors d'œuvre:[2] cold, without sauce, sliced into quarters. For picnics: cold, without sauce, whole. For family meals:[3] hot, with sauce.[4]
Time required to cool stock[1]	Hors d'œuvre:[2] cold, without sauce, cut into matchsticks. For family meals:[3] hot, with sauce,[4] cut into strips; or cut into slivers and sautéed with Chinese chives.
Time required to cool stock[1]	Hors d'œuvre:[2] cold, with little or no sauce, sliced thin. With wine or spirits: cold, without sauce, cut into chunks. For family meals: hot, with sauce.[4]
Simmer 15 minutes, cool in stock[1]	Hors d'œuvre:[2] cold, with little or no sauce, sliced very thin across the two halves to form figure 8's. With wine or spirits: cold, without sauce, cut into slices or chunks.
Simmer 1 hour	With wine or spirits: cold without sauce. For family meals: hot, with sauce.[4] Softened mushrooms or black fungus (40) may be added.
Simmer 2½ hours	With wine or spirits: cold, with little or no sauce, cut into strips. For family meals: hot, with sauce,[4] cut into strips.
Simmer 1½ hours	With wine or spirits: cold, without sauce, cut into small pieces. For family meals: hot, with sauce,[4] cut into chunks.
Simmer 2 hours	For family meals: hot, with sauce.[4] Chunks of plain spongy bean curd, prepared as directed in (102) may be added during the last 15 minutes.
Simmer 2½ hours	As a rich main dish: hot, with sauce,[4] shelled, hard-boiled eggs. bean curd, blanched bean sprouts (83) or Chinese chives (84) may be added during the last 10 to 15 minutes.
Simmer 1½ to 1¾ hours	As a rich main dish: hot, with sauce,[4] chopped up. Hors d'œuvre:[2] cold, with a little sauce, chopped up.
Simmer 2 hours	With wine or spirits: cut into dice and served cold. As a confection: drained very thoroughly, cut into dice or bean-size pieces and wrapped individually in paper (like candy).

[3] This ingredient may also be added to spare ribs, short ribs of beef or belly pork during the last 15 to 30 minutes.

[4] The quantity of sauce varies with the dish, ranging from 2 to 12 tablespoons. The remainder of the stock sauce is stored.

FUKIEN

閩
菜

There lies a village whose name is Chu Ch'en—
A hundred miles away from the county town,
Among fields of hemp and green of mulberry trees.
Click, click goes the sound of the spinning-wheel;
Mules and oxen pack the village streets.
The girls go drawing water from the brook;
The men go gathering firewood on the hill.
So far from the town Government affairs are few;
So deep in the hills, man's ways are simple.
Though they have wealth, they do not traffic with it;
Though they reach the age, they do not enter the Army.
Each family keeps to its village trade;
Grey-headed, they have never left the gates.

Alive, they are the people of Ch'en Village;
Dead, they become the dust of Ch'en Village.
Out in the fields old men and young
Gaze gladly, each in the other's face.
In the whole village there are only two clans;
Age after age Chus have married Ch'ens.
Near or distant, they have kinsmen in every house;
Young or old, they have friends wherever they go.
On white wine and roasted fowl they fare
At joyful meetings more than "once a week".
While they are alive, they have no distant partings;
To choose a wife they go to a neighbour's house.
When they are dead, no distant burial;
Round the village graves lie thick.
They are not troubled either about life or death;
They have no anguish either of body or soul.
And so it happens they live to a ripe age
And great-great-grandsons are often seen.

Long have I envied the people of Ch'en Village.

part of a poem by PO CHU-I

The knowing sophistication of Chekiang and Kiangsu faded away abruptly in the smaller villages and hamlets farther south. Avenues of trade and exchange narrowed and seemed to come to a full stop. Finally, it was only the little town (or, in our eyes, the big town), the surrounding hamlets, the family and the household. In a way, this was not a narrowing of the world, for the man of little learning, regarded as a scholar, and the girl with good facial contours, regarded as a beauty, were indeed not less learned nor less pretty than the renowned professor and the film star of Shanghai. It would not be false to say that each small event had as much weight, or even more, in the minds of these insular people, as the national events have in the daily lives of the more worldly. For, after all, they had some control over what was happening in their own households.

The daintiness of central China gave way to loud-voiced heartiness (or was this only in our family?), and life was never for a moment quiet, unembarrassed by the wish for anything else. All meals were punctuated by the call to "Eat! Eat! [*Chiah! Chiah!*]" Gossip was the main hobby and eating came a close second. The cooking of elaborate dainties was an excuse to indulge in both at once. In the earlier part of this century, women in the South were less sophisticated and seldom went out about the town. The home and kitchen were their domain. In the daytime, while the men were away, the house bustled with women, chattering and chopping, quite comfortable in their work. A silence descended in some households when the men returned, for while the men, eating at their own tables, might say a word or two, they preferred to give the food their undivided attention. The women ate silently at another table, or after the men. Aunts padded about the kitchen in slippers, making their specialities. Some were sloppy, others energetic. One aunt had learnt how to make scones from a woman missionary stationed in our home town. Arrivals and departures were incomplete without the harassed traveller having to bear the best wishes of his maternal great-aunt to his paternal cousin, sent with a heavy basket of tangerines. He would leave carrying a box of "pillows", a local pastry made in the rectangular shape of the Chinese pillow. The salty-sour-sweet (*kiam-sng-ti*) dried plums for which Fukien was famous were pressed into his hands, to ward off seasickness, and he was given packets of dried salted olive meats to help him endure his voyage.

It was the women who made life go. A wedding could keep one busy for months. Wealth was to be displayed if one had it, and this was carried out in the food, clothes and jewels. Although women had no say in the decisions, it all came back to them in the end. Matchmakers and midwives were important. Their occasional silence did not mean lack of attention. Lack of education only sharpened their other senses. Each person coming to the house was scrutinized by the women, to be discussed while they chopped and slivered. In their small world all things were definite, and the slightest deviation was remarked on.

Several decades ago, when there was a wedding in Fukien, the groom would go to the bride's house to fetch her, taking with him the bridal chair, which was completely covered with red satin and fresh flowers. He himself made the journey there and back in a blue and yellow teak sedan chair. For the journey to the bride's house, the place under the bridal chair was occupied by a quarter of a freshly slaughtered pig, and on the footstool on which she was to rest her feet was placed the "drum" of firecrackers. This symbolized the life at home, for food was important on important days, and on unimportant ones too. It was under the control of the women of the household, not the renowned chefs famous for their specialities and bad tempers. One worked and planned for these days, which marked the passing of time.

When the groom arrived at the bride's home he was offered sweet *longan* (dragon's eye, a sweet nut like lichee) tea, two hard-boiled eggs in syrup and transparent noodles cooked in thick stock, all for display. The groom who actually ate the eggs was never forgotten by those who had watched him at a distance. When the bride left, there were the firecrackers to be lighted, each igniting its neighbour in a procession of sulphurous pops, and the huge piece of pork to be cooked and given to the beggars.

So the bride went to her new home, where her new relatives stood, waiting to meet her. Perhaps they looked at her more closely than the groom, as women will look at women. All the household had been marshalled. Even at the feast, in the earlier part of this century, the men and women sat at different tables. The menu was studded with expensive things, fins and bird's nest supplied by a relative from the South Seas and brought by another relative paying a visit home. The bird's nest became a soup sweetened with candy sugar (rock candy), and red dates made another sweet, with pigeon eggs making the third sweet soup.

It was an insular world, yet generations lived and died in it. The cultures of northern and central China had not really penetrated it. It grew by the sea, in easy fashion. The flavour of the cuisine was just local, with a great deal of seafood, oysters, clams and fish. We liked the fat-free taste of seafood, and we used the word *tien*, literally meaning sweet, instead of *hsien*. The cleverness of the Cantonese had not reached Fukien, nor the forced simplicity of Peking, nor the laboured delicacy of Chekiang cuisine. All we knew of Szechuan was that its food was very hot, but we could not see the sense in it. After all, even five miles in the baking sun is a long walk. Why alter the taste of anything, when it is already so good?

Specialities of the Region: Shredded Fish; Shredded Pork

People sometimes fail to see the whole point of cooking, which is to amuse oneself, in the preparation as well as in the eating. According to Parkinson's Law, work expands to fill the time in which to do it, and in our home town there were a large number of women in the household, with a great deal of time. The food of Amoy was famous for its painstakingly cut slices and shredded fish, and all the trimmings that require pounding, chopping, grinding and cutting. The best thing is to be busy being idle, or to be idle being busy. We amused ourselves cooking and called it work.

The following recipe requires little attention in the stewing of fish, but constant stirring during the second part, the drying out. Not half a minute's rest can be tolerated, or it will burn. The shreds are made from salt-water fish with which the coastal city abounded. Muscular and fibrous, the fishmeat shrivels into wool-like curls, tasty and fluffy, to be served with congee and peanuts for breakfast, or on bread and butter, imported delicacies.

79. Shredded Fish (魚 鬆)

4 lb. prepared mackerel
  or porgy (see method)
4 fluid oz. (½ cup) light soy sauce
5 tablespoons pale dry sherry
2 oz. (¼ cup) sugar

1 tablespoon pressed ginger (juice)
1 head garlic, crushed or pressed
8 fluid oz. (1 cup) oil
½ oz. (½ cup) dried parsley

Remove fish heads and discard them. Weigh out 4 lb. fish. Steam the fish for 20 minutes, then bone and skin it. Mix the fishmeat with soy sauce, sherry, sugar, ginger, garlic and half the oil. Bring to the boil and simmer for 1½ hours, until the liquid is absorbed and the flakes start to come apart.

For the drying out, use a large shallow pan about 10 inches by 14 inches. Pour in the remaining oil and place the pan over low heat. Add the stewed fish and, when heated through, reduce the heat to very low. Stir the fish constantly for about 1½ hours, so that it dries out very, very gradually. *Do not leave the pan unattended.* Towards the end, the fish will appear to consist entirely of curly fibres, like unspun wool. The slow drying out is continued until the fibres have a slightly toasted flavour, and are crisp and brown but not burnt. At this point you may add the dried parsley and stir the fish for 10 minutes more. Cool it thoroughly, then store it in tightly closed containers. It will keep for months. If the fibres become too soft, dry them out in a 250°F. (Mark ½) oven for about 20 minutes, stirring occasionally.

80. Shredded Pork (肉 鬆)

4 lb. pork fillet (tenderloin), trimmed of fat, sinews and bone
1 head garlic, peeled and crushed to a paste
5 fluid oz. (⅔ cup) soy sauce

2 oz. (⅓ cup) red fermented bean curd (紅 豆 腐 乳)
6 fluid oz. (¾ cup) water
3 level tablespoons medium or dark brown sugar

Cut the pork into 1¼-inch cubes. Stew it for about 2 hours over very low heat together with the remaining ingredients. The pork must be stirred during the stewing to prevent burning. Keep the pot covered at intervals. During the course of the stewing try to separate the fibres with a wooden spoon. When all the liquid has evaporated, and some oil has collected at the bottom of the pot, and the fibres are beginning to fall apart, transfer the contents to a very large frying-pan, or to a 10-inch by 14-inch pan. Over very low heat, constantly stir and separate the meat fibres with a wooden spoon. This process requires 1½ to 2 hours. The meat will begin to resemble matted wool, and smell a little toasted (but not burnt!). The drying out is continued until the fibres are fluffy and woolly, and taste dry yet succulent. Place the fibres on a large sheet of paper to cool them. As soon as they are perfectly cold, pack them into containers, which should be tightly closed or sealed. The shredded pork will keep for months at room temperature. Reheat in the oven if, after a while, the fibres lose their crispness, following directions given under Shredded Fish (79).

Speciality of Amoy: Popia, *consisting of the Great Pot, Thin Crêpes and the side dishes and sauces to go with it*

Popia, the great crêpe which is the speciality of Amoy, our home town, in a way sums up the flavour of life at home. The reader will see that it requires several people a few days' work to prepare it, a large gathering of people to eat it, and that its flavour, sweet and dainty, is offset by the impressive and hearty manner in which they fall to. *Popia* consists of three parts: the great pot of filling, the thin crêpes, and the half-dozen or more side dishes without which the flavour is incomplete. The three parts take about equal time to make. As a rule, the main pot is put together first, the crêpes made second, and the side dishes, especially the crisp ones, made last. Each part requires almost a day's work, and it should be remembered that the great pot must be slowly stewed and allowed to cool down and mellow before perfection of flavour is reached. After all is ready, one likes to spend some time setting the table. As each guest will be reaching for things from a dozen plates, all must be within reach. Each place is set with napkins, plate, chopsticks and spoon. Then everyone is summoned to the table.

81. Popia: The Great Pot (to serve 10–12 persons) (薄 餅 料)

3 lb. (12 cakes) bean curd	Oil
2 lb. prawns (shrimps)	Light soy sauce and soy sauce
6 spring onions (scallions)	Salt
2 cans (about 1½ lb.) bamboo shoots	Sugar
	Pale dry sherry
2 lb. pork fillet (tenderloin)	¼ pint (½ cup) chicken stock or
2 to 2½ lb. snow peas	water

Press the bean curd as directed (71). Cut curd into slivers and reserve them. Shell and clean the prawns. Dice them and reserve them. Chop the spring onions very finely. Sliver the bamboo shoots, pork and snow peas, keeping them separate.

Each of the ingredients is slowly sautéed to bring out its fragrance, then combined with the others to fuse the flavours.

(1) Pork, spring onions and bamboo shoots: Sauté pork and spring onions with 3 tablespoons oil and 1 tablespoon light soy sauce to bring out toasted flavour. Then add bamboo, 2 tablespoons oil and 1 level teaspoon salt, and sauté until the mixture appears a little dry. Reserve.

(2) Bean curd: Sauté bean curd with 4 tablespoons oil and 1 tablespoon soy sauce until very lightly toasted. This may take about 15 minutes. Continue until you can smell the fragrance of the bean curd. Reserve.

(3) Prawns: Sauté prawns with 2 tablespoons oil, ½ level teaspoon salt, ¼ level teaspoon sugar and 2 teaspoons sherry. Continue mixing and tossing the prawns until all the liquid has evaporated.

At this point all the ingredients have been sautéed except for the snow peas. Select a large pot which will accommodate all the ingredients with room to spare, or use two pots. Reheat the pork, spring onions and bamboo in it, then add the bean curd, then the prawns. Finally, when all these ingredients are simmering together, add the slivered snow peas. The pot is cooked over very low heat for 2½ to 4 hours, with occasional stirring. No liquid is added, therefore the ingredients cook in their own juices, achieving perfection of taste. *At no time should the great pot be subjected to high heat,* otherwise the ingredients will burn, the meat juices and the prawn juices will coagulate, and all the *hsien* will be lost. If you think the pot threatens to burn, you may add the chicken stock or water. Stir the pot every 15 minutes for about 2½ hours. If possible, let it cool down.

* * *

On the following day, reheat it over low heat, adding a little liquid if necessary. The reheating will take about 45 minutes. Correct the seasoning, adding more salt if necessary. This is served piping hot.

82. Popia: Thin Crêpes (薄 餅 皮)

3½ pints minus 4 tablespoons (8½ cups) water

3½ lb. (16 cups) plain flour, sifted

These delicate crêpes are strong, pliable and elastic, and light. They are made by touching a toffee-like dough of flour and water to an ungreased hot griddle or heavy frying pan. The portion of the wet dough which adheres to its surface forms a translucent crêpe. This recipe requires about 4 hours' hard work, and makes 250 to 300 six-inch sheets.

Pour the water into a large mixing bowl. Add half the flour and beat until very smooth. (This part may be done in an electric mixer.) Add the remaining flour and work it in by hand. *The dough must be absolutely homogeneous at all times.* Knead it for about ½ hour until it is smooth, elastic and toffee-like. When pulled out of the bowl in which it is kneaded, it should fall back in thick sheets and strands. If possible, let it rest in the refrigerator for several hours, the bowl covered with a damp cloth.

* * *

To make the crêpes, use a cast-iron pancake griddle or heavy frying pan. Have ready a clean damp cloth or paper towel, two plates with clean damp cloths over them, and a sharp knife. Heat the griddle over low heat. It must be free of grease and of even temperature. To even out the temperature, pour about 1 teaspoon water over the heated surface. It will boil all over. Wipe the surface with a clean damp towel. The levelling out of the griddle temperature is repeated from time to time. Take a handful of dough, replacing the damp cloth on the bowl, and work the dough so that it is centred in the palm of your hand, though it tends to flow. Press it to the centre of the griddle. Immediately pull back on the dough, so that a fine film adheres to the griddle. While the dough in the one hand is kept in slow constant motion by working it with the fingers and palm, the thin crêpe adhering to the griddle cooks in about 30 seconds, peeling from the outer edge as it dries. Loosen it with the knife edge. With the other hand peel it off the griddle, and place it on the plate between two folds of a damp cloth. There must be no dough left adhering to the surface of the griddle. If there is a patch, scrape it off and smooth out the griddle temperature with a wipe of the damp cloth.

*   *   *

After an hour or two, the remaining portion of uncooked dough may be moistened with about 1 tablespoon water to keep it at the proper consistency. Work the added water in thoroughly. Crêpes keep well for a few days in the refrigerator if arranged in a high stack and closely wrapped in a clean damp cloth. Crêpes are served at room temperature, in stacks, covered with a clean damp napkin. They do not stick to one another.

HINTS

Holes appear. Griddle is too hot. Wipe it with the damp cloth.

Crêpes are too thick. Dough is too dry. Add a little water to the dough and work it in thoroughly.

Crêpes are lumpy. Dough is too dry and not homogeneous. Add a little water and work it in thoroughly.

Crêpes are lacy. Dough is too wet. Swing it about on the palm to evaporate the moisture. The quality will improve. Do not attempt to work in flour.

Crêpes brown at edges and break in centre. Griddle is unevenly heated. Add 1 teaspoon water to griddle and wipe it with a cloth.

Dough fails to stick to griddle. Griddle is too dry. Wipe the surface with a damp cloth.

Side dishes: Arrange each of the following in separate dishes and serve them at room temperature.

83. Blanched Bean Sprouts (豆 芽)

½ lb. bean sprouts
3 pints (8 cups) boiling water

Blanch the bean sprouts in boiling water for 2 to 3 minutes. Drain immediately in a colander and rinse with cold water. Drain well.

84. Blanched Chinese Chives (韭 菜)

½ lb. chives
3 pints (8 cups) boiling water

Cut off the white stalks and wash chives in quantities of cold water until free of earth. Blanch in boiling water until deep green. Drain and rinse with cold water. Cut the chives into 1-inch lengths.

85. Dried Seaweed (紫菜)

2 tablespoons oil
6 sheets (1½ oz.) dry seaweed

The best green seaweed for this purpose can be obtained only on the Amoy coast. Japanese laver, a purple seaweed, has a similar taste after being fried briefly and crumbled.

Heat the oil in a frying pan or wo. Fry the sheets of seaweed one at a time for 5 seconds each. Drain and crumble them into bits. They contribute an indescribably delicious toasted flavour.

86. Egg Slivers (蛋絲)

5 eggs   *½ level teaspoon MSG*
2 tablespoons water   *Oil or fat*

Beat the eggs, water and MSG together. Pour 2 to 3 tablespoons of the mixture into a heated, greased frying pan, and tip it to make the thinnest possible layer. Stack the layers on top of one another, roll them up, and cut them into the thinnest possible slivers.

87. Dried Flatfish (鯿魚)

2 dried flatfish
Fat for deep-frying

Strip the skins off the flatfish. Break them into pieces and fry in deep fat until a deep peach colour, then drain the pieces and chop them into a fine meal.

Peanuts

Toast 7 oz. (1¼ cups) peanuts, and chop them into a very fine meal.

Chinese Parsley (芫荽)

Use only the tender leaves and stems, discarding stalks and roots. Wash and drain 4 oz. (3 cups) Chinese parsley. (Very tender, young coriander may be used.)

Relishes

Make the following brushes with which to paint on the sauces, which consist of hot red mustard (Tabasco, hot sauce), yellow mustard, Hoisin sauce (海鮮醬) and plum sauce (酸梅醬).

88. Spring Onion (Scallion) Brushes (葱 花)

Wash and cut into 1½-inch lengths the white and light green stalks of spring onions, one for each person. Slash the sections to a depth of ½ inch, as finely as possible, to make the brushes, and soak these in iced water for a few hours. Then drain and place neatly around the dishes of relishes.

Each person put a crêpe or two on his plate, then painted them with sauces. Heaped spoonfuls of the steaming hot filling were put in the centre, then we added the crunchy bean sprouts, fragrant parsley, peanuts, crunchy sun-dried fish, delicious seaweed, bland egg slivers, and pungent chives, and rolled them into a cylinder, tucked in at one end.

It is observed that each year, when we made *popia* and gathered the clan together, the same things were said, the same stories told, the same comments made. It elicited the thought that the size and shape of each person's crêpe was a reflection of his personality. All the comforts that resulted from the clan speaking the same dialect, gathered together at the same time and helping themselves to the same pot, softened our feelings, producing contentment, encouraging *gourmandise*. We almost never finished the anecdotes or the comments, for all lapsed into the silence of glorious eating, with an occasional contented groan.

Note that in the great pot the snow peas are deliberately overcooked to bring out a flavour not to be found in the usual crisp sauté. The pot is made on the first day, mellowed during the second, and best on the third day, after it has been reheated once or twice. By then, all the juices and flavours have softened and run into one another. Since little or no water is added, the flavour is very concentrated. On the fourth day, if any remains, the leftovers are rolled into the remaining crêpes, sealed with a little beaten egg and fried like egg roll. These are also delicious.

*Quick Lunch at the Stalls: Pork Liver and Noodles
in Soup, including a recipe for Cheap Stock*

The local version of the quick lunch or snack was made in the
stalls by the harbour, or in the untidy streets. At the stalls, the pots
of cheap stock were always kept steaming, and all the vendor had
to do was to drop in some very thin parboiled vermicelli (*misua*)
and add a few slices of pork liver. In less than a minute, a big bowl
of this was served. The liver was actually crisp. While the little
boats bobbed up and down, perhaps waiting to take one of us
across the water, we perched on a rickety wooden stool, sat by a
table none too clean, and ate Pork Liver and Noodles in Soup. Add
plenty of black pepper, and do not overcook the liver.

89. Cheap Stock (經 濟 湯)

1½ pints (3½ cups) water
½ level teaspoon MSG
½ level teaspoon salt
½ level teaspoon sugar
2 teaspoons soy sauce

¼ level teaspoon black pepper
*1 spring onion (scallion), cut into
   2-inch lengths*
2 slices ginger

Make a cheap stock by bringing the water, seasonings, spring onion and
ginger to the boil. Then add the noodles and liver prepared according to
the following recipe.

90. Pork Liver and Noodles in Soup (豬 肝 麵 線)

3 oz. vermicelli, parboiled
¼ lb. pork liver, thinly sliced

Black pepper
Vinegar

Heat the noodles gently and, when heated through, stir in the liver. When
the liver is just cooked (30 to 60 seconds), serve the dish at once, adding
pepper and vinegar to taste.

*Gastronomic Favours: Pig's Knuckles and Transparent
Noodles; Rich Glutinous Rice*

Within the home, the serving of food was subtly geared to the
status of the person in the family. The elderly were given better,
soft and nourishing food. The killing of a chicken was an event.

In a household of perhaps two or three dozen people, only the more important and elderly people were privileged to eat it. Favours and gifts and insults were expressed gastronomically. A visiting relative from afar returned to be given *vegetable* soup, with not a piece of meat in sight! He would think he had been insulted, or that the family was acting poverty-stricken in order to prepare him for a small loan. Daughters-in-law and female cousins sought the favours and approval of the old lady and the head of the house by appearing in mid-afternoon with a bowl of chicken soup, or a fragrant bowl of transparent noodles cooked in a rich and nourishing soup of pig's knuckles.

91. Pig's Knuckles and Transparent Noodles (豬 脚 粉 絲 湯)

3 lb. pig's knuckles	2 level teaspoons salt
3 spring onions (scallions)	½ level teaspoon sugar
4 slices ginger	½ level teaspoon MSG
4 to 6 dried Chinese mushrooms	¼ lb. transparent noodles

Bring the knuckles to the boil with 5 pints (12 cups) water, 1 spring onion and 2 slices ginger. Keep at a rolling boil for 3 minutes to remove the scum. Discard the water, spring onion and ginger. Bring the blanched knuckles to the boil again in 2½ pints (6 cups) water with the remaining spring onions, cut into 2-inch lengths, and ginger, and the mushrooms, salt, sugar and MSG. Simmer the mixture for about 2½ hours, until the bones come loose. Remove them. Remove stems from mushrooms.

Meanwhile, soak the noodles in a large quantity of cold water to soften them. When the soup and knuckles are ready, drop in the softened noodles and cook them for about 10 minutes.

In the earlier part of this century, a daughter-in-law's status within a great household rose immediately after she had produced a grandchild. There was a common saying that

> *Father eats the chicken,*
> *Mother drinks the soup,*
> *Son has the pickings,*
> *Daughter-in-law just looks.*

But the principle contained therein was put aside especially when the daughter-in-law was nursing. Young women became fat and smooth, enjoying comforts that had often been previously denied.

Rich Glutinous Rice was considered particularly nourishing, and was made specially for women after childbirth, for convalescents and the elderly. The rich rice was also a fancy dish that could be served on occasions when it was right and proper to feel quite heavy and stuffed. The baby's first month was celebrated with dyed red eggs, a huge, rich feast, and the tiny child, dressed in red, was displayed like a great doll, each guest pressing a packet of silver dollars on it. Then one would have a feast and the rich rice.

*92. Rich Glutinous Rice (油 飯)

⅜ oz. (2 level tablespoons) dried prawns (shrimps)
6 large or 10 small dried Chinese mushrooms
½ pint (1 cup) water
4 oz. lean pork
2 spring onions (scallions)

4 tablespoons oil
¼ level teaspoon salt
1½ teaspoons soy sauce
¼ level teaspoon MSG
¼ level teaspoon sugar
10 oz. (1½ cups) glutinous rice, washed

Soak the dried prawns and mushrooms in water. When the mushrooms are softened, remove the stems and sliver them very finely. Remove the prawns and reserve them, keeping the liquid apart. Sliver the pork and spring onions separately.

Heat 3 tablespoons oil in a frying pan and add the spring onions, sprinkling them with the salt. Sauté for at least 3 minutes over low heat. Add the softened dried prawns and sauté until their flavour is added to that of the spring onions, about 5 minutes. Add the mushrooms and 1 teaspoon soy sauce, and sauté until all the juices have evaporated, and the fragrance of the mushrooms is brought out. Then add the pork, and sprinkle the mixture with MSG, sugar, and the remaining ½ teaspoon soy sauce. Stir the mixture continuously with chopsticks, tossing the ingredients about. When the flavours all come together in the air, but not before, add the rice and the remaining tablespoon of oil. Stir until the grains are evenly coloured. Make the prawn-mushroom water up to 1 pint (2½ cups) with water, and add it to the frying pan. Bring to the boil with rice, stirring. Cover the pan closely and reduce the heat to very low. It will be ready in 20 to 25 minutes.

KWANGTUNG

The fields are chill; the sparse rain has stopped;
The colours of Spring teem on every side.
With leaping fish the blue pond is full;
With singing thrushes the green boughs droop.
The flowers of the field have dabbled their powdered cheeks;
The mountain grasses are bent level at the waist.
By the bamboo stream the last fragment of cloud
Blown by the wind slowly scatters away.

LI PO

The exotic quality of Kwangtung cooking comes not from the taste but from the choice of material. It lies farther south of Fukien, along the sea coast. Mushrooms grew in the mountainous terrain. The sparrows and wild ducks were beaten out of the reeds, huge snails picked up. The squirming snake and slithering eel were highly regarded as food. Huge oysters were picked out of the sea, frogs, turtles and winkles from the watery rice fields, by the side of which grew quantities of green and leafy vegetables. Plump chickens and pigeons were raised specially for the table.

The natural variety of ingredients and the perhaps uncommon character of this regional cuisine developed naturally as the result of its climate and the temper of its people. The natural taste of these foods was not altered, and all the art was concentrated on texture. It may be true that when things are too easily come by, they are not worked over. The climate is warm the year round, and fresh food was available at all times. Cooking of vegetables was casual, their flavour taken for granted, and no labour went into their preparation that could be compared to the cooking of Spinach in Cream Stock (20). Vegetables were sautéed with snails, or chicken or fish, lacking the touch that makes flavours complementary. Their handling of flavour lacked the depth which comes from much thought on gastronomy. What they excelled in was the control of the crisp and tender textures. They cooked duck's web better than the duck itself, chicken better than anybody. This is because they knew when to leave things alone. The cutting and chopping were coarse, in keeping with an impatient people. The character of their cuisine was marked by artful speed and variety of texture.

Artful Speed: Dipped Snails;
Blanched Greens in Oyster Sauce

The fast but studied technique of Kwangtung cuisine is illustrated by the preparation of snails in the manner called "dipping". The same technique may be applied to kidneys, with good results. The problem lies in cooking snails without destroying their texture, which when properly done is crisp, like that of fresh clams. One makes very thin slices of the edible, scallop-like portion of the snails, dips them in boiling acidified water and finishes them in simmering sauce. If the water were not acidified, the slices would be tough. On the other hand, if the dipping were not fast, the snail would also lose its sweetness. Frankly, the preparation of the snails themselves is not for the squeamish, for in order to be assured that the snails are fresh they must be manifestly alive. But one can get used to it, and the result is worth the effort.

93. Dipped Snails (白 灼 蚵 螺 片)

3 live snails (about 1 lb. each)
5 pints (12 cups) water
1 piece ginger
1 spring onion (scallion)
1 teaspoon vinegar

SAUCE
3 tablespoons pale dry sherry

1 tablespoon oyster sauce
1 teaspoon light soy sauce
2 tablespoons chicken stock
¾ level teaspoon sugar
¼ level teaspoon MSG
2 slices ginger, finely slivered
1 spring onion, slivered
3 tablespoons oil

Press the foot which lies along the curve of the shell of the snail. If it retracts the snail is alive. Place it between several folds of newspaper and crack the shell with a hammer until all of the snail is exposed. The scallop-like muscle attached to the disc is the edible portion. This greyish and ivory-coloured portion tapers to a narrow strip. Cut off the muscle at the narrow strip, and free it from the soft tissue next to it. Discard the remainder of the snail. Cut off the foot, the reddish tubule, the bony cartilage, and the gelatinous material surrounding the cartilage. Slice off the disc and the greyish outer layer of the scallop. Discard all of these portions, saving only the ivory-coloured scallop. Slice it very thinly, gripping the muscle with a cloth to prevent it from slipping about. Three snails yield enough thin slices to measure 12 fluid oz. (1½ cups) if packed in a measuring cup.

To make the sauce: Mix all the ingredients together in a small saucepan and heat gently.

Have ready a large square of cheesecloth placed over a bowl, a slotted spoon and a pair of chopsticks. Bring water to the boil with the ginger and spring onion. Remove the ginger and spring onion. Add vinegar to the boiling water, keeping it at a rolling boil. Bring the sauce up to simmering point.

Throw the snail slices all at once into the acidified water. Almost immediately remove all the slices with the aid of the slotted spoon and chopsticks, and place them in the cheesecloth. Wring the water out of the slices, and drop the slices into the simmering sauce, which must now be brought to high heat. Sauté for 15 to 20 seconds, and serve immediately.

The most elusive flavours are the natural ones, which like moving spirits have to be caught. The way to catch the natural flavour of vegetables is to blanch them, thereby removing some of the acrid taste without destroying the flavour. The following dish is a standard item in the short-order restaurants of Hong Kong.

*94. Blanched Greens in Oyster Sauce (蠔 油 芥 蘭)

¾ lb. mustard greens, celery,
asparagus or Chinese cabbage
stalks

6 tablespoons oyster sauce
4 level teaspoons sugar

Use mustard greens or a similar vegetable (see above) with thin, crisp stalks and not too many leaves. Blanch the greens in 4 to 6 pints (12 to 16 cups) boiling water for a few minutes. When the stalks turn a deeper colour, turn the contents into a colander, and rinse them very thoroughly under the cold tap. Cut the stalks into 2- or 3-inch sections and place them on a plate in a neat stack.

To reheat the greens, scald them with about 2½ pints (6 cups) water, tipping the plate to drain. Stir oyster sauce with sugar until dissolved and pour over the greens.

Two Cantonese Recipes for Chicken:
Brown Chicken; Lemon Chicken

The Cantonese excelled in cooking chicken, timing the cooking precisely so that the sweet marrow was just barely cooked. Plain Chicken (3) is a Cantonese recipe. Since the climate was too warm to permit air-drying, chickens were barely cooked, then rubbed with vinegar and sugar, and hung up to dry. When it was fried, the skin was crisp and brittle. In Swatow, chicken was wrapped in rice paper, then packed in very hot salt to cook it. Only a little salt dissolved in the juices of the chicken, which was rich and fragrant. Still another way was to wrap the chicken in mud and bake it, cracking open the clay to get at the juicy hot bird (Beggar's Chicken). The most popular is still the chicken cooked in a crock of soy sauce. Many people attempt to make this, but fail to get the skin a rich brown. The secret is to use a freshly killed chicken, one whose skin has not yet contracted. Once the latter has occurred, the fat comes to the surface and the colour will not penetrate. In a freshly killed chicken, the outer surface of the skin is still moist and will take in the soy sauce. These subtle changes taking place after death are, of course, hardly noticeable to the eye.

95. Brown Chicken (鼓 油 鷄)

A 4-lb. freshly killed chicken
6½ pints (16 cups) soy sauce
1 lb. candy sugar (rock candy)

6 cloves or 1 star anise
2 pieces dried tangerine peel
6 slices fresh ginger

Clean, pluck and draw the chicken. Bring the remaining ingredients to the boil in a large pot and add the chicken. Bring to the boil again, cover the pot and let it cool to room temperature. This will take about 5 hours. Remove the chicken, chop it into pieces and serve it with a little of the sauce. The remaining sauce is saved and used again.

The following recipe does not call for a very freshly killed chicken. Its flavour is excellent.

96. Lemon Chicken (檸 檬 鷄)

A 3- to 4-lb. chicken
1 level teaspoon salt
2 tablespoons soy sauce
2 tablespoons gin, vodka or other
   strong alcohol

5 tablespoons oil
½ teaspoon pressed ginger (juice)
1½ to 2 tablespoons lemon juice
   (juice of 1 lemon)
1 tablespoon sesame oil
½ level teaspoon salt
½ level teaspoon sugar
4 tablespoons chicken stock

Wipe the chicken dry and rub its body cavity with salt. Place it in a dish, and rub soy sauce and gin, vodka or other strong alcohol over its body (*meikweilu*, an aromatic liqueur made from roses, is excellent for this purpose). Let the chicken stand in the dish of alcohol for about 4 hours, turning the chicken occasionally to let it soak into the skin.

*　　　*　　　*

Heat oil and ginger juice in a wo. Brown the chicken in the wo over moderately low heat, reserving the marinade. The browning of the chicken must be thorough for the flavour to be right. After the chicken is browned, reduce the heat and remove 4 tablespoons of the oil. Add the remaining ingredients together with the reserved marinade. Bring to the boil, cover the wo closely and simmer it for about 35 minutes, turning the chicken so that the liquid coats it. Chop the chicken into small pieces, and place it on a serving dish. Warm the sauce and pour it over the chicken.

Pure Flavour of the Region:
Sautéed Mushrooms; Mushrooms in Broth

Chinese mushrooms can be almost perfect in shape, texture and flavour. Their only flaw is a slightly bitter aftertaste. This can be corrected with sugar, or with a meaty stock. People tend to misuse mushrooms, slivering them finely to spread out their flavour, but to their detriment. They should be left whole or cut in half, juicy, fragrant and smooth. Do not add other things to them, for it takes away from the pure enjoyment of mushrooms. Do not talk when eating mushrooms, or you spoil the flavour. Chew a mushroom as little as possible, only press out its hidden juices between tongue and teeth. The best mushrooms are patterned on top, and have thick curled caps. Rather spend more money on these and buy less than try to find the sublime flavour in the chipped and thin caps of the cheaper variety.

*97. Sautéed Mushrooms (炒 香 菇)

24 large dried Chinese mushrooms
1 tablespoon oil
½ level teaspoon sugar
¼ level teaspoon salt
1 teaspoon soy sauce
1 tablespoon sesame oil
1 tablespoon oyster sauce

SAUCE
¼ pint (⅔ cup) chicken stock
2 tablespoons oyster sauce
½ level teaspoon sugar
2 level teaspoons cornflour

Soak mushrooms in water to cover until they are softened and have increased their volume by one-third (30 minutes to 1 hour). Trim off the stems and discard them, or add them to a stock pot. Reserve the soaking liquid. Sauté the caps in oil, adding sugar, salt and soy sauce. Add the mushroom water, sesame oil and oyster sauce, and heat the mixture to simmering point. Simmer over low heat, covered, until the water is absorbed. Place the mushrooms in a mound, caps facing upwards.

Sautéed Mushrooms are served either with or without sauce. If a sauce is desired, mix the ingredients together and cook until thickened. Pour the sauce over the mound of mushroom caps.

To make a broth with mushrooms, remember to (1) add a little sugar, to round out the taste; (2) simmer the mushrooms until they sink to the bottom of the pot; (3) open the pot as little as possible, so that the vapours will not escape. Some people seal the pot with a paste of flour and water.

142 | **Regional Cooking**

*98. Mushrooms in Broth (清燉香菇)

12 dried Chinese mushrooms
Generous ½ pint (1½ cups) water
1½ pints (3½ cups) best chicken
   stock
1 spring onion (scallion)
1 slice ginger
1 tablespoon soy sauce
½ level teaspoon sugar
¼ level teaspoon salt

Soften mushrooms in water. Remove the stems, reserving the caps and
the soaking water. Put the caps in a saucepan together with the reserved
mushroom water and the remaining ingredients. Bring to the boil and
simmer for 1 hour, with the pan closely covered. Remove the spring onion
and ginger.

5. Curiosities

Éléphant: *La chair de l'éléphant est comestible, mais coriace; la trompe et les pieds passent pour les morceaux très délicats.*

Ours: *Les gourmets un peu excentriques prisent fort les pattes de l'ours qui, après avoir été marinées (pendant 3 jours au moins), sont mises à braiser dans un fond fortement aromatisé et servies dans un coulis preparé avec leur fonds de cuisson.*

Rat: *Rongeur qui a été élevé au rang de comestibles pendant le siège de Paris en 1870, et qui est consommé dans certaines regions.*

LAROUSSE GASTRONOMIQUE

DURING THE WAR in the 1940's, the rats of Chungking grew so large that cats cowered before them, afraid to challenge them. At this time there appeared at certain tables dishes of red-cooked meat which people hesitated to identify, and some dared not eat. It is true that necessity and economy led people to explore all things. But this is only part of the story. The great cuisine, like a broad river, was constantly breaking up into side streams and eddies, each pool whirling about itself in ever smaller circles. These eccentric foci were occasionally drawn into the main stream, while others remained on the periphery. This would not be a world in itself, but for the fanatics and the lunatic fringe. The special character of the cuisine comes not from hunger or need, but from the cult of gastronomy. Were it not for the cult, such exotic experiments in search of taste would not have been made. One can see their point of view. Each thing is an entity, and its perfection of taste should be an end in itself. The more you taste it, the more tastes it has. The more closely you look, the finer the pattern; small differences loom as wide gaps. Were it not for the cult of gastronomy, the cuisine would not have its present depth and range.

In this chapter we discuss some interesting extremes which

exaggerate the particular point of view of Chinese gastronomy. That point of view is part taste, part knowledge, part habit and part prejudice. It differs from the French idea of cuisine and the American type of cooking. The most elegant French cooking makes use of the breast meat of chicken, the fillet of fish. The difference between Chinese and French gastronomy is that to the Chinese the enjoyment of *sole meunière* extends from the fillet to the crunchy little bones around the side of the fish. Chinese gastronomy would have made a speciality of the tiny crisp parts, but for the fact that flatfish are generally absent from fresh water. The "oyster" of the turkey, located in the pelvic bone, would have made a contribution to Chinese cuisine, but there are few turkeys in China. Artichoke leaves would have been better liked than the hearts, bread chosen for the crust.

The finer graduations of texture are appreciated in the parts of fish. Brain, lips, jowls, ventral fins, underbelly and tail each form the main ingredient in a number of dishes. These recipes are part of classic cuisine. Necessity may have led to the eating of all parts, but gastronomy made it a sign of refinement. The cult of gastronomy promoted the bizarre and recherché to the level of sophistication. It gave a definite cast to the development of the cuisine. Yuan Mei said:

I often see that in the preparation of turtle only the mantle is used; actually the flavour is concentrated in its flesh. When shad is steamed, only its belly is used, but the sweetest part is the back. There is nothing cheaper than salted [duck] eggs. The best part is the yolk. But if you served only the yolks, would it not be insipid? I do not say this because I am afraid of using my good fortune too fast, as common people might put it. Supposing I said that all this waste made for better cooking, then it might be tolerated. In fact it has its disadvantages, so why go to all the trouble?

It is not really a case of bad taste, but gourmandise. For, if fish lips have that special gelatinous quality when braised, why not have a whole dish of them? Another famous dish of Chekiang-Kiangsu was called "Paddles" (划水), consisting of the ventral fins and soft belly of the fish. The cabbage also has parts.

99. Soochow Cabbage Stew (爛 糊)

1½ to 2 lb. Chinese cabbage
2 tablespoons chicken or duck fat
Generous ½ pint (1½ cups) good
  chicken or duck stock
½ level teaspoon salt

Carefully separate the cabbage stalks. Brush, wash and drain them. Each stalk is cut into three sections about 3 inches long. Each section is stacked in neat piles with others of its kind. A. *Base of stalks:* Slice the stack lengthwise into ⅜-inch widths, keeping the lengths parallel. B. *Middle sections:* Slice this stack lengthwise, into ⅜-inch-wide pieces, keeping them parallel. C. *Leafy tips:* Slice this stack radially with the grain into ⅜-inch widths. Sections A, B and C are cooked in that order. *Do not stir the stew at any time.*

Bring the chicken or duck fat and stock to the boil in a large pot. Add section A, laying the lengths so they remain parallel, and sprinkle with half the salt. Cover the pot and keep it at a vigorous boil for 15 minutes. Add section B, laying the lengths in the same direction as A. Boil it, covered, for 10 minutes. Add section C, more or less parallel to A and B, and sprinkle with the remaining salt. Reduce the heat and simmer for 1 hour. Total cooking time is 1 hour 25 minutes. Invert the cabbage on to a dish of soup-plate dimensions. Its ribbed dome shape somewhat resembles that of a melon.

Concerning the eating of parts there is a horror story. Bram Stoker's *Dracula* tells us that we all have individual tastes, but should not make them known. Some gastronomes unfortunately did make their preferences known. "No gentleman would do it," wrote Yuan Mei about the following practice. Li Liweng had described this method in his notes. "I shall tell you of a person who was good at preparing goose feet. Every time a fattened goose was to be killed, he plunged its feet into a pan of boiling oil, and let it go again into the pond. Then he repeated this four times in all. The feet of the goose were sweet and luscious, at least an inch thick, really an unusual delicacy. I said, 'I have heard about this and don't wish to hear it again.' " This is an example of sadism, but perhaps not worse than the raising of poultry for market. These fowl are huddled together, force-fed, and their feet are never allowed to touch the ground. One thinks that they must have a buried desire for one good long pull at a worm and a peck at the earth, which they may look at but not touch. Is not their life a prolonged moment of frustration? "Animals were made for man's use," said Yuan

Mei, "so they may be killed, but they should never be made to wish for death."

The cult of gastronomy talked into prominence the texture of foods which by their very nothingness were a challenge. One is reminded of a balloon, inflated by hot air, which rises into the air and becomes an enormous attraction and curiosity. Other absurdities have been sent aloft, but only these remain airborne. This makes one think that there is something more to the launching of a balloon than a lot of air.

There were many elements which entered into the cult. One was the cook, who had to be a skilled technician. "To make deer sinew tender requires three days. First pound it, then boil it several times to rid it of its rank smell. Stew it in beef broth, then in chicken broth. Add a little sesame oil to round it off. Serve it plain, pure white, and sprinkle crushed wild pepper on it." Secondly, these curiosities of the table may have a little merit. Gastronomy is a lifetime avocation, in which progress is marked by the discernment of ever more subtle differences. Perhaps the most sophisticated palate will place texture above flavour, since it requires more training to appreciate the qualities of texture. Bear's paw, elephant trunk and veal tendons were brought into the menus because of the cult of gastronomy and because of the food snobs. "Food snobs are merely those people who covet expensive things. Their tastes are influenced by hearsay, not by their own judgment. They do not know that bean curd tastes better than bird's nest, and seaweed, unless it is of the best quality, does not compare with bamboo shoots. Chicken, pork, fish and duck can stand upon their own merits, but bêche-de-mer and bird's nest depend on other substances for their taste." This snob element brought the fins and the bird's nest into the cuisine, where they are now so common as to be contemptible, no longer curiosities.

Gastronomy is a series of experiments, and some experiments were total failures. Eggs were tampered with. Even the great Yuan Mei tried to improve on them, but the idea was too belaboured. "Make a tiny hole in an egg, pour out the yolk and egg white and discard the yolk. Mix the white with thick chicken stock, and beat the mixture with chopsticks until thoroughly blended. Replace it in the shell and seal the egg with a piece of paper. Steam it on top of rice which is cooking. Then peel off the shell and you have the perfect egg." A variation on the same idea comes from Chekiang.

One takes both white and yolk and mixes them with minced pork fat, mushrooms, bamboo shoots, dried prawns (shrimps) and seasoning, pouring the whole back into the shell to steam it. In a way, these bumbling experiments are rather charming, for in our wild enthusiasm we pursue the taste of things, all rushing off in different directions. Some of us return with sparkling eyes and a secret smile, others, bespattered with their idiotic adventures, return only to set off in another direction, spirits undiminished. Let us spend a while exchanging adventures, both good and bad.

"I have been tasting water wherever I go. Mountain water rushes forth, bubbling and foaming. It surges through stone-banked pools. Drinking too much of this often gives people diseases of the throat. People may have to go far for river water, so most draw is from wells. Lu Yu says in his *Book of Tea*, 'Mountain, river and well water in that order.' As another says, there are twenty different grades of water," wrote Ouyang Shiu. He listed his twenty preferences in order.

There has been a story in circulation for a long time concerning live monkey brain of Kwangtung. We had almost dismissed it as pure fiction until by diligent questioning of the people who spread these stories, of which there were a number, we finally found one who had actually tasted it. The table did have a hole in the centre, and the monkey's head was shaved and cracked open. As there were a number of people at this table, each person had only a spoonful. After all, a monkey's brain is only so big. "Any sauce?" we asked. He just shrugged. "The usual soy sauce and ginger," he replied. He went on to the description of another small horror called "Three Peeps"—a descriptive name which requires no further elucidation. It was served with the same sauce.

The two items mentioned above are not commonly met, but in the Yangtse lake regions the small live river shrimps were a speciality which would have merited a mention in a Chinese Guide Michelin. They were flavoured with wine and slivers of spring onion. Thinking back on how they jumped about, this must have been a dish that tossed and mixed itself. We had these with warmed wine, and the effect was rather like that of oysters and champagne.

A speciality of Szechuan was called "The Nine Twists"— light, rich and delicate intestines cooked in broth, unforgettably delicious. Speaking of intestines, we are reminded of the homely charm of large intestine stuffed with glutinous rice, sliced cold and sprinkled either with sugar or with soy sauce, a dish of Amoy. We in Amoy were incapable of much sophistication, and could never match the geometrical intricacy of Chekiang, where an intestine was stuffed with several others, cooked and sliced to form circles within circles.

The search for flavour led to the oddest corners, some of which, in retrospect, one wished one had never visited at all. But the joyous surprises of our wayward journeys were remembered for a long time. This is in a way how the somewhat odd quality of the cuisine came to be. It explains the dish called "Happy Family" which is slightly bizarre and rather common. Were it bizarre and uncommon we could dismiss it. But it is well within the main body of classic cuisine. The charm of the dish lies in knowing each of the ingredients separately and seeing them all together, in a gastronomic Ark. Each species is represented. If each one seems to have been pulled out of its native habitat to be put among strange company, it is only because an intelligent hand has put it there.

100. Happy Family (全 家 福)

Generous 1½ pints (4 cups) Cream Stock (16)

¼ oz. fish maw, softened and cut into ½-inch chunks (42)

6 Pearly Meat Balls, uncooked (76)

4 oz. (½ cup) uncooked chicken, very finely chopped (see 2)

6 Fish Balls, poached (31)

2 oz. (½ cup) Blanched Kidneys (124)

3 oz. (½ cup) cauliflower, blanched

4 oz. (1 cup) mustard greens, blanched

2 oz. dried bêche-de-mer, softened and cut into ½-inch chunks (41)

¾ pint (2 cups) meat stock

4 oz. whole prawns (shrimps), sautéed (25)

Prepare the first eight ingredients, keeping them separate. Prepare the bêche-de-mer as directed and simmer the chunks in meat stock for about 2 hours, until very tender. Drain the chunks and reserve them. Prepare whole prawns and drain them well.

Heat the Cream Stock gently, and place the bêche-de-mer, fish maw and Pearly Meat Balls in it. Simmer them for 15 to 20 minutes. Add the prawns and the two vegetables. When these are heated through, add the finely chopped chicken and stir very gently, then add the fish balls and the kidneys, keeping the stock just simmering, not boiling. Heat through and serve immediately.

This recipe sums up all the exquisite absurdities of the cuisine. The cult of gastronomy went very far and very deep not only in the choice of food but in its preparation. Its excesses showed how far one could go in the study of taste and texture.

6. Plain Cooking

If you like good food, cook it yourself.

LI LIWENG

IT MAY be interesting in later years to know what kind of food was commonly eaten in China, but to us it is more important to concentrate on what is best about plain food, and to know how to achieve excellence through plainness. The cooking of plain food is based on economy, simplicity and speed. There are those who eat plain food because they are poor; others cook it because they do not know any better. But plain cooking can also be appreciated as a matter of choice.

In this chapter we discuss the qualities of home cooking and country-style food; and what the very poor people ate. We go on to discuss the affected simplicity and coarseness in food as practised by sophisticates. We consider the essential qualities of the best of plain cooking, which involve a breaking of certain habits which the well-trained cook has learnt. The last part of this chapter is devoted to a description of the interesting array of pickles and preserved meats, an important block of ingredients in the daily fare of the Chinese.

HOME COOKING

What the Very Poor Ate:
Salted Spring Onions (Scallions) in Lard
(with rice), including a description of other meats

Gastronomy must be the hobby of the wealthy; otherwise the question of food is not so amusing. Gastronomy is a matter of choice, and the poor have no choice. But the gastronome could wander about. He realized that the poor man's food was monotonous, but that in itself the taste was not so bad.

There were poor, dirty, bright-eyed children, staring at him from behind the big bowls of rice; beggars, their professionally useful, painful expressions inscribed across their faces; peasants. They did not care for subtleties of texture and flavour carefully composed —rather, a big bowl of firm rice, with just soy sauce and a fried egg over the rice. The impoverished aunt, who had the chance to come to her rich relatives' home occasionally, sat at her doorstep, wishing she had been born more fortunate. She loved the taste of luxurious foods, soft and rich and gliding (*neng-tseng-tseng*, in our dialect), like the transparent noodles cooked with pig's knuckles (91).

We speak of the poor, not necessarily of the miserable. In the very poorest cooking there is no more artifice. As they grow older, some people become sated, bored, and lose the joy of eating. It is a constant effort to discover something new. But see the very poor child, scrambling about barefoot all day, now sitting on his stool, eating supper before the others. He shovelled in big mouthfuls of rice, discovering to his joy that buried under the mound of rice was a square of meat cooked in soy sauce and garlic.

Eating is very much a matter of habit, and not of intellect. A country woman brought up on rice and red peppers would eat little else, though the great meats and vegetables and fish were all available to her. The taste of red pepper sauce was like a drug to her, and she could not do without it, though it wrecked her digestion and made her nose bleed. "Huang-ma, eat something else," we said. She was addicted to red peppers. Nothing could have whetted her appetite and refreshed her as the taste of hot red peppers. The very poor ate rice mixed with soy sauce, the sauce having within it a quantity of salt and monosodium glutamate (MSG) to add flavour. The food of the very poor was not without taste, though it was very monotonous and one had to be extremely hungry to enjoy it. On the other hand, one should not be hungry when sitting down to a long and tedious banquet consisting of the standard dishes of classic cuisine. Go back to the original idea of eating— chew, swallow, taste, smell the food. Forget the subtleties, enjoy fat and salt, and the heady fragrance of spring onions. Forget Li Liweng, who hated spring onions. He was wrong. The poor and simple people ate them browned in lard with salt, solidified into a preserve which would keep for weeks. A dab of it on rice was tasty.

*101. Salted Spring Onions (Scallions) in Lard (炒 油 葱)

½ lb. pork fat
6 spring onions
2 level tablespoons salt

Dice the fat and render it over low heat. Chop the spring onions very finely and sauté them in the lard, adding salt. When the onions are browned, pour the mixture into a small crock or dish, and let it cool. Use as a relish with rice or congee.

Anyone who cooks congee will realize that, unless the timing is precise, the grain swells and divides repeatedly until there is apparently no more liquid left. Half a cup of dry rice could therefore be made into a huge potful of rice to feed a family. This was economical, and the peasants lived on it. It is said that a poor student, wishing to save money in order to study, lived on congee and one salted duck's egg per year. He picked at it a little at a time. When it was finished, it floated away, shell almost intact. In China one ate congee for breakfast and had with it peanuts cooked in brine and some bean curd cheese, pressed by hand. We returned always to these simple things, even though one could well afford to leave them. A Chinese monk living in a Belgian monastery, devout in all his ways, in his old age thought only of these things: congee, and pickles, and little chewy peanuts. He told us of this wish, which we could not satisfy.

The plainest kind of cooking, which we have described, cannot be judged according to the criteria of the gastronome. But it forms the background against which all the quirks and artifices and nuances of refined cooking are shown up.

Rustic Simplicity: Spongy Bean Curd, including Yuan Mei's comments on the serving of food; Pig's Foot Jelly; Chicken-flavoured Cabbage

The crude and simple things of the poor man's fare were as a rule outside the pale of classic cuisine, but they influenced the course of Chinese gastronomy by introducing the element of rustic simplicity. It is often the case that the sophisticated develop definite tastes, which they can indulge in with some effort. Thus the rich man may genuinely like peasant food, but when served in his house it becomes pseudo-rustic. In order to make things more harmonious, he has simple food served on plain dishes, but guests will see that the dishes are carefully textured so as to appear coarse, and his simplicity will appear an affectation. On the other hand, a farmer's wife may have gloriously expensive tastes which she can only appease by a single extravagance, which in its loneliness appears even ugly. It is better to act consistently with one's means, than be accused of too humble or too expensive airs. But few people ever do it, except the very poor.

In the vein of simple elegance Yuan Mei said, "I think it may be more sophisticated to use cheap bowls and plates." On a cheap plate, one would have placed an artfully prepared bean curd. This lowly ingredient becomes full of holes when boiled rapidly, and its spongy texture soaks up all the sauce, so that when one bites into it the juices spurt out. Arrange the slices so they form a mound, and without garnish, so it looks like coarse, common food.

There are people who find this pretence at coarseness loathsome, but this is the argument against it. What is the difference between real rustic simplicity and pseudo-rustic style? The difference lies in awareness. For a person too keenly conscious of style can barely help observing himself, his style. It is impossible to do anything without style, good or bad; even those who are without style inflict their actions on others, and are equally loathsome. Therefore it is better to be consciously coarse, than be without sensitivity; to be playful, than heedless; to eat, than to feed; even to affect roughness, than to be brutish; to be critical, than not to think at all. One cannot help but be deliberately casual, to practise plain cooking with studied carelessness, to be rigorously lax. So be it.

*102. Spongy Bean Curd (滷 豆 腐)

12 oz. (3 cakes) bean curd	5 tablespoons stock
3½ pints (8 cups) cold water	¾ level teaspoon sugar
2 tablespoons oyster sauce	1½ level teaspoons cornflour
1 teaspoon soy sauce	(cornstarch)

Place bean curd and water in a pot and bring to the boil. Keep it at a rolling boil for 30 minutes. Remove the curd. When it is cool, slice each cake into seven pieces.

Bring the remaining ingredients to the boil in a shallow frying pan. When the sauce is smooth, lay the bean curd slices in it evenly, lower the heat, cover the pan and let it simmer for about 12 minutes, covered, until all the liquid is absorbed.

The intelligent housewife will eventually realize that she cannot produce a great banquet at home, and must concentrate on those simple and cunning country-style dishes much admired by gourmets. This is the solution of choice, suitable to the household kitchen and to the facilities available, and in keeping with good taste. Then she can indulge in all the fine points of coarse cooking mentioned earlier under the mask of simplicity, and achieve a homely elegance rarely found. Under the guise of country-style cooking and limited facilities, make what is perfectly suited to the surroundings, neither too common, nor too showy—something which resembles coarse food, but is later shown to be fine cooking of a rather high order. Be quiet in your cleverness, and make no noise about it. Make a jelly, slice it very finely, and serve it without fuss. Then the only thing you can be accused of is a certain deadly good taste.

*103. Pig's Foot Jelly (豬 脚 凍)

3 lb. pig's feet (3 or 4), split
   in half
2 level teaspoons salt
2 tablespoons light soy sauce
½ level teaspoon sugar

¼ level teaspoon wild pepper,
   crushed
¾ level teaspoon MSG
½ lb. very lean pork, minced
   (ground)

Blanch the pig's feet for 5 minutes in 5 pints (12 cups) boiling water. Rinse the feet well with cold water, and brush them clean. Stew them for about 2¾ hours in 1½ pints (3½ cups) water, together with salt, soy sauce, sugar and crushed wild pepper, until the bones just come loose. Let the mixture cool to lukewarm, and remove all the strips of skin. Lay them skin side out, lining a bowl with straight sides. Remove all the bones in the feet, feeling with the fingers to make sure every bone is out. This is essential if neat slices are to be made later.

Add MSG and another ¼ pint (⅔ cup) water to the pot. Bring it to the boil and reduce the heat. Stir in the minced pork and continue to stir gently until the pork is cooked, about 5 minutes. Pour the mixture on top of the skin, and smooth it out. Let it cool until set, then unmould it and cut it into very thin slices.

This is excellent served with Ribbon Rolls (52) or Pinwheels (51), and Wild Pepper Mix (36). After the jelly, serve a little dish of cabbage and some rice. It is enough.

*104. Chicken-flavoured Cabbage (鷄 油 菜 心)

1 lb. cabbage hearts
¼ pint (⅔ cup) chicken stock
¼ level teaspoon MSG
½ level teaspoon sugar
½ level teaspoon salt

1 tablespoon oil
3 tablespoons chicken fat
1 level tablespoon cornflour
   (cornstarch) mixed with ¼ pint
   (½ cup) chicken stock

Use only hearts of Chinese cabbage or small green cabbages. Include a leaf or two for the colour, but let it look as if it got in there by mistake.

Cut the cabbage hearts lengthwise and crosswise into 3-inch sections. Mix the chicken stock, MSG, sugar and half the salt together in a bowl. Sauté cabbage with remaining salt and oil, keeping the whole thing in a high mound in order to avoid burning the cabbage. Add the chicken stock mixture, bring it to the boil, and toss it with chopsticks, always keeping the cabbage in a heap. When the cabbage is almost done, add the chicken fat and the cornflour mixed with chicken stock. Stir until smooth and hot and thick.

Rules of Plain Cooking:
Leave bones in (Chicken 4-4-4-4)
Do not beautify the dish (Duck Fried with Onions)
Add no seasoning but salt (Steamed Cucumbers)

It actually takes a certain amount of discipline to do plain cooking, for its unique charm rests on some tenuous and questionable practices which must be observed with rigour. The flavour of some of the best household dishes rests on the offhand method of preparation.

*105. Chicken 4-4-4-4 (三杯子鷄)

A 4-lb. chicken   4 tablespoons soy sauce
4 tablespoons wine   1 slice ginger
4 tablespoons oil   1 spring onion (scallion)

Chop the chicken up and place it in a pot together with all the remaining ingredients. Bring the mixture to the boil, give it a stir, cover the pot and simmer it for 30 minutes without further stirring.

An attempt to bone the chicken before cooking it in rough and tumble destroys the flavour. Why? The reason is that the marrow contributes a great deal of flavour to the sauce. Prolonged stewing ruins the flavour. Sometimes the coarsest food is the tastiest, mainly because the cook is too lazy, too tired, or doesn't know enough to remove those inedible parts. The more refined cooking becomes, the more delicate its flavours; finally, one may go from subtlety to insipid flavour, and much of the joy of eating is lost.

The cook must also resist any attempt to beautify the following recipe, such as extracting the flavour of the onions without serving them, or some such idea. Its virtue is that the onion juices run into the duck, and the duck fat runs into the onions. There is no way to serve it neatly, but the flavour is superb.

*106. Duck Fried with Onions (葱 燜 鴨)

Half a duck (about 2½ lb.)	2 tablespoons oil
1 lb. Spanish (yellow) onions	Salt

Remove the fat pads from the duck. Break its thigh, drumstick, wing and back bones, so that it will lie snugly in the curve of the wo. Peel and quarter the onions and sauté in oil for about 3 minutes, adding ¼ level teaspoon salt. Remove the onions, and place the duck skin side down in the wo. Pile the onions in the body cavity and sprinkle them with ¼ level teaspoon salt. Cover the wo and fry the duck over moderately low heat for 40 minutes. Push the onions aside into the juices and remove the duck. Chop it into chunks and sprinkle with another ¼ level teaspoon salt. Remove most of the fat overlying the juices. Pour the onions and juices over the duck and serve it immediately.

The charm of plain cooking lies in its simplicity of flavour. The third rule which the cook must know is this tricky business of being simple in keeping the seasoning plain. In the following recipe, resist the desire to add MSG, sugar, chicken stock, etc. You need only salt.

*107. Steamed Cucumbers (蒸 青 苽)

2 or 3 cucumbers
½ level teaspoon salt

Peel and core cucumbers. Slice them lengthwise into strips about ⅜ inch wide, and cut them into 2½-inch lengths. Place the strips on a soup plate and sprinkle with salt. Cover the dish closely, and steam it for about 25 minutes.

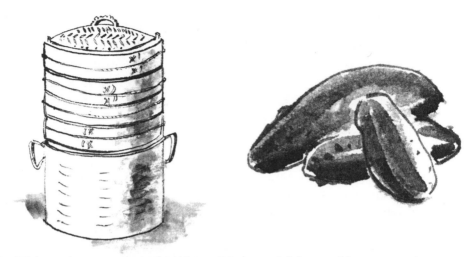

This recipe sums up the idea of *hsien*, which roughly means the spirit of the food. This is the flavour which is aimed at in meat and fish, and rarely achieved. The cook who attempts to tamper with it should be punished. But in recent times such attempts have been made. A court chef extracted about 30 lb. of bean sprouts to make a few bowls of soup. There is really nothing wrong with bean sprouts as nature made them. Too much art and trickery in cooking are to be avoided.

A Simple Meal:
Braised Chicken Parts; Fried Fish; Sautéed Liver;
French (String) Beans with Garlic; Spare Ribs Soup

There is form in home cooking, and we must recognize it. For a plain meal, four dishes and a soup, perhaps as contemptible as the familiar meat-and-two-veg of Britain, but there it is. In this modest frame, no one dish outshines the others by much, though they are all different. The economical housewife shows her guile by making the third and fourth dish from most inexpensive ingredients. Meat appears only once or twice, the rest of the dishes are made up from bits and pieces. It is a very cheap way of feeding a large household.

Household food has a different tone to it. The texture is firm, oil visible and separated, rice white and grainy, vegetables firm and fresh. The taste is to be chewed, not sensed, the flavours pronounced, not in the air, the substance solid, not gliding. The food is not elaborate. Each ingredient is recognizable. At a very superior banquet one tasted a custard or bean curd-like substance vaguely reminiscent of a familiar object, but could not quite place it. It was the disembodied flavour of chicken liver incorporated into a pudding-like delicacy, even further removed from the natural form than the finest pâté. The cook who has learnt the trick of making this exquisite thing has trouble keeping his hands off food. Learn to leave things alone, in their natural state. They may even taste better that way.

A housewife will collect all the odd parts of the chicken, and economically make a tasty and interesting dish out of them. The charm of household cookery lies in its appearance. All parts can be identified. Chicken feet, scalded to remove the outer skin and stewed first, may be added to the recipe.

*108. Braised Chicken Parts (紅 燜 三 件)

½ lb. chicken wings (3 or 4)
½ lb. chicken livers (about 6)
½ lb. chicken giblets (about 6)
3 tablespoons oil
½ level teaspoon very finely
   chopped ginger

3 tablespoons wine
2 teaspoons soy sauce
¾ level teaspoon sugar

Prepare the chicken parts: Chop the wings into 1½-inch sections. Cut the livers into lobes. Cut the giblets into sections. Heat oil and ginger in a pot. Add all the chicken parts and sauté them until they turn colour. Then add wine, soy sauce and sugar and mix well. Turn heat down and simmer, covered, stirring occasionally, for 25 minutes.

*109. Fried Fish (煎 魚)

Take little fish and clean them. Dip them lightly in flour, heads and all. Heat about ¼ pint (¾ cup) oil in a wo, and lay fish down side by side, so that they are all immersed in the oil. Fry gently and thoroughly until one side is browned. Turn them over and fry the other side until browned. Serve them simply with soy sauce.

The flavour of household cooking is geared to that of rice. Heavy, thick sauces are welcome, daintiness often goes unappreciated. In classic cooking, rice is all but left out of the menu, and a mantle of delicacy envelops the selections. Quite the opposite is wanted in plain, everyday cooking, for where banquets merely amuse the sated, home meals must satisfy the hungry. The hearty, robust quality of the following dish satisfies both the hungry and the critical audience. It is prepared and served in a casserole if possible, to emphasize its deliberate and savoury coarseness.

*110. Sautéed Liver (蠔 油 炒 肝)

¾ lb. beef or pork liver
1 teaspoon soy sauce
3 tablespoons oyster sauce
1 tablespoon sesame oil

½ level teaspoon sugar
1 spring onion (scallion)
2 slices ginger
2 tablespoons oil

Cut the liver into large chunks and marinate it for 2 to 3 hours in a mixture of soy sauce, oyster sauce, sesame oil and sugar. Sauté spring onion and ginger in oil for a few minutes. Remove the liver from the marinade, reserving the latter. Sauté liver for about 1 minute, depending on the size of the pieces. Add the marinade and stir well. When the liver is done and the sauce simmering, serve it immediately. Total cooking time is 2½ to 3 minutes.

Garlic, like hot red peppers, is excluded from classic cuisine, but comes into its own in the household kitchen. In cooking garlic with French (string) beans, aim for mellowness. Use low heat, wilt the beans, and slowly extract the flavour of the garlic. Then let it cool and stand for a while so that the juices blend. Instead of being sharp and acrid, the mixture is soft and mellow in taste, not unlike *haricots verts* as cooked in France.

*111. French (String) Beans with Garlic (炒青豆)

3 cloves garlic
1 lb. fresh French beans
2 tablespoons oil

4 teaspoons soy sauce
1 level teaspoon sugar
1 tablespoon pale dry sherry

Peel and crush the garlic. Wash the beans and snap them into 2-inch sections. Sauté garlic in oil for a few minutes. Add the beans and stir them quickly to coat them with oil. After 1 or 2 minutes add soy sauce and sugar. Continue to stir the beans for 2 minutes longer, then add sherry. Reduce the heat. Cook the beans, uncovered, for about another 10 minutes, until they are wilted, stirring occasionally. This is excellent served cold.

When you make the following soup, leave the long ribs in the stalks whole, and do not alter the natural texture of the bean curd. The gourmet will find this a relief from the minced food and slivers and pastes of the more elegant cuisine.

*112. Spare Ribs Soup (排骨湯)

2½ pints (6 cups) water
1 large stalk pickled mustard
    green, or 2 spring onions
    (scallions)
½ lb. spare ribs, separated

¾ level teaspoon MSG
½ level teaspoon sugar
½ level teaspoon salt
¼ level teaspoon pepper
½ lb. (2 cakes) bean curd

Bring water to the boil with the mustard green, spare ribs and seasonings. Simmer the soup for 1½ hours, then add the bean curd, each cake cut into nine cubes.

Homely Hospitality:
Chicken Soup; The Pieces of Eight; Pig Tripe Soup

We watched each other eat, modesty and humility shown in the minimal number of times we reached to the centre of the table with the chopsticks. At times, the grandfather would actually pick a choice piece to give it to a favourite grandchild, and this was observed by all. This is very different from the exquisite privacy of a Western meal, where the contents of one's plate are guarded and inviolate, a matter of choice and commitment. In the Chinese home an unexpected guest staying for dinner was no problem. One simply set out another bowl and pair of chopsticks for him. At meals and other times, we were constantly shifting ourselves to make room for and accommodate others. It was perhaps not a bad thing, but the daily wear and tear was quite real. There was a saying that

Kinfolk under one roof
Look daggers at each other.
Comes the cousin, long absent—
For him, kill the chicken, prepare the feast!

Cheapness and frugality were the rule, which one broke with fervour on occasion. The chicken, usually cut up into bits and pieces to serve in several dishes, went whole into the pot to greet the arrival of a long-absent relative, or a rich one. One remembers particularly the black-skinned and black-boned fowl used for soup, its feather-light and rich tenderness extending even to its feet, which were skinned and simmered in the soup until they almost fell apart. In the atmosphere of practised economy we women looked at food with a calculating eye, and meals were judged not so much by how they tasted as how much they cost.

*113. Chicken Soup (鶏 湯)

A 4½- to 5-lb. chicken, whole *2 to 3 slices ginger*
4 to 5 pints (10 to 12 cups) water *1½ level tablespoons salt*

Bring all the ingredients to the boil and simmer for 3 hours. Skim off most of the fat. Serve the chicken whole, in a large bowl with the soup.

*114. The Pieces of Eight (炸 八 塊)

2 chicken legs *3 tablespoons soy sauce*
1 pair chicken breasts *2 level teaspoons sugar*
Cornflour (cornstarch) *1 level teaspoon salt*
Fat for deep-frying *½ level teaspoon pepper*
  ½ level teaspoon MSG
MARINADE *1 level teaspoon ginger powder or*
¼ pint (⅔ cup) pale dry sherry *very finely chopped fresh ginger*

Cut the white meat and the dark meat of the chicken into eight pieces each, making sixteen pieces in all. Soak the pieces in the marinade for 3 to 6 hours. Dust them with cornflour, and fry them in deep fat until well browned.

Like those unused to extravagance, Chinese hospitality is excessive. At a feast, the only way to stop the steady stream of food arriving on one's plate is to let it pile up; otherwise, the host and hostess are not convinced that they are doing their duty. This is more exaggerated in entertaining guests at home. One is more likely to serve what would please the host than what the guest would like. In the matter of entertaining at home Yuan Mei said, "When serving a guest, the proper thing is to let him choose his own food. From each dish let him choose the lean, fat, savoury or crisp parts. Let him be comfortable. Why 'force-feed' him? I often notice a host piling food upon the guest's bowl and plate, to his annoyance. He is neither a child nor a bride enduring hunger pangs out of modesty. Do not be the provincial woman when waiting upon your guests."

Actually, what would please the distinguished relative returned home is that plain soup made out of pig's tripe, with the nutlike gingko to round out its sweet and mellow flavour. This is a little too coarse for elegant cooking; all the more reason to serve it at home.

115. Pig Tripe Soup (豬 肚 湯)

1 lb. prepared tripe (see method)
Coarse salt
Vinegar
8 fluid oz. (1 cup) pale dry sherry
2 teaspoons light soy sauce
1½ level teaspoons salt
½ level teaspoon MSG
¾ level teaspoon sugar
1 oz. dried bean curd, softened in water
1 can gingko, drained (5½ oz.) (optional)
3 oz. (½ cup) skinned unsalted peanuts (optional)

Tripe has a ridge of fat along its outer surface, while its inner lining is coated with a slippery film. Both of these must be removed. Trim off the fat, turn the tripe inside out and rub it vigorously alternately with coarse salt, followed by a rinse with cold water, and diluted vinegar, followed by another rinse. Continue until the tripe is odourless and almost entirely free of slippery film.

Blanch the prepared tripe for 3 minutes in 5 pints (12 cups) water. Discard the liquid, and rinse the tripe thoroughly under the cold tap until it is cool. Slice it into strips ½ inch by 2 inches. Simmer the tripe in 1¼ pints (3 cups) water, with the sherry, soy sauce, seasonings and softened bean curd, cut into ½-inch by 2-inch strips, adding gingko and peanuts if liked. Stew this mixture for about 2½ hours, or until very tender.

PICKLES AND CURED MEATS

Time was the key which made the household kitchen run. We stretched it by making preserves and pickles, and shortened it with simple recipes. In the making of preserves themselves there was anticipation, and in the tasting, recollection. "Wash pork liver and cut it into long strips. In each strip cut a gash along its length, and place a strip of fat pork in it. Run a string through the strips and hang them up in a cold windy place until they are dry and stiff. Then immerse the liver in *kaoliang* (sorghum) wine and seal it tightly. In the following year, steam it with sugar, salt and sesame oil, and serve it in slices, cold."

There was a garden of pickles, a sea of sun-dried fish, and a clutch of preserved eggs. Almost each fresh vegetable had its preserved counterpart. The plump flatfish eyed its sun-dried relative, who was only skin and bone and had sockets for eyes. The flavour of the two could not be compared. The preserves were like old people in whom individual traits had frozen and intensified. We would fry the dried fish and crush it to a meal (87) for sprinkling on fresh food, or soak it and make a soup with it, adding a turnip. It made the fresh fish seem insipid. Fresh squid is *hsien*, but dried squid is better. The most delicious way of eating squid is to take the leathery, peach-coloured sheet and grill it slowly over a fire. The tough fibres turn white and begin to separate from one another. One rolls it up and unrolls it, to soften it a little. After more toasting, one chews it slowly to get at the sweet aftertaste. These were some of the preserved fish of our native Fukien. In the Yellow River region, fish were salted and smoked, specialities of northern Anhwei and Honan. These were so tasty that in Chekiang copies of it, called "smoked fish", were made with fresh fried fish. The whole thing had gone a full circle.

A very old method for making fish preserve consisted of packing dried carp in a crock with salt and wine. On the second day the liquid was poured away, and hot pepper and spices added. Uncooked rice and salt and more wine were added. The liquid resulting from fermentation was poured off on the sixth day, and boiling sesame oil was poured in. This was called *kung cha* (貢 鮓), tribute or gift preserve.

Home-made preserves sometimes went awry. One recipe for bean pickle says, "If you lift the lid the smell will come up to meet you, but if you stir it on a clear day and it gives off hot gases, start all over again."

Eggs were preserved by packing them raw in alkaline ashes, until they were chemically cooked, the white turning a transparent brown, with a pine-needle pattern, and the yolk becoming greenish, often with a concentric design. Instead of the flat simplicity of fresh eggs, they acquired a depth and mellowness truly to be appreciated. Upon being pickled in brine, the eggs remained fluid, as they are when raw, but underwent a delicious change in flavour.

Home-made Preserves:
Salty Duck's Eggs; Pickled Vegetables, Spiced or Plain;
Salt-cured Duck; Directions on How to Grow Bean Sprouts

116. Salty Duck's Eggs (鹹 鴨 蛋)

4½ oz. (1 cup) coarse salt
1¼ pints (3 cups) cold boiled
  water
Duck eggs

Make a brine with the salt and water. Place several duck eggs in it, and leave them for at least 3 weeks with a plate on top of the eggs to keep them completely immersed in the brine. Hard-boil the eggs in plain water and serve one or two at a time, sliced in eighths or quarters through the shell. This is very good with Congee (2).

Juicy turnips were salted and dried until they were only a fraction of their original size, then chopped very finely and scrambled with fresh eggs, tasting like some delicacy a brilliant cook had invented. And one had, a long time ago. Great tubs of vegetables were sprinkled with rock salt, and jumped on, to work the salt in. Then slowly the flavour ripened, turning first salty and sweet, then a little sour. Its pungency showed up the bland bamboo or the little pork or beef in the household meal. Any common vegetables, like cabbage, turnips and cauliflower, can be preserved for several weeks in the following manner, without much alteration of flavour.

117. Pickled Vegetables, Spiced or Plain (泡菜)

18 fluid oz. (2¼ cups) water
1 oz. (¼ cup) coarse salt
2 level teaspoons sugar
½ level teaspoon crushed red
   pepper (optional)

¼ level teaspoon crushed wild
   pepper (optional)
¾ to 1 lb. vegetables, all of one
   kind or mixed

Bring water to the boil with salt and sugar. Let it cool. Add red and wild pepper, if desired. Cut the vegetables into large sections, put them in a jar and cover them with brine. Cover the jar tightly and store it in a cool place. It is ready to use in about 1 week, and can be used as part of hors d'oeuvre, in soup, in sautés, or as a pickle.

Against the winter's hardships there were salted and wined vegetables packed in a jar and buried in a pit, called "good-till-spring". Even bamboo was salted and dried. But the best solution to the lean season was beans. They sprouted in the dark and damp, providing fresh vegetables against the steady diet of pickles and preserved meats.

118. How to Grow Bean Sprouts (發豆芽)

Wash 6 oz. (1 cup) yellow sprouting beans and soak them overnight in 1½ pints (4 cups) cold water. Discard the water, and place the swollen beans on a flat woven mat or tray, so that air will get to the beans from above and below. Cover the beans with a wet cloth and store the tray in a dark place. Rinse the beans with water every morning and evening, and keep the cloth wet. In 5 to 6 days the sprouts are ready to be used. Rinse the sprouts, storing them in a closed plastic bag in the refrigerator.

An excellent method for preserving duck consists of soaking it in brine and hanging it to dry, during which time it loses 20 per cent of its weight in water. After the duck is boiled, it will keep for a few weeks in a cool place. Both the fat and the meat turn waxy and firm.

119. Salt-cured Duck (鹹 水 鴨)

BRINE
1¼ lb. coarse salt
Generous 2½ pints (6½ cups)
   water
1 star anise
6 cloves
1 teaspoon fennel
4 slices ginger

1 duck
2 level tablespoons coarse salt

Mix the brine ingredients together and stir for a few minutes (the salt will not all dissolve). Rub the cleaned and towel-dried duck with coarse salt. In order to permit easy handling and immersion in the brine, double the duck backwards on itself, breaking the spine. Truss it tightly, making a loop by which it may be hung later. Let it stand for about 1 hour, and pour off the liquid which runs out.

Place the duck in the brine for 4 to 18 hours, turning if necessary to immerse all parts evenly. Remove the duck (the brine may be re-used if kept saturated with salt). Drain the body cavity. Hang the duck in a cool, airy place for 24 to 48 hours, so that water may drip off and evaporate.

Bring 5½ pints (14 cups) water to the boil. Add the duck and simmer for 20 minutes. Discard the water, being sure to empty the body cavity. Repeat this procedure with a fresh portion of boiling water, cooking the duck for a total of 40 minutes. Drain and cool it very thoroughly before chopping it into thin segments. One duck is sufficient for two or three occasions. Serve it cold, arranged neatly on a small plate.

7. Classic Cuisine

Who does not know the measure of a man's foot had better not be a cobbler. Men's tastes are alike. Iya [a famous cook] knew my taste better than I. All men's tastes are alike; we are not dogs or horses. Were it not so, how would Iya have become famous?

MENCIUS

THERE IS ORDER in the world of gastronomy. That order appears with familiarity. Taste and form come from the recognition of orders of cooking. Often a meal will be composed of dishes, each one delicious in itself, but the whole will give the effect of being a hodge-podge. The principal reason for this is the mismatching of ingredients and dishes. The difference between hodge-podge and something better is taste, the recognition of form. A Chinese restaurateur in California once listed one of the dishes on the menu as "Miscellaneous, with Fried Rice" (*The New Yorker*, November 1962), a pithy definition of chop suey. Perhaps he was more conscious of form than his colleagues, and so acknowledged his break with it. By form we mean the carrying out of a consistent theme in the make-up of dishes and menus. This is one of the pleasures of the gastronome.

Classic cuisine is a summation of gastronomy, a gathering together of the best ideas in food. It takes its shape from these ideas. This is the cuisine of choice, not necessity, reflecting a liberal expenditure of time, labour, thought and money. The great feast is the product of classic cuisine, a collection of gastronomic jewels. Though the form of the menu may be standard, its individual selections reflect taste. This is where the gastronome can come into his own. Within the classic framework he can exercise his taste, drawing on various orders of cooking, sometimes deliberately crossing the lines in recognition of their existence. A great feast has style, form and rhythm.

Four or eight hors d'oeuvre. These must be amusing.
A fried dish. Delicate, without bones.
A rich, expensive, concentrated soup.
Shark's fins may follow.
Fowl, prepared in an unusual fashion.
For relief, an interesting but insignificant sauté.
A second soup, completely different from the first.
A texture-food.
A vegetable prepared in original fashion.
A roast duck or suckling pig.
A third soup, different from the first or second.
A whole fish.

It is up to the host to carry out the theme of subdued elegance, preciousness, deliberate simplicity or florid display, or dignity and grandeur, or all that is right and beautiful. These questions of taste are not developed instantaneously, or by intuition or compulsion, but by discipline. It would not be right, though elegant, to spend a huge sum of money on a mock rustic meal, or to have the chef and his assistants labour for days for the sake of display, or to be so perverse in your choices that you draw attention to your taste. Yet each of these occurs in our daily experience.

HORS D'OEUVRE

Five Selections in Various Styles:
Agar and Turnip Slivers; Glazed Duck; Drunken
Prawns (Shrimps); Old and Fresh Eggs; Blanched Kidneys

The hors d'oeuvre must set the tone of the dinner, like the overture to an opera. There are various styles to hors d'oeuvre, illustrated below.

EXAGGERATED SIMPLICITY
Dipped Snails (93)
Spongy Bean Curd (102)
Criss Cross Pork
Marinated Fresh Ginger

FLORID INDULGENCE
(Selected from the hors d'oeuvre of Li Hung Chang)
Duck Web Wrapped about Crab Roe
   Chicken Testicles
      Fried Sparrows
        Sautéed Prawns with Chicken

POLISHED ELEGANCE
Agar and Turnip Slivers (120)
   Glazed Duck (121)
      Drunken Prawns (122)
        Radish Flowers (28)

RUSTIC SIMPLICITY
Preserved Eggs
   Pig's Foot Jelly (103)
      Salt-cured Duck (119)
        Pan-roasted Peppers (67)

THE BEST
Old and Fresh Eggs (123)
   Blanched Kidneys (124)
      Vegetarian Ham (37)
        Jellyfish (44)

The hors d'oeuvre must look neat. They are best served in matched dishes, each containing one item. Many people like to garnish the dishes with parsley, and vegetables cut in the shape of birds, fish, bats, etc., or even to make baskets of flowers from food. These are all acceptable if kept under control, and if the rest of the meal is also in the same florid style. The worst offence would be to start with a florid display of food, and then suddenly change style midway, to the pseudo-rustic, for example. It is safer to underplay the hors d'oeuvre, taking care that they taste good and look immaculate. In the matching of colours as in the matching of flavours, a favourite device is to mix together similar but non-identical ingredients, a subtle compliment to the diner, in that such dishes demand a certain amount of discernment.

120. Agar and Turnip Slivers (荣 燕 蘿 蔔 絲)

½ oz. agar-agar
4 oz. turnip
1 tablespoon white vinegar
2 level teaspoons sugar

¼ level teaspoon MSG
1 tablespoon oil
½ teaspoon sesame oil
½ level teaspoon salt

Cut agar-agar into 1-inch sticks and soak in cold water for about ½ hour, until softened. Reserve. Peel and sliver turnip to match the size of the agar-agar. Blanch the turnip slivers in 2½ pints (6 cups) boiling water for 3 to 5 minutes, then rinse under the cold tap and drain well. Mix the remaining ingredients together to make a sauce. Drain the agar-agar, shaking it well. Toss it with the drained turnip slivers and the sauce. Serve cold.

The hors d'oeuvre must be attractive. Take only the breast of the Glazed Duck and slice it neatly. Place the pieces in a small, orderly mound. In the following recipe a roasted duck is literally painted with a spiced sauce. The flavours fuse with the duck upon standing for a few hours. The glaze is very durable, and the appearance is elegant.

121. Glazed Duck (糖 酱 鴨)

A 5-lb. duck
5 tablespoons soy sauce
¼ pint minus 2 tablespoons
  (½ cup) pale dry sherry

2 level tablespoons sugar
1 level teaspoon Mixed Spices*

Clean the duck, wipe it dry and truss it securely. Roast it for about 1½ hours in a 350°F. (Mark 3) oven. Pour out the liquid in the body cavity and let the fat drip off.

Bring the remaining ingredients to the boil in a large pan into which the whole duck will fit. Place the hot roasted duck in the pan and keep the sauce at a steady boil. Use a pastry brush to paint the duck with the sauce as it reduces, turning the duck so that all parts will be coated. Spoon the liquid into the body cavity, and pour it out again. Continue to paint the duck until the liquid thickens. Cut the strings and remove them. Turn the heat down to low, and resume painting the duck with the sauce, taking care that the colouring is even. As the glaze thickens, it becomes very thick and shiny. Use it all up. Transfer the duck to a rack and let it stand for at least 4 hours, or overnight. Serve it chopped, cold.

*Mixed Spices: 6 level tablespoons fennel, 3 level tablespoons wild pepper, and 1 level tablespoon star anise.

The hors d'oeuvre must taste clean. This means that their taste must be clear and definite, but not lingering. They must be like epigrams, pithy, amusing, light and brief.

*122. Drunken Prawns (Shrimps)—Recipe of Yuan Mei (醉 蝦)

½ lb. prawns
About ¼ pint (¾ cup) pale dry
  sherry

4 teaspoons water
4 teaspoons white vinegar
8 teaspoons light soy sauce

Wash the prawns and trim off the legs. Drain them well and place them in pale dry sherry to cover. Bring to the boil and poach the prawns for 3 to 4 minutes, turning them to cook them evenly. Remove the prawns from the pan and discard the sherry. Mix the prawns with the water, vinegar and soy sauce, and let them stand for 1 to 4 hours. Peel the prawns. Arrange them neatly on a small plate. Garnishes are unnecessary.

The hors d'oeuvre must be intriguing, but not so mysterious as to make every item a matter for discussion. If mysterious new combinations are to be served, they must be accompanied by clearly recognizable dishes. Do not serve four mysteries at one time or you will attract an undue amount of attention to the food. The following is a puzzle for gourmets. The mellowness of preserved eggs is rounded out by the addition of fresh eggs.

123. Old and Fresh Eggs (皮 蛋 鮮 蛋 糕)

2 preserved eggs
2 fresh eggs
1 tablespoon chicken stock
⅛ level teaspoon salt

Oil or fat
2 teaspoons soy sauce
2 teaspoons sesame oil
½ level teaspoon MSG

The preservation of eggs by alkaline ash turns the white to brown and the yolk to green. This colour change is actually very beautiful.

Gently crack the shells of the preserved eggs and remove the egg white (brown) carefully, reserving it. Mash the yolks and combine them with the fresh eggs, chicken stock and salt. Grease a bowl and pour in the egg mixture. Steam it for about 20 minutes. When cool, loosen the egg from the bowl, slice it in half and cut each half into thin slices. Chop the egg white (brown) very finely, and arrange the slices around it. Mix the soy sauce, sesame oil and MSG together, and carefully spoon this sauce over the slices only. The sauce will gradually seep into the egg.

The hors d'oeuvre must be light. In the choice of ingredients, seafood, eggs, vegetables and parts are preferred over the important meats, fish and fowl. But this is a matter of taste. In the Chekiang-Kiangsu region the dinner begins with a large platter of assorted meats and pickled vegetables, cut into geometrical shapes. We think it is better to avoid this, for in the subsequent courses the pork and chicken and duck appear again. It is more cunning to avoid the great meats assiduously, and use artfully simple, unimportant little dishes; for example, crisp kidneys on a bed of crisp bean sprouts.

The kidney consists of two different layers of tissue. The outside is edible, the inside is not. The object in cooking kidneys is simply to make them crisp, *tsuei*. Two things stand in the way: formation of scum within the slices, which makes the consistency mealy instead of crunchy, and overcooking. The extraordinary procedure outlined below takes care of both problems, salt being used to draw out the scum, wine to solidify it. Salt, wine and scum are all rinsed away by repeated scalding, during the course of which the kidneys become cooked.

124. Blanched Kidneys (白 灼 腰 片)

¾ lb. pork kidneys (3 or 4
   kidneys)
Salt
4 tablespoons pale dry sherry

SAUCE
2 tablespoons wine
2 teaspoons oil
½ teaspoon sesame oil
½ level teaspoon salt
½ level teaspoon MSG
¼ level teaspoon sugar

Wash the kidneys and sprinkle them with salt. Remove the membranes. Rinse off the kidneys. Carefully pare off large slices, avoiding the hard core. Rinse and drain the slices very thoroughly. Place the slices close together in a single layer on a chopping board. With a cleaver, lightly slash the slices about every ⅟₁₆ inch. Turn the board around one-quarter of a circle and make slashes ⅟₁₆ inch apart in the opposite direction, forming a grid or diamond pattern on one side of the slices. Place all the slashed slices in a heatproof 2-pint (4-cup) measuring cup. They will fill it up to the 8 fluid oz. mark. Add the sherry and 1 level teaspoon salt and mix lightly with chopsticks. Let the kidneys stand in the mixture for about 5 minutes, during which time a great deal of scum will be thrown out by the slices.

Meanwhile, bring 6½ pints (16 cups) water to the boil. Have ready a large mesh sieve. The slices are scalded with five successive portions of boiling water, and drained after each scalding. After draining, replace the slices in the measuring cup and add the next portion of boiling water. The total time of immersion in scalding water is 25 to 30 seconds.

PORTION	FILL TO MARK	COUNT TO
1	32 fluid oz. (4 cups)	5
2	32 fluid oz. (4 cups)	5
3	16 fluid oz. (2 cups)	10
4	16 fluid oz. (2 cups)	10
5	32 fluid oz. (4 cups)	15

Stir the sauce ingredients together until dissolved. Mix half of the sauce lightly with the kidneys, and serve cold, on a bed of Blanched Bean Sprouts (83) which have been mixed with the remaining sauce.

MAIN COURSES

The tone set by the hors d'oeuvre should be developed in the rest of the menu. What belongs to classic cuisine? A certain number of tastes and textures. Understand that it is a gathering together of the best ideas, hence a creation of the mind. It therefore contains a preponderance of those total creations of texture and flavour. It consists of the sophistications of the cuisine, but is not necessarily the best of the cuisine. To it belong all the plays on texture. The mild, mellow, bland, rich and convoluted flavours are emphasized to the exclusion of the very salty, sour and hot. Red peppers are not allowed. Coarseness is excluded; minces and pastes, tender, suave substances that glide down the throat, have a central place. It is the ultimate in gastronomy, as far removed from savage cooking as can be imagined. That is why this creation of the mind is considered in gastronomy as the highest order of cooking.

No item in classic cooking is brought in casually. Each one is the result of perhaps an exorbitant amount of thought and labour. Considering all these things, why is it that many feasts are so unsatisfying? It is because they lack style, because the host has little taste. Taking the most expensive things and putting them together on a menu is foolish. We encounter it so often that we call it "the usual". It consists of the fins, the nest, the duck, the squab, *ad nauseam*. It is possible to stay well within the boundaries of classic cuisine and escape common vulgarity. The art of making up menus, like the art of dress, is not what you put on, but how everything is put together.

OPULENT
(suitable for visiting dignitaries, merchant princes and rich relatives)
Shark's Fins with Crab Sauce (125)
  Happy Family (100)
    Stuffed Duck (127)
      Whole Chicken Stuffed with Bird's Nest (126, 38)
        Pastry Peaches (134)

PSEUDO-RUSTIC
(suitable for artists, gourmets, noted authors)
Black Hen Soup, with Black Mushrooms
  Tungpo Pork, with Pinwheels (8, 51)
    Soochow Cabbage Stew (99)
      Duck Steamed in Wine (128)
        Sweet Bird's Nest (39)

RECHERCHÉ
(for entertaining good cooks and distinguished company)
Bêche-de-mer Gourmet (130)
  Crisp Spiced Duck, with Buns (35, 53)
    Bird's Nest with Bean Sprouts (129)
      Carp in Lamb Broth (13)
        Silver Fungus with Candy Sugar Syrup (40)

THE BEST
(neither too showy nor mock simple, it is excellent for all occasions)
Velvet Chicken I (29)
  Prawn (Shrimp) Balls (131)
    Peking Duck (57)
      Minute Beef (132)
        Steamed Fish (133)
          Peking Dust*

*A mound of chestnut purée covered with whipped cream.

Opulence:
Shark's Fins with Crab Sauce; Stuffed Duck,
including Directions on How to Bone Fowl

The idea of opulence is very important in classic cooking, as it always has been in the art of older cultures. Only in America is this idea played down, to be expressed in the make and model of the cars Americans drive, cryptic to the uninitiated. Opulence is the key to the splendour of European palaces, to their grand churches: a display of sentiment, pomp and grandeur buoyed up by what some people hold most dear, money. The opulent feast is proof of the esteem in which one holds one's guests, uncomplicated by subtle compliments to their real tastes, which are intangibles. When you eat a mouthful of shark's fins, you can almost price the entire dinner. There is no greater comfort than to know that your host has spent a great deal of money on you.

In the most expensive cooking the shark's fins are blanched a few times in water, and then cooked several times in chicken stock, the stock being discarded each time. The purpose of this is to replace the water in the fins with stock. In this way, each fibre is tasty because it is impregnated with stock. The fins, which are almost completely tasteless, acquire a positive, rich flavour which enables them to take on other ingredients without being overshadowed. Yuan Mei thought that the cooking of fins with crab was "vile and vulgar in the extreme". Nonetheless, it is common practice to combine the fins with crabs roe or crab meat so that the mixture is unctuous and the appearance gilded. There are those who always forsake splendour for mock simplicity. It is refreshing to be vulgar once in a while.

125. Shark's Fins with Crab Sauce (蟹 肉 扒 翅)

½ lb. dried shark's fins
About ¾ pint (1¾ cups) Cream
   Stock (16)
1 level tablespoon cornflour
   (cornstarch)
5 oz. (¾ cup) crab meat
1 teaspoon sesame oil
½ level teaspoon MSG
½ level teaspoon salt

3 egg yolks, beaten
2 whole eggs, beaten
5 tablespoons oil

Prepare the shark's fins as directed in recipe 43. Use Cream Stock for this dish, if possible. If not, use the best chicken, chicken-and-duck, or chicken-and-ham stock. This is essential; otherwise one should omit the dish from the menu. Place the softened fins in a deep dish and pour in sufficient stock to keep the fins moist. Cover the dish and steam it for about 2 hours, until the fins are tender. Then pour off the stock, and thicken it with the cornflour dissolved in ¼ teaspoon stock. Stir the sauce until smooth and hot, and pour it over the fins. Cover the dish and steam it again for 5 minutes.

Meanwhile, remove the transparent bones from the crab meat. Mix the crab with sesame oil, MSG, salt and the beaten yolks and whole eggs. Heat oil in a wo, and sauté the crab and egg until creamy. Invert the shark's fins on a dish, and make a depression in the centre. Fill the depression with the egg mixture, letting some of the fins show around the edge of the dish.

The idea of opulence is not only in the expense of a feast, but in the rich and gorgeous flavours of the food. Opulence is to be enjoyed without restraint, with unabashed zest. A whole stuffed duck invites gourmandise. The original form of the following recipe ("eight-jewelled duck") contained five kinds of nuts, fungi and seeds: lotus seeds, seeds of *Euryale ferox* (a kind of water-lily), seeds of *Coix lachryma* (Job's Tears), tiger lilies, and a flat, nut-like bean. These five ingredients were added to provide some relief for this heavy and unctuous combination, so that there was a kind of balance in the resulting contest of flavours. For practical reasons we have left out these five ingredients. The essential point in this dish is to have the flavour of the duck fat penetrate the glutinous rice, and for the rice to soak up all the flavour, in a rich, soft consistency. Another name for glutinous rice is sticky rice, or better still "glutton's rice". The duck must first be boned.

126. How to Bone Fowl (怎 樣 去 掉 骨 頭)

This process is quite simple, taking only about 20 minutes. The only difference between boning a duck and a chicken is in the removal of thigh bones. The duck's thigh bones are set well within the frame of the body; they are removed from the inside. The chicken's thigh bones are set away from the body, and are pulled out from the outside, after the drumstick.

(1) Spine: Place the duck breast side down. Free the duck skin from the spine by cutting your way in with a pair of blunt-tipped scissors, starting at one end and working towards the middle. Turn the duck around and cut the skin and meat loose from the other end of the spine, working towards the middle. When the spine has been cut free of skin and bone, the hand is slipped in between them, freeing the skin of membranous filaments.

(2) Wings: Turn the duck breast side up. Cut off the wing tips. Bend the wings away from the body to break the joint. The single bone is removed later. The double bones are left in.

(3) Legs: Slit the skin at the shin, and cut through all the tendons, freeing the drumstick bone. Pull the bone forward, and at the same time draw the skin and meat of the drumstick back with the other hand, exposing the joint. Bend drumstick backward, breaking the joint. Cut the drumstick bone free of the joint. Remove the thigh bone by carefully slashing the flesh next to it from inside the body cavity. Cut it loose. Ignore the cartilaginous knee joint, which is removed later.

(4) Breast: The cartilaginous ridge along the middle of the breast is attached to the skin. The meat on either side of it is carefully freed from the bone before the ridge is carefully cut free of the skin.

With the body cavity towards you, insert scissors or knife between the breast bone and the flesh, working always with the cutting edge against the bone, to avoid piercing the skin. When the meat has been freed midway, slip in the hand between meat and breast bone, freeing the meat all the way to the collarbone. Repeat the procedure for the other side of the breast bone. Turn the collarbone towards you and cut it free of the flesh. Carefully cut along the midline ridge, freeing the skin of the cartilage. Slip the scissors inside the body cavity and cut the ribs on each side. Remove the breast bone.

(5) Back: Turn the duck inside out, and cut the bones in the back free of the flesh. Slash the flesh along the single large bone in the wings, and cut the bone free at both ends. Remove the wishbone, the cartilaginous joints at the knee, and all other pieces of bone or cartilage previously overlooked.

(6) Finishing Steps: Turn the duck right side out. The whole duck is now boned except for the double bones in the wings. The boned duck is stuffed, firmly trussed, pulled and tucked into shape, and finally blanched to set the shape and remove the scum.

127. Stuffed Duck (糯 米 鴨)

A 5- to 5½-lb. duck
10 dried Chinese mushrooms
2 oz. (5 level tablespoons)
  glutinous rice
1 spring onion (scallion), very
  finely chopped
4 oz. bamboo, diced (¾ cup diced)

1 teaspoon soy sauce
¼ level teaspoon sugar
Oil
2 oz. cooked ham, diced
  (⅓ cup diced)
½ level teaspoon salt

Bone the duck as directed above. Soak dried mushrooms in water to cover. When softened, remove the stems and dice the caps. Wash and drain glutinous rice.

Sauté mushrooms, spring onion and bamboo with the soy sauce, sugar and 1 tablespoon oil. Add the ham and sauté for a few minutes longer, then add the rice and mix them all together. Place the stuffing inside the body cavity of the boned duck. The duck is trussed as follows (needle, thread or skewers are unnecessary). Bring one leg across the opening and overlap the other with it. Bring the wings close to the body, and tuck the skin of the collar under the body. Truss the duck securely across the wings, around the sides, down the midline and across the thighs. This sturdy package will not spill its contents. Pull and tuck the duck so that the breast appears smooth and plump, and the shape of the duck is a symmetrical oval.

Bring 5 pints (12 cups) water to the boil. Blanch the duck in it for 3 minutes, then rinse it under the cold tap, rubbing the skin free of scum. Dry the duck and sprinkle it with salt. Place it breast side down on a rack, and steam it for 1½ hours. Wipe the duck dry and fry it in a wo, using about ½ pint (1 cup) oil, for about 5 minutes, until evenly browned all over. Remove the strings. Place the duck on a plate, cut all the way around it with scissors, like a melon, then down the midline and from midline to side. The shape of the duck is retained after the skin is cut.

Simplicity: Duck Steamed in Wine

In the course of a feast, the host may say repeatedly, "There is nothing to eat! This is just a home meal." He continues to deprecate the talents of the cook. "He cannot cook. He can only make coarse food." When a magnificent, expensive, great bowl of duck appears, he says, "This is only a little duck, cooked with a little wine."

The following recipe is an extraordinary combination of duck and wine, in which each spoonful of wine tastes of duck, and each fibre of duck tastes of the wine. The duck is cooked in the rice wine *Shaoshing* (from Chekiang), resembling pale dry sherry, in a sealed casserole placed in boiling water; in other words, a *bain-marie*. The boiling point of wine is lower than that of water, so after a while the wine will begin to boil. For this reason, the casserole must be sealed or covered tightly to prevent undue evaporation. The second important point is the clarification of the soup. Every trace of oil must be removed so that the soup attains the clarity of brandy. Every bone must be removed. The wine causes the meat to separate into fibres, so that finally it resembles a bowlful of unearthly noodle soup, consisting of very fine strands of duck meat in a crystal-clear broth. A small bowlful of this would be strong enough to revive the dead.

128. Duck Steamed in Wine (酒 蒸 鴨)

A 5- to 5½-lb. duck　　　　　*2 pints (5 cups) or 2 bottles*
½ level teaspoon pepper　　　*Shaoshing wine or pale dry*
2½ level teaspoons salt　　　 *sherry*

Clean the duck, removing the fat pads on either side of the body cavity. Wipe the duck dry inside and out. Rub it both inside and outside with the pepper and 2 level teaspoons salt. Let it stand for 4 to 16 hours (preferably overnight) in the refrigerator. The bloody liquid should be discarded.

Wipe the duck dry and place it in a casserole with a close-fitting lid. If necessary, double the duck back on itself, breaking the spine, so that it will be a compact body completely immersed in wine. Pour over it 1½ pints (3¾ cups) *Shaoshing* wine or sherry, reserving the remaining ½ pint (1¼ cups). Place the casserole in a pan of water, and cover the casserole with its lid. If the fit is not tight, cover the lid with overlapping lengths of cellophane or foil, tied securely with string. Add water so that it will come to within 2 inches of the edge of the casserole. Bring the water to the boil, keeping the lid of the pan on tightly. Keep the water simmering for 3½ hours, adding boiling water to the pan as necessary. Without undoing the casserole, let it cool overnight to room temperature.

The duck meat is loosened from its skin, fat and bones. The meat is fibrous and has a pinkish tinge. Gently remove all the skin and all the bones, by hand. The meat falls into delicate fibres, which should be moved aside, and the bones lifted out. Remove every bone and every bit of skin. Gently rake the fibres to reveal odd bits of fat, bone and skin. Remove these. Remove the floating fat, and skim off the oil until a clear stock is distinctly visible beneath a thin layer of oil. With a ladle, pass the top portion of the soup through a very fine-meshed sieve, or through cheese-cloth placed over a coarse sieve. Let the strained broth fall back into the casserole. Gently rake the duck meat again by hand or with chopsticks, so that pieces of fat will float to the top and can be sieved out. This step is of crucial importance to the final quality of the soup. Add the reserved

½ pint (1¼ cups) wine or sherry and the remaining ½ level teaspoon salt. Seal the casserole again, bring the water around it to the boil and simmer for 1 to 1½ hours. Serve in the casserole.

Recherché:
Bird's Nest with Bean Sprouts; Bêche-de-mer Gourmet

Classic cooking generally gains in comparison with the objects around it. A good deal of thought has gone into it, and a good deal of fun may be had in return. We can trace the convolutions of thought, like the channels and grooves of the human brain, for the sheer adventure of it, just as the eye joyfully follows the dips, waves and curls of baroque architecture. In the deeper reaches of sophistication there are amusements and diversions. Yuan Mei suggested combining "the cheapest and the most expensive"—a rich man's fancy. "The soft with the soft, the pale with the pale," repeating the idea of putting together ingredients similar but not the same. What one really has attempted to do is to hang a cheap bauble on an expensive bore, and so provide a few moments' amusement.

129. Bird's Nest with Bean Sprouts (芽 菜 燕 窩 湯)

2 oz. dry bird's nest	½ level teaspoon MSG
1½ lb. bean sprouts	¼ level teaspoon salt
1½ pints (3½ cups) good, fat-free chicken or ham stock	8 level teaspoons cornflour (cornstarch)
1 teaspoon light soy sauce	8 tablespoons (½ cup) cold stock

Soften and prepare the bird's nest as directed in recipe 38. Pick over the bean sprouts, discarding root and bean, and saving only the stems. Blanch them for 1 minute in boiling water, then drain them and rinse them with cold water.

Bring stock to the boil with soy sauce, MSG and salt. Add the stems and the nest, and simmer for 30 minutes. Dissolve cornflour in cold stock, and stir it into the soup until thickened and smooth.

The bêche-de-mer easily degenerates into a spineless nothingness. The slug must be livened by a number of little prawns (shrimps). In the following recipe the prawns are boiled to yield a zesty, supercharged essence, far too electric if taken alone. When the slug is cooked in it, the combination is just right. The combination of black fungus and black mushrooms with the black slug is reminiscent of the "chicken in mourning" of French cuisine. A recipe of Yuan Mei: "All will be black."

130. Bêche-de-mer Gourmet (花 菇 海 参)

STOCK
3 oz. (1 cup) dried prawns
  (shrimps)
1 tablespoon sesame oil
Sugar
6 small (white) onions
3 slices ginger
2½ pints (6 cups) half chicken
  or beef consommé and half
  water
1 tablespoon soy sauce

½ lb. dried bêche-de-mer
½ oz. (½ cup) dried black tree
  fungus
2½ oz. (¾ cup) dried Chinese
  mushrooms

Prepare the stock: Place the prawns in a 2-pint (4-cup) heatproof measuring cup together with sesame oil and 2 level teaspoons sugar. Fill the cup to the 24 fluid oz. (3-cup) mark with boiling water, and let it stand for 10 minutes. Drain the prawns well, discarding the liquid. This treatment removes the fishy and salty taste of the dried prawns. Place the rinsed prawns in a pot and simmer them with onions, ginger, diluted consommé, soy sauce and ¾ level teaspoon sugar for 1 hour. Strain the stock, discarding the pulp. You will have about 2 pints (5 cups) stock.

Soften bêche-de-mer as directed in recipe 41, cutting it into ½-inch chunks. Soften tree fungus as directed in recipe 40 until three times its original volume. Place the mushrooms in a measuring cup and cover with water to the 8 fluid oz. (1-cup) mark. When softened, trim off the stems.

Simmer the bêche-de-mer, fungus and mushroom caps in the mushroom water and just over 1½ pints (4 cups) stock for 2½ to 3 hours, adding more stock when necessary. The final texture should be one of tender resilience. The stock becomes a little thickened as the bêche-de-mer is stewed.

The Best: Prawn (Shrimp) Balls;
Minute Beef; Steamed Fish

But what is the best? We say that what is the best is not too obvious, but apparent; not esoteric, but well considered; not common, nor vulgar nor exaggerated, but excellent of its kind. The taste of food is not to be shared by anyone, except those who already agree with you. So the cook should not pay attention to his audience, but only to himself, or to his patron. The gift of taste is something too rare and inexplicable, and too personal to be disseminated. This being so, perhaps the most difficult thing to achieve in cooking is general appreciation. The best is what is not only excellent, but also easily recognized to be so. For in cooking, as elsewhere, it is best not to be outstanding, to bring one's talents within the boundaries of common recognition. The plays on texture should not be recognized as such. If this were so, popcorn would be the favourite of gastronomes only, and it is not; or potato chips, all plays on texture, such as *rösti* or sausage, or bread, or Red Delicious apples. The following recipe is a popular dish and also a play on texture.

In order to achieve the correct texture the prawn fibres must be destroyed. This is achieved by chopping or by scraping, to minimize inclusion of the fibres in the paste. We prefer chopping, as it is less time-consuming and a little fibre does not hurt the texture. The addition of water, cornflour (cornstarch) and egg white is essential to provide lightness. Indeed, the trick in making meat balls is to include non-meat, and in making prawn balls it is to add a lot of ingredients which are not prawns. In contrast to a common Western method of using egg whites, they must be kept bubble-free, so that it is impossible to tell where the prawn ends and the egg begins. They are chopped into the paste, as are the water and the cornflour. The addition of fat pork makes the texture gliding and tender, and keeps the balls moist. Otherwise the dried yet wet quality of overcooked prawns resembles moist blankets.

Serve this dish with a small dish of Wild Pepper Mix (36) on the side. The balls are best made by hand, like fish balls; ballers and pastry tubes are useless. With a little practice, perfect balls can be made out of prawn or fish paste (31).

*131. Prawn (Shrimp) Balls (炸 蝦 球)

1 lb. prawns	3 egg whites
¼ lb. pork fat	4 level tablespoons cornflour
3 to 4 tablespoons water	(cornstarch)
½ level teaspoon salt	Fat for deep-frying
½ teaspoon pressed ginger	Wild Pepper Mix (36)
(juice)	

Shell the prawns, wash them and pat them dry. Chop the pork fat very finely, then add it to the prawns and chop them together, gradually adding water, salt and pressed ginger. Continue to chop, adding the 3 egg whites and the 4 tablespoons cornflour one by one. When all the ingredients are well mixed by chopping, take a handful of the paste, and squeeze it through index finger and thumb into hot fat, tipping the ball into the fat with the aid of a spoon. Fry the balls in fat for about 3 minutes, until a golden brown colour. Because of the high moisture and fat content, these balls take longer to cook than plain prawns. When fried to a golden brown, the inside is still moist and tender. Serve them immediately with a dish of Wild Pepper Mix.

A feast is like a symphony. The rhythm of the great feast comes from the pauses. A pause is very important, and must in itself be tasteful. A feast is like a walk along straight streets, until one comes to a quiet square, where it is possible to rest a moment. Here comes one of the pleasant moments.

The little dishes to fill in the pauses are cooked in a matter of minutes. One of the best of these is the "two passes" method for kidneys, pork, beef or seafood. The meat slices, passed quickly through hot fat, go directly into the simmering sauce, are given two or three stirs, and served immediately. Hence the name for the method, which takes longer to describe than to do. This method requires two pans, one readied with the sauce, the wo heated and used for deep-fat frying.

*132. Minute Beef (抓 搶 牛 肉 片)

¾ lb. rump steak (or flank steak)
4 teaspoons soy sauce
1 level tablespoon cornflour
  (cornstarch)
½ pint (1 cup) oil
½ teaspoon vinegar

SAUCE
1 level tablespoon peeled
  chopped ginger
2 tablespoons pale dry sherry
¼ pint (⅔ cup) stock
2 level teaspoons cornflour
1 teaspoon soy sauce
1 teaspoon oyster sauce
¼ level teaspoon sugar

Trim the steak of all solid fat and any membranes, sinews, or ligaments. Make very thin slices across the grain about ½ inch wide and 1½ inches long, and coat them with soy sauce and cornflour.

Mix the sauce ingredients together in a frying pan, saucepan, or wo. Bring to the boil and stir until smooth. Heat the oil in a wo. Have ready a pair of chopsticks and a slotted spoon. Heat the sauce to simmering point.

1st pass: When the oil is very hot, add the slices and stir immediately with chopsticks. As soon as the slices are browned (over 30 seconds), remove them with the chopsticks and the slotted spoon and transfer them directly into the simmering sauce.

2nd pass: Stir the slices in the sauce, turning the heat up. After 10 seconds, add the vinegar. Give it a few more stirs and serve at once.

The best is to fit into the standard form. We know very well that the taste of odd things has charms. "When I was a child," someone wrote, "I crawled about the garden, putting little stones in my mouth as if they were eggs." We have never ceased to do so, and so discovered many things. But the most important of all is to see the whole shape of the thing, to carry out the standard form, but to do it better than anyone else. A fish is the traditional end to a great banquet.

133. Steamed Fish (清 蒸 魚)

A 2½-lb. pike, carp, sea bass or
  small flounder
¼ pint plus 2 tablespoons
  (¾ cup) chicken stock
1 level tablespoon cornflour
  (cornstarch)

½ level teaspoon sugar
½ level teaspoon salt
1 tablespoon wine
1 teaspoon sesame oil
¼ level teaspoon MSG

Clean the fish and brush out all the blood. Blanch it for 1 minute in boiling water, then rinse it under the tap and pat it dry. Place it on a dish to fit the length of the fish, with sides to hold in the sauce. Mix the remaining ingredients together in a saucepan and cook gently until thickened. Pour this sauce over the fish. Cover the dish closely with cellophane, foil or an overlapping plate, and steam it for about 25 to 30 minutes. Serve immediately.

The standard form is rather amusing to think on, for the serving of fish (*yü*, 魚) at the end means that there is more (*yu yü*, 有 餘). In the inland provinces, where fish were scarce, the feasts sometimes closed with the presentation of a wooden fish. Those who knew the language of food had also put puns into it.

8. A Gastronomic Calendar

He casts his nets midstream his
*   haul to take;*
She drops her line and waits her
*   catch to make.*
When all the day's catch is changed
*   again for wine,*
They row the boat homeward in the
*   shower's wake.*

CHANG CHUNSHOU

THE SILENCE of the landscape was broken by the boat's paddles, and the calm faded away. Human voices interrupted. The sound of life was in the festivals, the restaurants, the temples. Some men wrote about how things ought to be, but were interrupted by people. We would not do justice to the great subject of Chinese gastronomy if we did not describe how it was, as well as how it should be.

Life was a jumble, but there was order in it. Familiar objects had their place. Real life was made up of things, and not of ideas. We went to the market, traded in eggs, felt and held between thumb and fingers, ate sweet fried noodles cut in "elephant eye" (diamond) pattern, weighed the squawking chickens and squabs, were indifferent to their pains, chewed thin wheat cakes wrapped about fried egg and spring onions, and green bean noodles sprinkled with pepper oil and hot sauce. Life was real. The passing of time was marked by weddings, birthdays and funerals. Each thing had its place. Though nothing important really ever happened, the days swung from the whites of death to the reds of marriage and birthdays. Hemp and yards of white cloth, unhemmed smocks and the wailing of men and women mixed with the smoke from burnt gilded multi-coloured paper objects, as offerings to the dead.

Which of us was dissimulating, which of us only unable to give evidence of grief? We shied away from looking at the photograph of the deceased, placed directly in front of the enormous coffin. Only the joy of birthdays and weddings could wipe out those horrors. At those times we all went through the well-known paces, and the wheel of time went round. For a month-old anniversary of a baby, two, four or eight silver dollars were wrapped in red paper and dropped on the tiny child as it was brought around. Eight or sixteen hard-boiled eggs, dyed red, were given away in announcement, and more lay in pyramids on raised dishes, beside the candles.

On those days the great words "Happiness" and "Longevity" were brought out in golden characters on red scrolls. This was how much we valued life, that rather than sweet and short, we wanted it to be long, even if difficult. The fairy immortal was pictured in all the drawings as being bearded and stooped, holding a peach in one hand, and a staff in the other. It was good to grow old and have a glorious seventieth or eightieth or ninetieth birthday, with all the smooth-faced grandchildren gathered about. Gold and red candles, fat and big, burned in pairs. If the hall was dim, it was not gloomy because of all the red hanging about. All the things were in pairs, and red. On birthdays of elderly persons the little children were ushered in to pay their respects and receive packets of dollars. Pyramids of fresh noodles, with cut-outs of red paper placed upon them, and *paotse* made in the shape of peaches (longevity peaches called *shoutao*), their pale and doughy surfaces speckled with red, stuck with green leaves, stood on stands. All the peaches were put in a mound by the candles. Without this pyramid of pastry peaches, something would be missing.

134. Pastry Peaches (壽 桃)

1 recipe Basic Yeast Dough (47)
Green, red and yellow food
   colouring

FILLING
4 oz. (¾ cup) sesame seed
4 oz. (½ cup) peanut butter
1½ oz. (3 level tablespoons)
   butter
10 oz. (1½ cups) light brown
   sugar

Make the dough and set apart 2 oz. (3 level tablespoons) unrisen dough. Tint it green to make leaves, working the colouring in well.

To make the filling: Toast the sesame seed gently in an ungreased heavy frying pan until a light brown colour, then crush the seed to bring out the flavour. Mix it with peanut butter, butter and light brown sugar.

To make the peaches: Let the dough rise as directed, then punch it down and roll it into two long cylinders. Cut each into twelve pieces. Roll each piece into a circle. Place a heaped tablespoon of the filling in the centre, and pinch the circle together by making pleats, all but for one-eighth of the circle. Leave this portion unpleated, and pinch together the remaining free edges of the circle to make the peach with the pointed tip. Lightly score the smooth side of the peach with the dull edge of a knife from the tip upwards, to make the seam characteristic of peaches.

To colour peaches: Moisten the bristles of a pastry brush with red and yellow food colouring, and flick it with the thumb towards the pointed tip of the peach, to give it a rosy tinge. Place the peaches aside on squares of foil or paper to rise.

Next, make the leaves: Punch down the risen green-tinted dough and roll it into an oblong. Lightly score it three or four times lengthwise, and from these slashes make parallel diagonal slashes lightly, sloping away from each long score mark. Cut long, oval shapes along each lengthwise gash to make the leaves. Make 48 leaves, transfer them to a clean plate and place them in the refrigerator, so that they will remain flat and not undergo a second rising.

Assembling peaches and leaves: After peaches have risen (about 30 minutes), moisten bottoms of leaves with a little water and place them on to the top of the peach, opposite the pointed tip. Stick two leaves on to each peach. Steam the peaches for 15 minutes and serve immediately, or let them cool and place them in a pyramid on a plate for display, to be steamed again later. Though they turn stone hard when cold, they will soften when steamed again.

Cooks took care never to cut birthday noodles. At table the guests lifted them with chopsticks, rising to clear them of the dish. The noodles could be half as tall as a man, and take him one long breath to suck them in. The longer the noodles, the longer would be the life. Do not speak of the sauces or stocks or soups in which these were presented. They are unimportant. The main thing was for each person seated at the table to eat noodles, in celebration of the birthday.

Gifts were wrapped in red paper. This could be a whole cooked chicken, or fruit in season, or an imported delicacy. Usually brought in a basket, it was received with a tip to the servant, and a gift in return to "weight the basket". Holidays were in a way a means of equalizing wealth, the poor relatives coming for a big feast and the dole, and the wealthy branch of the family spending a good deal on display of wealth as a way of celebration. Servants received extra pay on holidays, the size of the tips being geared to the wealth of the family. The rich were expected to be generous, so gifts went out by basketfuls, or as bolts of material, all wrapped in red. Unaware of time's passing, we went through the paces, the same at each time of the year.

On the coming of spring, the weather turned warm at *Chingming* (清 明) and a day in April was set aside for the visit to the graves. There were few cemeteries as such, and graves were placed at sites chosen at will, where the configuration of trees, rivers and fields was considered fortuitous. Rice fields which belonged to private families were dotted with the raised mounds of graves. On the day before Chingming, only cold food was served. One did not light fires. The offerings were composed of cooked bamboo shoots and boiled fish. Dumplings and cooked red lotus root were sold in the streets. The outing to the graves was rather like a solemn picnic. Food was brought to the graves, to which one travelled by boat or on foot. In earlier times a son-in-law and daughter had two visits to make, the day before Chingming for the visit to the daughter's family graves, on the day itself to his family graves. The graves were swept, and the incised letters on the stone, worn down by the weather in the past year, once again filled with red ink paste. The food was presented, arranged with the orderly symmetry which one observed on these serious occasions, and then eaten by the relatives. This marked the coming of spring.

The frogs had begun to croak, and one could not be sure whether it would rain or not. At the end of April, the flavour of tea was at its best, and offered an excuse to go into the mountains for the day. The mountains were thronged with visitors. Tea connoisseurs were repelled by the sight of so many people, preferring to sip tea made with mountain water in the grand silence of the mountains. This was hard to get. "The secret of good tea lies in the water, which should be taken from a good spring. How can this be obtained in an ordinary home? By special carrier, or by storing spring water or snow. When water is new it is raw. Aged water is sweet. Perhaps the best tea in the world is to be found at the top of Wuyi mountain. It is almost colourless. The party should not consist of too many people, or it begins to resemble Lungching [a famous place for tea] before Chingming. If the leaves are tightly curled the flavour will be subdued. Then you must use a lot of leaves. The best time is before the rain, a great expanse of jade. Collect about four ounces in each paper packet, and place it in the ash incubator for ten days. When you change the ashes, cover the tea with paper. When you come to brew the tea, bring the water to the boil over a low fire. Do not boil it too much, or the water will change flavour (the best point at which to stop is when tiny bubbles called 'crab's eyes' appear to stream from the sides of the pot). Drink a cup immediately, then cover the pot. The flavour will change again." (Yuan Mei) The appreciation of tea lies in the same vein as the enjoyment of food— the manifold, complex, convoluted flavours being of special interest to the connoisseur.

The spring and early summer rains were collected for tea. Setting out great jars in the courtyard, we listened with delight to the *plop!* of the rain accumulating. This would keep for a long time without spoiling, but one was rarely given the chance to wait so long. "The sky clears after the rain, and the moss is wet. The jars are full of rain water, and just as tea is made, guests arrive." (Ku Tieh Ching)

Fresh tea was picked and, in those peculiar exchanges of nearly or completely identical gifts, families presented tea to one another. Dried tea leaves, steeped and drained, are excellent sautéed with prawns (26). Yuan Mei cooked ham with tea leaves. A salted steamed duck which is smoked over camphor wood shavings and tea leaves, and then fried, acquires a beautifully mellow taste (Szechuan); hard-boiled eggs, with shells cracked and steeped in strong tea, acquire a marble-ized look and an interesting flavour; fresh eggs beaten with a little water are excellent steamed with tea or with chopped orioles (Yuan Mei).

As the weather grew warmer, some country houses would be hung with rush swords, peach branches, thorns and strings of garlic to ward off evil spirits. Children went about with sachets of incense hung about their necks. Bugs and insects began to appear at windows and in the cracks. Vermilion cinnabar (mercurous sulfide, HgS) and orange realgar (As_2S_2) were taken in wine to clear the system. The last of the home-made wine, aged over the winter, was finished off in the evening of a warm spring day. In the economical household nothing was wasted, and the dregs, which were mild and non-alcoholic, and somehow turned rose-red in the ageing process, were used in cooking. The red colour of a number of Southern dishes comes from the wine dregs, whose mild and subtle flavour improves the taste of bland foods. Potted capon was made by sealing a steamed capon between two layers of red wine dregs mixed with wine and salt; in Swatow, an excellent dish is made from the first tripe of the cow, and red wine dregs.

During and after the spring rains, the bamboo put forth shoots, leaves shot forth and the bamboo grew almost visibly. The biggest leaves were plucked and sun-dried, to be used as cones for glutinous rice dumplings (*tsungtse*, 粽子) filled with meat or red bean paste, then enclosed by a further twist of the cone, and tied with string. The arrival of these pastries coincided with the dragonboat festival, a noisy exercise of decorated boats racing down a river. Originally, sacrifices were made to Ch'ü Yuan, the poet-statesman of long ago, with offerings of rice thrown into the river. But now it remained a festival, with soggy pastries in evidence everywhere, but not thrown into the river, where they would have sunk quickly. These formed neat little packages, good for gifts. In the Soochow region, the leaf-wrapped delicacy was made into cones of varying dimensions, resembling hammer, horn, water chestnut, tube, figure nine or the awl. But it was generally a crude pastry, wrapped so it would hold together and not stick to anything, and dropped into boiling water to reheat it.

The summer grew ripe, and the round watermelons, the gourds and marrows, trailed from the dainty vines, large and absurd appendages lying on the earth. A watermelon was scooped out, steamed chicken soup with ham and mushrooms poured in, and steamed again. Watermelon juices mingled with chicken soup, imparting a sweet taste to it. Bamboo shoots were cut in the early morning, before the sun grew warm, and cooked for lunch. Cucumbers plucked off the vine were peeled and went directly into the steamer and to the table.

Now at the height of summer, the insects chirped, moulted, leaving their past selves in odd corners of the garden or on the branches of a high tree. As children, we crunched these, finding them quite tasty. What confectioner would have been able to achieve the delicacy of form and detail? When we were children we considered almost all small objects playthings, particularly insects, keeping silkworms in matchboxes as pets, holding them to the ear to listen to the little creatures as they munched noisily through several mulberry leaves a day. The braver of us would let a silkworm crawl on the tongue for the fun of it, while others looked on in admiration. We roasted silkworms in their cocoons and cut them open for a look. Fresh plums, peaches and gingko, lichee and mango—fruits well remembered in winter— suddenly descended on us by bushelfuls, so that one had to salt them quickly and dry them, making the "salty-sour-sweet" (in Amoy dialect, *kiam-sng-ti* 鹹 酸 甜) preserves for which the semi-tropical South was known. Meanwhile, we gorged ourselves on luscious fresh fruits, whose heady fragrances added to the summer's languor.

"On a hot summer's day, you sit in a rattan chair, with a bowl of cold plum juice beside you, and fan yourself lazily." We were careful to choose plums from Tientsin, the sweetest and darkest, then stew them with candy sugar and cinnamon. We had time to choose between several kinds of nuts and half-a-dozen varieties of olives. As children, we would pass the time watching dried olive pits burn with forked blue flames. Adults preferred the sour and salty to the sweet, the hot to the cold. The cold sweets were for children: agar-agar and the imported gelatine, known as "glass powder"; lotus root smothered with syrup. Women would sit and fan themselves, quite content. One made cold sweets with boiled green beans, crunched juicy and sweet sugar cane. The household was without refrigeration, but one could make a delightful sweet with imported Japanese seaweed, agar-agar, which set at room temperature. Its gelatinous, slippery texture was a favourite with children.

*135. Agar-Agar in Syrup (燕 菜)

¼ oz. dried agar-agar
1¼ pints (3 cups) water
6 oz. (¾ cup) white sugar, or
   about 4 oz. (4 level
   tablespoons) candy sugar
   (rock candy)

SYRUP
½ pint plus 4 tablespoons
   (1½ cups) water
4½ oz. (⅔ cup) brown sugar, or
   2 oz. (2 level tablespoons)
   candy sugar

Cut the sticks of agar-agar into 1-inch lengths. Bring water and sugar to the boil. Add agar-agar and simmer for 20 minutes, uncovered, until the agar is almost dissolved, stirring occasionally. Pour it through a coarse sieve into a dish or pan, and let it cool to room temperature. Cut it into diamond-shaped pieces and serve in cold syrup, made by bringing water and brown sugar to the boil. Allow to cool and, if possible, chill the syrup and the agar.

The days were easily passed with an occasional excitement. If someone got heat prostration, an aunt was always ready to give the treatment, consisting of scraping the neck and the tender skin at the elbow with a penny or a silver dollar, so that the victim howled, and so stimulated, rapidly got over what was ailing her. Another consisted of plucking the shoulder muscles, like stretching a rubber band and letting go. This made the patient sit up right away. A combination of the two treatments had the victim nursing the welts for days afterwards. We entertained each other with minor mishaps and were never without an audience.

As autumn came, gastronomes, having spent a few weeks in the mountains tasting some vegetarian food, descended to the lowlands, where the crabs had begun to appear in the marshes. Blinded by the lights in the dark, they clumsily swam to captivity and the table.

The best way to eat crabs is to have them plain, boiled in salt or sea water, and to pick them apart oneself. You may also steam them, but this makes them a little too bland. For crab soup cook crab in its own broth. Mind you do *not* put in chicken stock.

YUAN MEI

Every year before the crab season starts, I begin to save money. People say crabs are my life, and my hoarded money is the ransom. From the first day of the season until the last, I do not miss a single day. People know I have a weakness for crabs and invite me. I call September and October the crab autumn. It is easily used up, and expensive to keep up. I tell the servants to scour the bottles and brew wine, both raw and clear, so that I can get tipsy, and I call those wines the crab wine and the crab brew, and the bottles crab bottles. I also used to have a maid servant whom I called the crab maid, but she is now dead. Her sole job was to attend to the crab feast.

LI LIWENG

When the crab season ended, people were loath to give up the idea of being without crab. The following is an excellent dish, but a poor substitute for the heady concentrate of roe found in the furry-clawed crabs of the Yangtse lakes.

136. Mock Crab Roe (賽 蟹 黃)

¼ lb. fresh fillet of sole, plaice
 (flounder) or cod
6 egg yolks
2 level tablespoons chopped spring
 onions (scallions), white parts
 only
1 teaspoon sesame oil

¼ level teaspoon MSG
¼ level teaspoon salt
⅛ level teaspoon white pepper
Fat for deep-frying
5 tablespoons soy sauce
3 tablespoons vinegar

Steam the fish for 10 minutes and flake it gently. Mix the egg yolks together with the spring onions, sesame oil, MSG, salt and white pepper. Add the fish and mix it in. Fry tablespoons of the mixture in fairly deep fat, until the sides are almost brown or a pinkish gold. The fat will foam, but this cannot be helped. The final texture must be firm. Serve hot with a separate dish of soy sauce mixed with vinegar. Excellent with warmed wine.

The arrival of autumn sent some people into orgies of crab eating, giving crab dinners with plenty of wine. "We were drunk by sunset, and reached home as the sun rose over the thicket." (*The Book of Wine*, Sung dynasty)

> At the third cup I penetrate the Great Way;
> A full gallon—Nature and I are one . . .
> But the things I feel when wine possesses my soul
> I will never tell to those who are not drunk.
>
> LI PO

Gastronomic Calendar | 195

When a gentleman has one drink, he becomes mellow; when he has had two, he talks but his speech is literate. When he has had three he is drunk and retires (*The Book of Wine*). Drink when happy, sing when drunk, sleep when tired (Tung Cheng-feng). A sober man knows right from wrong and good food from bad. It is said that the subtleties of flavour are lost by talk. But if one did not talk, how would those noisy drunks know what they were eating?

YUAN MEI

Others felt they had to give and receive moon cakes. The full moon, the crab, chrysanthemums and wine formed a poetic complement with some indulging in one, and others in the cakes shaped like the moon. Once again families exchanged near-identical gifts, buying these cakes from shops making essentially the same cakes, and giving them to each other. The fillings were of red bean paste, or crushed lotus seeds embedded with a salted cooked duck's egg. These cakes are like the plum pudding and fruit cake which make an annual appearance, often unpalatable, heavy and soggy. Recently, a modern note was introduced into gift-boxed moon cakes when the traditional fairy in flowing silks was shown astride a rocket missile on her way to the full moon. But the celebration of mid-autumn (*chung ch'iu*, 中 秋) would be incomplete without stacks of these weighty delicacies.

The eighth day of the twelfth month (approximately 14 January) was marked by a special sweet called *lapacho* (臘 八 粥). The simplest form had eight ingredients, but the number could be increased to sixty-four. It was a hot, sweet soup made of the seeds of Job's Tears, red, green and yellow beans, red and brown dates, lotus seeds, chestnuts, almonds and peanuts, the meat of watermelon seeds, dried longan, walnuts, raisins and dried lichees, stewed together with glutinous rice.

The best time of all was the New Year festival, lasting two weeks. This was a general holiday for everyone. The servants, who had no days off, could take a few days' holiday to visit their relatives. Others stayed behind, collecting tips from the stream of courtesy callers, and from the guests who stayed to gamble and gave a share of their winnings *pour le personnel*. The joy of New Year came from many directions. Creditors looked forward to getting their debts paid, debtors to settling the accounts somehow. Madams of certain houses were paid at New Year. Children were given new clothes made specially for New Year's Day, and some entered in close alliance with the servants in their expectation of red packets of money, counting the number of visitors, shrewdly assessing their generosity. Housewives were not required to cook, and, in fact, were inviting bad luck if they did so. For this reason, the preparation for the holidays could begin a month ahead to supply the house with food for at least the first few days of the New Year. Great crocks of *chiaotse* (54) were made and stored uncooked, frozen in the chill weather. Restaurants and butchers' shops cooked whole farmyards of chickens, ducks and pigs in tubs of soy sauce, and hung them up to drip, the juices half running out. Women were fond of gathering together in a circle, making little balls out of glutinous rice flour for dumplings, and discussing the coming holiday, taking care to say only the good and lucky things as they rolled balls of dough between their palms. The aura of the New Year extended a month afterwards if one still had sweet *nienkao* lying about the kitchen, and the chances were very good that this heavy, steamed cake, made from brown sugar and glutinous rice flour, would still be there. It had remarkable lasting and keeping qualities. Sweet *nienkao* came in various sizes, each stamped with a lucky word in red on top, and were exchanged in quantity during the holidays. Cut into slices and fried in oil, they became crusty and even palatable. Their somewhat elastic and rubbery texture was little altered by time, and they appeared indestructible, nor could they be thrown out without qualms. The other gifts, fresh fish, pig's knuckles and cold chickens, and tangerines, symbols of good luck, were received and rapidly disappeared down our throats, but we had to look at the *nienkao* for a long, long time before it went away.

On the morning of New Year's Day (about 5 February) one did not sweep, light fires or pour out water, these being unlucky. Fragrant candles were lit, everyone put on his best new clothes, still stiff from never having been washed, and with smiling faces received callers. Housewives settled down at the mahjong table, refusing to budge, telling people to help themselves to cold food. The clatter of mahjong chips mingled with the constant explosions of firecrackers, whose sulphurous fumes mingled with the light of the flickering candles. Children scampered about, for once freed from watchful mother's eyes, and went with their fathers to the fair. The devout chose to go to the temples, shaking out their fortunes for the next year by tipping out one stick from a large bundle. The sticks, each bearing a coded fortune, were tapered. The slight protrusion of one from the bundle caused the others to nudge it out even further with each shake of the cylinder, so that eventually it fell to the ground. The coded fortune was translated for a small fee by a gentleman sitting in a booth, to the side. The temple was permanent, but at New Year the fair would be set up close to it, so that the throngs going to each eventually milled about each other, and it was impossible to tell which was which.

The fortune-tellers were next to the physiognomists, and these were close to the main square where the jugglers and acrobats, sword-swallowers, magicians, boxers, animal trainers and story-tellers entertained the people. One listened to tales, told by the rhythm of the wooden fish, the *pipa* and the *huchin*. One goggled at the magician producing a steaming bowl of noodles from beneath a quilt, squinted into the Foreign Mirror, a kind of peepshow, and gazed at the pictures of magnified objects, more remote, it seemed, than the pictures of fairies and wise men. Farmers bought pictures of the farmer and the ox, and sugar animals for their children. Wineshops and teashops were jammed. Poor people, to make a few pennies, would fill waterpipes. About the lakes, people would throw pieces of steamed bread to the turtles and fish, or feed them pieces of orange. So it continued, with some marathon gambling games, until the sixteenth of the month, when the students went back to their books, and farmers and artisans went back to work. Then the housewife returned to her kitchen, and the chef to his cleaver and chopping board and his bottles of sauces. Now all things were back in their proper places.

Glossary of Cooking Methods

The Sautés

Simple Sauté (炒): A wo or frying pan is prepared by heating in it a few tablespoons of oil. Ingredients in the form of dice, slivers or slices are added and stirred, seasoned, and mixed very briefly.

ILLUSTRATIVE RECIPES:
Sautéed Pork (11); Bamboo with Pickled Mustard Green (12)

Sauté, Finished in Sauce (燴): A sauce is added to a simple sauté before the substances are completely cooked.

ILLUSTRATIVE RECIPES:
Sautéed Liver (110); Chicken-flavoured Cabbage (104)

Sauté over Very High Heat (爆): The substances are seared or sautéed over very high heat for a short time.

ILLUSTRATIVE RECIPES:
Diced Chicken in Sauce (68); Hot Red Pepper Chicken (69)

Dry Sauté (乾 燒 or 乾 炒): A liquid is added to a simple sauté before the ingredients are completely cooked. It is absorbed by the substances and evaporated away, so that the dish as served appears to have no sauce.

ILLUSTRATIVE RECIPES:
Bamboo Dry Sauté (10); Sautéed Mushrooms (97); Spiced Tangerine Chicken (62); Spongy Bean Curd (102)

Braising and Stewing

Braising (燜): Meat is browned before being stewed with seasonings and a little liquid.

ILLUSTRATIVE RECIPES:
Lemon Chicken (96); Braised Chicken Parts (108)

Stewing (煨): Meat is stewed without first browning it, in a moderate amount of liquid.

ILLUSTRATIVE RECIPES:
Chicken 4-4-4-4 (105); Beef Yuan Mei (7)

Stewing (燉): Meat is stewed in a large amount of liquid until very tender.

ILLUSTRATIVE RECIPES:
Duck Steamed in Wine (128); Knuckles and Transparent Noodles (91)

Frying

Pan-fried (煎): Substances are fried in shallow fat.
ILLUSTRATIVE RECIPES:
Fried Fish (109); Fried Bean Curd (45)

Deep-fried (炸): Substances are fried in deep fat.
ILLUSTRATIVE RECIPES:
The Pieces of Eight (114); Crisp Spiced Duck (35); Fried Slices (61); Prawn (Shrimp) Balls (131)

Soft-fried (Two Passes Method, 抓 搶): The ingredient, coated with cornflour (cornstarch) and seasoning, is passed through deep fat, then directly placed in a simmering sauce, where it is finished.
ILLUSTRATIVE RECIPES:
Sautéed Lamb Slivers (60); Minute Beef (132); Whole Prawns (Shrimps) (25); Fish Fillets in Tart Sauce (59)

Roasting

Simple roasting (烤): The meat is roasted without basting.
ILLUSTRATIVE RECIPE:
Peking Duck (57)

Roasting with Sauce (燒): The meat is repeatedly painted with sauces in the course of roasting.

Dipping, Blanching, Poaching and Scalding

Dipping (灼): The thinly sliced or slashed substance is thrown into a large quantity of boiling water to which a spring onion (scallion), a slice of ginger and a small quantity of vinegar have been added. It is removed in less than 5 seconds.
ILLUSTRATIVE RECIPE:
Dipped Snails (93)

Blanching (浸): Vegetables are thrown into a large quantity of boiling water, stirred, and removed as soon as they turn deep green, or after they have lost their acrid taste (30 seconds to 2 minutes, depending on age and kind of vegetable). After draining, the vegetables are rinsed immediately with cold water, until cold to the touch. This step fixes the colour and texture.
ILLUSTRATIVE RECIPES:
Blanched Greens in Oyster Sauce (94); Blanched Bean Sprouts (83)

Poaching (川): The substance is placed in a large quantity of boiling water, which is then kept simmering (not boiling) until the substance is cooked.

ILLUSTRATIVE RECIPE:
Carp in Lamb Broth (13)

Scalding Followed by Slow Cooling (燙): Cantonese method for cooking chicken, young pigeons (squab). The meat is scalded by plunging it into a very large quantity of boiling stock or seasoned sauce. The heat is momentarily brought up, then turned off. The meat is cooked in the process of cooling the liquid.

ILLUSTRATIVE RECIPES:
Brown Chicken (95); Plain Chicken (3); See also *Chicken Livers in Brown Stock Sauce (78)*

Steaming

Simple Steaming (蒸): The substance is cooked by hot water vapours.

ILLUSTRATIVE RECIPES:
Steamed Cucumbers (107); Plain Buns (48); Steamed Fish (133)

Steamed, and Served with a Sauce (扒): The steamed substance is combined with a sauce made separately.

ILLUSTRATIVE RECIPE:
Shark's Fins with Crab Sauce (125)

Terms for Soups

Clear Soup (清 湯): Stock or consommé which you can see through.

ILLUSTRATIVE RECIPE:
Mushrooms in Broth (98)

Cream Soup (奶 湯): These are of two types: those to which milk has been added, and those which are made by extraction of fat droplets from the ingredients, producing the "milky" quality.

ILLUSTRATIVE RECIPES:
Fish Head in Casserole (9); Cream Stock (16); Duck Soup (58)

Half-soup (湯 菜): The other "half" of the dish being occupied by solid ingredients. The two substances are taken together by means of a spoon.

ILLUSTRATIVE RECIPES:
Spinach in Cream Stock (20); Happy Family (100); Carp in Lamb Broth (13)

Purée (羹): Soups made from finely divided ingredients. May be made from crab meat, vegetables, or curd; or from fruits and nuts. The latter are sweetened.

TABLE OF EQUIVALENTS

U.S. MEASURES

1 tablespoon =	*3 teaspoons*	= *½ fl. oz.*
1 cup =	*16 tablespoons*	= *8 fl. oz.*
1 pint =	*2 cups*	= *16 fl. oz.*
1 quart =	*4 cups*	= *32 fl. oz.*

BRITISH MEASURES

1 cup		= *10 fl. oz.*
1 pint =	*2 cups*	= *20 fl. oz.*
1 quart =	*4 cups*	= *40 fl. oz.*

The following table relates the weight of the ingredient (first and second columns) to its volume at the indicated stage of preparation (third and fourth columns). Thus, ¼ oz. of dry agar-agar, cut into 1-inch lengths and packed in a measuring cup, would come up to the ½ cup level (U.S. measure). The same weight when softened would occupy ⅞ cup and when cooked (135) yields 3 cups of jelly.

Ingredient	*Weight*	*Volume measured as*	*Volume equivalent or number of pieces (U.S. measures)*
Agar-agar, dry	¼ oz.	1-inch sticks, dry	½ cup
		1-inch sticks, softened	⅞ cup
		jelly	3 cups
Bamboo shoots	½ lb.	finely chopped dice	1½ cups
		slivers	1¾ cups
Bean curd, fresh	4 oz. (1 cake)	chunks	⅔ cups
		(pressed) slivers	½ cup
Bean curd sheets	2 oz.		3 sheets
Bean curd, fermented	2 oz.	drained cakes	⅓ cup
Bean sprouts	1 lb.	whole sprouts	6 cups
		stems only	1⅔ cups
Beans, French (string)	1 lb.	1½-inch lengths, cooked	2 cups
Bêche-de-mer, dry	½ lb.	½-inch chunks, softened	2½ cups
Beef, fresh	½ lb.	slices	1½ cups
Bird's nest, dry	2 oz.	dry flakes	1½ cups
		softened flakes	2½ cups

Ingredient	Weight	Volume measured as	Volume equivalent or number of pieces (U.S. measures)
Cabbage, Chinese	½ lb.	finely cut shreds	2 cups
Candy sugar (rock candy)	1 oz.	small pieces	about 1 tbs.
Carrots	4 oz.	slivers	1 cup
Chicken breasts	¾ to 1 lb.	skinned, boned dice	1 cup
		finely chopped paste	⅔ cup
Chicken giblets	1 lb.	quartered lobes	1 cup
Chicken legs	1 lb.		1 pair
Chicken livers or wings	1 lb.		about 10 pieces
Crab meat	6 oz.	flakes	1 cup
Fish fillets	¼ lb.	cooked flakes	½ cup
Fish maw, puffed dry	1 oz.	½-inch chunks, softened	2 cups
Flour, plain	4½ oz.	sifted flour	1 cup
Ham	2 oz.	dice	⅓ cup
Kidney, pork	¼ lb.	thin slices	⅓ cup
Lamb stew	1 lb.	(boned) chunks	2 cups
Lamb, loin meat	½ lb.	slivers	1½ cups
Liver, pork or beef	¾ lb.	½-inch slices	2 cups
Longan	5½ oz.	drained cooked nuts	⅔ cup
Mushrooms, Chinese (dried)	2½ oz.	whole dried pieces (about 12)	¾ cup
		softened, trimmed caps	1 cup
Mustard greens, pickled	½ lb.	shreds	1½ cups
		slices	2 cups
Noodles, dry	¾ lb.	cooked, drained noodles	5½ cups
Noodles, fresh	1 lb.	cooked, drained noodles	5½ cups
Noodles, dry transparent	¼ lb.	uncooked, softened threads	2½ cups
Parsley, Chinese	4 oz.	trimmed edible sprigs	3 cups
	1 oz.	dried flakes	1 cup

Ingredient	Weight	Volume measured as	Volume equivalent or number of pieces (U.S. measures)
Peanuts	3 oz.	shelled, blanched nuts	½ cup
Pig's feet	3 lb.		3 feet
Pike, whole	2½ lb.	raw scraped fish meat	2¼ cups
Porgy, whole	2 lb.	cooked flakes	1⅞ cups
Pork, lean	½ lb.	slivers	1⅓ cups
Pork, spare ribs	1 lb.	1½-inch chunks	2 cups
Prawns (shrimps)	½ lb.	8 to 12 whole, shelled prawns	1 cup
		dice	¾ cup
Radishes	½ lb.	trimmed whole pieces	1⅔ cups
Rice, plain	12 oz.	uncooked grains	2 cups
		cooked rice	6 cups
Rice, glutinous	3½ oz.	uncooked grains	½ cup
		softened, uncooked grains	1 cup
Salt, coarse	1 lb.	dry grains	3½ cups
Seaweed, purple	1 oz.	dry sheets	approx. 4 sheets
Sesame seed	4 oz.	grains	¾ cup
Shark's fins, dry	4 oz.	softened, uncooked fins	2 cups
Shrimp, dried	3 oz.		1 cup
Spinach	¼ lb.	leaves only	2 cups
Spring onions (scallions)	2 oz.	finely cut shreds	1 cup
Snails, whole	1 lb.	thin slices	½ cup
Snow peas	5 oz.	trimmed pods	1 cup
Sugar, brown	5 oz.	firmly packed granules	¾ cup
Tree fungus, dry	¼ oz.	dry flakes	¼ cup
		softened flakes	about 1 cup
Tripe, pig	1 lb.		1 tripe
Turnips	½ lb.	slivers	2 cups
Water chestnuts	4 oz.	finely chopped shreds	¾ cup
Vermicelli, dry	3 oz.	parboiled, drained threads	2 cups

Mail Order Sources for Chinese Food and Cooking Utensils

EAST

Connecticut

Richard Sanders
China Bowl Trading Co., Inc.
PO Box 454
Westport, CT 06881
(203) 222-0381

China Trading
271 Crown Street
New Haven, CT 06511
(203) 865-9465

Massachusetts

Joyce Chen, Unlimited
Acton, MA
(800) 828-0368
(508) 263-6922

Legal Sea Foods Market
5 Cambridge Center
Kendall Square
Cambridge, MA 02139
(617) 864-3400

Sun Sun Co.
18 Oxford St.
Boston, MA 02111
(617) 426-6494

New York

Katagiri and Co.
224 East 59th Street
New York, NY 10012
(212) 755-3566

Mon Fong Wo Company
36 Pell Street
New York, New York 10013
Fax: (212) 962-5418

Kam Man Food Products
200 Canal Street
New York, NY 10013
(212) 571-0330

MID-ATLANTIC

Washington, D.C.

Mee Wah Lung Company
608 H Street, N.W.
Washington, D.C. 20001
(202) 737-0968

Wang's Company
800 7th Street, N.W.
Washington, D.C. 20001
(202) 347-2447

MIDWEST

Illinois

Oriental Food Market
7411 North Clark Street
Chicago, IL 60657
(312) 274-2826

Treasure Island
3460 North Broadway
Chicago, Illinois 60657
(312) 327-3880

SOUTH

South and Eastern Food Supply
6732 NE 4th Avenue
Miami, FL 33138

WEST

California

Chong Kee Jan Company
838 Grant Avenue
San Francisco, California 94108
(415) 982-1432

Wing Chong Lung Co. Grocery
922 South San Pedro Street
Los Angeles, California 94108

The Wok Shop
718 Grant Avenue
San Francisco, CA 94108
(415) 989-3797

RECIPES